No Man's River

Farley Mowat

KEY PORTER BOOKS

National Library of Canada Cataloguing in Publication

Mowat, Farley, 1921–
        No man's river / Farley Mowat.

ISBN 1-55263-624-0

1. Inuit—Manitoba, Northern. 2. Metis—Manitoba, Northern. 3. Manitoba, Northern—Description and travel. 4. Mowat, Farley, 1921– —Travel—Manitoba, Northern. I. Title.
E99.E7M8588 2004   971.2'710049712   C2004-902316-0

The Canada Council | Le Conseil des Arts
for the Arts | du Canada

ONTARIO ARTS COUNCIL
CONSEIL DES ARTS DE L'ONTARIO

The publisher gratefully acknowledges the support of the Canada Council for the Arts and the Ontario Arts Council for its publishing program. We acknowledge the support of the Government of Ontario through the Ontario Media Development Corporation's Ontario Book Initiative.

We acknowledge the financial support of the Government of Canada through the Book Publishing Industry Development Program (BPIDP) for our publishing activities.

Key Porter Books Limited
70 The Esplanade
Toronto, Ontario
Canada M5E 1R2

www.keyporter.com

Text design: Jack Steiner
Electronic formatting: Jean Lightfoot Peters
Maps: Lightfoot Art & Design Inc.

Printed and bound in Canada

04 05 06 07 08 09 6 5 4 3 2 1

For Justin Mowat,

who will, I believe,

travel far and do

good things

CONTENTS

THE WHY AND THE WHEREFORE 1

PART ONE — THE INCOMERS 17

Chapter One THE INCOMERS 19

Chapter Two LIVING ON THE LAND 31

Chapter Three BROTHERS 41

Chapter Four A SPRING TO REMEMBER 57

PART TWO — WINDY POST 71

Chapter Five WINDY POST 73

Chapter Six MAN AND LEMMINGS 87

Chapter Seven SCIENCE LOSES ONE 97

PART THREE — IDTHEN ELDELI   111

Chapter Eight   SOUTHBOUND   113

Chapter Nine   MANY ISLANDS LAKE   123

Chapter Ten   TELEQUOISIE   136

Chapter Eleven   BROCHET   147

PART FOUR — KASMERE'S RIVER   163

Chapter Twelve   CLIMBING THE COCHRANE   165

Chapter Thirteen   TWO TO REMEMBER   174

Chapter Fourteen   KASMERE'S GRAVE   185

Chapter Fifteen   KASMERE'S BIRDS   196

Chapter Sixteen   PUTAHOW   207

PART FIVE — ARCTIC PRAIRIE   219

Chapter Seventeen   HOMECOMING   221

Chapter Eighteen   LAND OF LITTLE STICKS   232

Chapter Nineteen   THE DEER'S WAY   244

PART SIX — NO MAN'S RIVER 255

Chapter Twenty   BIG RIVER   257

Chapter Twenty-one   RIVER DOGS   268

Chapter Twenty-two   ESKIMO CHARLIE   277

Chapter Twenty-three   KUMIUT   291

Chapter Twenty-four   TAVANNI NOT   302

PART SEVEN — AFTERMATH   317

Chapter Twenty-five   CHARLES   319

Chapter Twenty-six   RITA   331

AUTHOR'S NOTE   341

INDEX   343

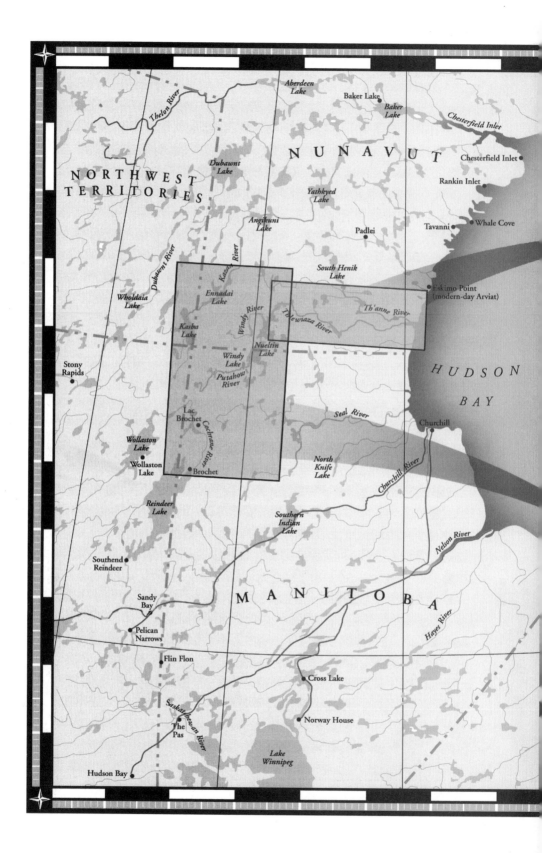

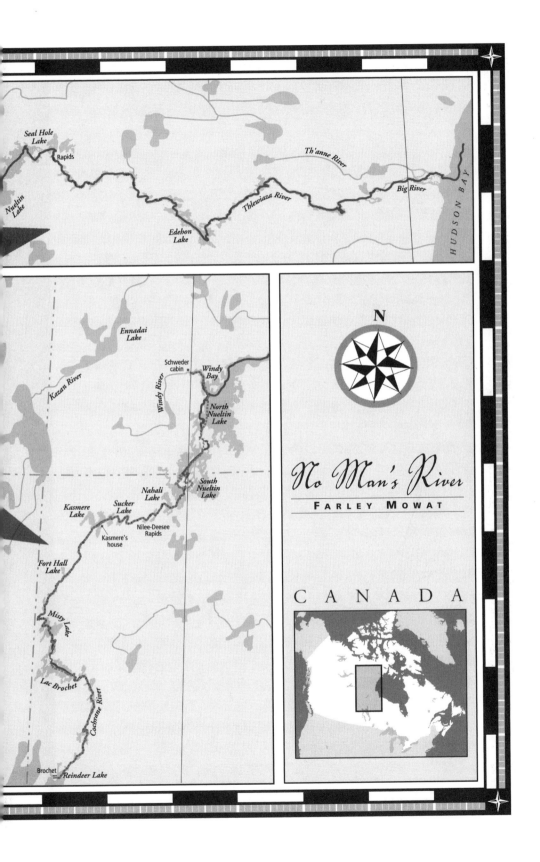

THE WHY AND THE WHEREFORE

ISPENT THE BEST PART OF MY CHILDHOOD ROAMING the central Saskatchewan prairie with dogs, coyotes, gophers, horned owls, garter snakes, and salamanders as my principal companions.

Living largely outside of civilization's pale, I was totally unprepared for what awaited me when in 1940 I stepped inside to become an infantryman in the Canadian army. I found myself hurled into a world apparently created and run by maniacs—a nightmarish construct, dark with auguries of death and destruction, which it became my task to help turn into bloody realities in Sicily, Italy, Belgium, and Holland.

By the time the war ended I had heard enough gunfire, seen enough dismembered corpses, smelled enough putrefaction to shatter many illusions, including the belief that we are the only species to practice compassion and to venerate life. I had learned instead that we are the killer species without peer.

Whereas most Canadian combat veterans hoped to be absorbed into the country's frenetic burst of post-war prosperity, I wanted no part of what I perceived to be a kind of fungal growth consequent upon the deaths of millions of people. So when I was "demobilized," I headed for Saskatchewan in a desperate attempt to return to the world I had lost.

Throughout the summer of 1946 I worked my way north

across the prairies into verdant boreal forests. The animals I sought were still there, but now there seemed to be an invisible barrier between us. I had become an alien in their world.

It was in no happy frame of mind that I returned to Toronto, where, for want of anything better to do, I went to university to study biology. My heart wasn't in it. And neither was any other essential part of my being. Pining for what I had lost, my psyche skittered off to seek refuge in a transcendental memory of ten years earlier.

In the spring of 1936 my great-uncle Frank Farley had taken me along on an "ornithological field trip" to the subarctic settlement of Churchill on Hudson Bay. Frank collected the eggs of rare birds. Though he did this in the name of science, the truth was that the eggs mostly ended up in the cabinets of wealthy collectors in the United States.

My rangy, weather-beaten uncle and I went by rail from Winnipeg to a frontier village mysteriously named The Pas. Here we changed to a ramshackle train known half-contemptuously and half-affectionately as the Muskeg Special, which ran north to the shores of that vast arctic sea misleadingly called Hudson *Bay*.

Passenger accommodation consisted of a single pioneer car of 1890s' vintage fitted with hard wooden seats, a coal stove, and a hole in the floor for a toilet. The passengers were mainly Indians, Metis, and white trappers. Uncle Frank thought they were "a mite too earthy" for the likes of me, so he prevailed upon the train crew to let us travel in the caboose at the end of what was principally a grain train carrying wheat to Churchill for transshipment to Europe.

The monotony of that two-day journey at an average speed of less than twenty miles an hour through a seemingly interminable evergreen forest still deep in snow was monumental. To pass the time, I amused myself counting the numbered mile boards nailed to telegraph poles along the right-of-way that marked off the miles.

I was sitting high up in the cupola of the caboose when, near mile 400 (counting northward from The Pas), the engine unleashed a full-throated shriek of warning. Looking forward over the humped backs of freight cars, I saw what appeared to be an undulating brown river flowing across the snow-covered roadbed ahead of us.

Viewed through the murky lenses of my old field glasses, the flood resolved itself into a multitude of long-legged, heavy-headed deer.

"*C'est la Foule!*" cried the train's French-Canadian brakeman, who had climbed up beside me.

La Foule—the Throng—was the name coined by early French explorers to describe one of the most impressive spectacles on earth—the mass migration of the barrenground caribou.

Although the whistle continued screeching, the surging tide of animals did not deviate from its course. After a while the engineer gave up, and with a resigned whiffle of steam the train drew to a stop. We remained stationary for nearly two hours while the living river flowed unhurriedly across our path. By the time the Muskeg Special had gathered its strength to continue on its plodding way, the image of la Foule was indelibly imprinted in my mind. That initial meeting with the deer (as caribou are universally known throughout the north) was to become a determining influence in my life.

During the final months of 1946 I gave myself over to enlarging upon that memory. I read everything I could find about the caribou, the country they lived in, and the other beings who shared it with them. I learned that the so-called barrengrounds encompassed nearly two million square miles of tundra (most of Canada north of the timberline) and that these vast arctic plains and the thin taiga forests immediately south of them provided a home and sustenance for a plethora of living creatures, including millions of caribou and several thousand native people.

I was astonished, but delighted, at how little seemed to be

known about the deer or the people of the deer. It appeared that only a handful of outsiders had traveled in the vast reaches of taiga and tundra shared by the aboriginal people and the caribou. In particular, the interior of Keewatin Territory, which, together with the adjacent northern reaches of Manitoba and Saskatchewan, amounted to nearly three hundred thousand square miles, seemed to be virtually *terra incognita*.

I could find only two accounts of white men having traversed this enormous region. The first was written by a young Hudson's Bay Company trader named Samuel Hearne, who, between 1770 and 1772, *walked* more than twenty-five hundred miles from Churchill to the mouth of the Coppermine River and back—in company with a band of northern Indians. The second concerned a canoe journey made in 1893 by the brothers Joseph and James Tyrrell, who encountered la Foule in such abundance that James wrote: "They could only be reckoned in acres and square miles." Joseph estimated that one herd alone contained as many as two hundred thousand animals.

This was only one of the brothers' remarkable discoveries. The second was a previously unheard-of population of inland-dwelling Inuit who lived in the Kazan and Dubawnt River watersheds. These were truly people of another time and place. Most had never seen a white man. They knew little or nothing about the sea, which nurtures most Inuit. *Their* sustenance was derived almost in its entirety from *tuktu*, as they called the caribou. Joseph Tyrrell noted that they were a natural people living almost unaffected by civilization.

In December of 1946, intrigued and heartened by the prospect (however unlikely) that a community of human beings uncontaminated by the murderous aberrations of civilized man might still exist in my own country, I decided to try to find these People of the Deer.

The first difficulty to be surmounted was how to get myself into the barrengrounds. I visited a zoologist friend at Toronto's

Royal Ontario Museum in hopes he might know of some expedition I could join. Early in February he called me on the phone.

"In case you're still interested, I've heard from a zoology prof at a Yankee university who says he wants to spend the summer in Keewatin collecting everything that walks, flies, swims, or crawls. He's looking for a Canadian associate. There's no pay, but we'd buy any specimens you could collect—at our usual princely rate of fifty cents per skin."

I wrote to the address my friend gave me and after some rather stilted correspondence found myself accepted as half of the Keewatin Zoological Expedition, whose other half was Dr. Francis Harper.

This was to be a scientific attempt to "investigate, inventory and catalogue the wildlife of the southern District of Keewatin in the Northwest Territories of Canada." I was to pay my own way, although the expedition was being financed by the U.S.-based Arctic Institute of North America and, rather surprisingly, I thought, by the United States Office of Naval Research. Perhaps I should not have been surprised. Although peace had only just come back into fashion, the Cold War was already heating up.

The plans Dr. Harper outlined in his elegant but spidery handwriting were somewhat vague. We were to establish our camp at "a suitable place in the interior of southern Keewatin or in an adjacent district of Manitoba," then spend the summer collecting animals and plants.

That prospect did not excite me. Having been involved in a few collecting trips before the war, I knew that they were little more than high-grade plundering ventures devoted to slaughtering everything non-human or non-domesticated that came under the gun, in order to produce "study skins" for deposit behind sealed doors in endless rows of steel cabinets. In 1947 the Royal Ontario Museum alone possessed more than a hundred thousand such "study skins." The idea of adding more mummies to these scientific catacombs had no appeal, even though I would be paid for doing so.

What I *wanted* to do was look for the People of the Deer and, if any still survived, live and travel with them while learning what they could teach me about Man Before the Fall.

Our first task was to find our way into the Keewatin interior. I had heard of a small charter outfit at Churchill calling itself Arctic Wings, so I wrote to see if it could fly us to the upper reaches of the Kazan River, which seemed to have been the heart of the inland Inuit country in the Tyrrells' time. In due course a scrawled reply informed me the fledgling company could not fly to the Kazan without first establishing gas caches along the way. Even more to the point, Arctic Wings would be wingless until its sole aircraft—a single-engined Norseman bush plane—returned from Winnipeg where it was undergoing an engine overhaul. Just when it might become available was problematic.

Harper and I nevertheless concluded Churchill should be our jumping-off point. There we could at least study the wildlife on the surrounding tundra until Arctic Wings was flying again, or we might even find an alternative means of getting into the interior.

I did not meet my partner in the flesh until mid-May, when he joined me in Toronto. A stickler for protocol, he introduced himself as *Doctor* Francis Harper and insisted on addressing me as *Captain* Mowat until I asked him to drop the military honorific.

Tall, lean, and slightly bowed, he wore round steel-framed spectacles and a broad-rimmed felt hat of the *Raiders of the Lost Ark* genus. His expression was a stern one, reflecting an almost Jesuitical infallibility which, however, reflected an allegiance not to Jehovah but to Science.

Dr. Harper was a naturalist of the old school whose specialty was taxonomy, the classification of animals and plants into species, subspecies, and races. He collected living things of all kinds by means of nets, traps, guns, even poison, then minutely examined their corpses to determine their correct positions in the taxonomic hierarchy.

He and I had both collected birds' eggs and butterflies in our juvenile years, but what had been a hobby with me had become his life's work. During the First World War, he had served as a second lieutenant in the Rodentological Control Branch of the U.S. Army in France, waging war on rats. While so employed, he had discovered and described a hitherto-unknown color phase of the Norway rat, an achievement that probably did not help the Allies win the war but that considerably enhanced Harper's stature in his chosen profession.

The generation gap between us (he was older than my father) was exacerbated by other differences. In the words of one of his peers: "Francis Harper had a strong antipathy toward socialism, labor unions, and civil rights movements." He was also a vehement teetotaler who believed the only legitimate use for alcohol was as a solvent or as a preservative of scientific specimens. And he loathed smoking with a fervor that would have won him plaudits from the anti-smoking puritans of today. Profanity of any kind profoundly offended him, and he was phobic about matters of hygiene.

On May 17 Dr. Francis Harper and I boarded a train at Toronto's Union Station bound for Winnipeg. There were some amongst my friends who suspected the expedition might be "fraught with rue," but I harbored no such reservations, for was I not bound north to see la Foule again?

Early on the morning of May 20 we reached The Pas, a little frontier community three hundred miles northwest of Winnipeg consisting of a sprawling collection of frame and log buildings inhabited by a heterogeneous mixture of whites, Indians, and Metis.

Learning that the Muskeg Special would not depart for several hours, I went for a walk. Crossing the broad Saskatchewan River on a primitive swing bridge, I made my way to a log school-house on the adjacent Cree Indian reserve, a place I had visited with my uncle Frank in 1936.

The school was an unusual one. Instead of being run by a missionary order as were most schools for natives in the north, this one was in the charge of Sam Waller, a shy, sandy-haired man in his fifties who professed no religion at all.

Foreshadowing my own experience, Sam had returned from three years overseas during the First World War and, appalled by what he had witnessed during that holocaust, had gone searching for a saner world.

"After I was demobbed in 1919," he told me over a pot of black tea in his snug little cabin, "I found I simply couldn't adjust to life on civvy street. There'd been a couple of Cree gunners in my old battery. Fine fellows, though they got treated pretty rough, being Indians. They told me a bit about their life in northern Manitoba, and it stuck in my mind. So when the mess in France was over, I came here to look around. There was a school—a hovel, more like—but it had no teacher so I sort of drifted into the job.

"The Cree took to me and I to them, so here I stayed. Great people. Don't have much, but what they have is yours when you need it. Sometimes they drink too much. Who wouldn't, when you're treated like niggers of the North! They made me welcome and let me teach their kids what I could, with lots of time left over to watch the birds and other animals."

Sam was a true naturalist, one who had long since rejected the collector syndrome and would no longer kill anything if he could avoid it. Talking with him did much to strengthen my own growing aversion to blood-and-guts science. Time went quickly by and I was into my third cup of tea when I heard the hoarse vibrato of a steamboat whistle.

"Better hop it!" Sam advised. "Bridge'll swing open now and Lord knows when it'll close again. You could miss your train, and the next one don't go north for a week."

I ran for the river bank. Sprinting ahead of me was a crowd of young Crees. The first four men to reach the bridge would get the job of pushing the wooden bars that turned a big capstan and opened the span.

By the time I reached the bridge, it had begun to swing and I had to jump a widening gap on the far side. Winded, I sat on the guardrail and watched one of the last working sternwheelers in the north come sweeping downstream pushing a string of barges loaded with sawlogs. The pilot had to aim his shot from nearly a mile upstream and thereafter could not alter course without the risk of losing his string. Since there was always a possibility he might miscalculate and hit the bridge, a good many people usually turned out to watch.

When the show was over, I went looking for the Muskeg Special and found it waiting on a siding. It had changed its spots since I had been a passenger aboard it eleven years earlier. Although the pioneer car still survived, it had yielded pride of place to half a dozen shiny Pullman sleepers filled with U.S. soldiers being transported to a huge military camp at Churchill, there to be trained to defend the arctic against the Red Menace.

Harper and I cornered a wood-planked, uncushioned seat in the ancient pioneer car, where we were soon accosted by a cadaverous, beak-nosed white man of late middle age accompanied by a dark-skinned young woman and an extraordinarily shy little boy. Both youngsters were clearly of mixed Indian and white parentage.

The man introduced himself as Fred Schweder, sometime trapper and trader bound for Churchill hoping to find work at the army base. The girl was his daughter, Mary, and the boy his youngest son, Norman.

The mysterious moccasin telegraph had done its stuff, for Schweder seemed to know almost as much about the Keewatin Zoological Expedition as we did. Furthermore, he was prepared to tell us exactly where we ought to go and how to get there. He even had a ready-made base to offer: a cabin at the mouth of Windy River, which flows into the northwestern arm of Nueltin Lake, and which was currently occupied by three of his sons.

Very little was then known about Nueltin Lake except that it was a vast body of water straddling the Manitoba-Keewatin border some two hundred and fifty miles northwest of Churchill. It had never been surveyed and much of it was represented even on the most recent maps by dotted lines. Schweder told us his sons had been trapping there for several years, but this year, once the ice melted from the lakes and rivers, they planned to come "outside" for good.

Schweder now proposed that Harper and I base ourselves at the Windy River cabin and that his sons fly out to Churchill on the plane that flew us in. Whose plane would that be? I asked. Arctic Wings, said Schweder. According to him, Gunnar Ingebritson, chief and only pilot of Arctic Wings, had flown to Windy once before and doubtless could find his way there again.

"Place'd be all yours. Cabin, stove, two canoes, dogs if you want 'em. Traps. Whole damn outfit. None of us is likely to go back. The boys'll get jobs outside from now on. So you can stay so long as you want. Do as you please. Wonderful fine country. Full of all kinds of birds and animals, 'specially caribou."

Schweder made the offer irresistible to me by adding: "Once the ice is gone, you could paddle north to the Kazan where the Eskimos got their camps. Charles, my oldest boy, he'd draw you a map to show you how to get there.

"Best time to go in is right now. Don't you wait 'til break-up. Right now a plane on skis can land most anyplace. With the cabin to live in, you'll be well fixed no matter what the weather. Ja! You should go right away. Ingebritson soon be back from Winnipeg. He take you in."

This seemed like such a complete and wonderful solution to our problem that I was ready to accept on the instant. However, after Schweder had returned to his own seat, my partner expressed reservations about dealing with a "squaw man"—a term I had previously encountered only in pulp fiction. At first I thought he was joking, and I laughed. He responded with a tight-lipped little lecture on the evils of miscegenation, the gist of which was that white men who married "lesser breeds" weakened their own race and deservedly became outcasts from it. He preferred to have no dealings with any such. It took a good deal of persuasion to convince him that the advantages of having a well-equipped base outweighed his prejudices. In fact, he remained dubious until I pointed out that the Schweder clan would not be present in the flesh and any baleful influence they might be able to exert from distant Churchill must be negligible. Finally he agreed that Windy Bay should be our objective.

The rest of the journey to Churchill was relatively uneventful for us, though a revelation to pretty Mary Schweder, who found herself being swarmed by what must have seemed like half the U.S. army. Her father was kept so busy defending her that he had little time to spare for us. I kept a sharp eye open for la Foule but, although we saw some small herds of caribou, the great multitudes of 1936 did not materialize.

At 10:00 p.m. two days after our departure from The Pas, the Muskeg Special puffed in to Churchill in broad daylight, for we were now in the Land of the Long Day.

We had outrun spring. Churchill's sprawl of mostly unpainted shacks and shanties still lay half-buried under winter drifts. Hudson Bay, stretching to the eastern and northern horizons, remained solidly icebound. So did the broad Churchill River. Over all hung a dusting of new snow.

A raw wind blowing off the bay ice cut deep into the flesh of the hundred or so GIs who stumbled out of the Pullman cars. They seemed to think they had been transported to some kind of frozen hell. Certainly their language as they climbed into a row of army trucks was colorful enough to send Harper hurrying off the platform with averted gaze.

There had been no real roads and few vehicles in Churchill in 1936. Now a wide graveled highway ran from the station several miles inland to the military camp. Eight-wheeled army trucks, jeeps, personnel carriers, and half-tracks snarled along it, rousing unpleasant memories of times and places I had come a long way to forget. When, in casual conversation with an army driver, I learned that the colonel who had commanded my regiment in Italy now commanded the Canadian section of Fort Churchill, I felt a disturbing sense of déjà vu and an urgent desire to put the place behind me as soon as possible.

"Soon" was not possible.

Harper and I went to the Hudson Hotel, a fragile frame box divided by matchboard partitions into tiny cells so well ventilated that drifts of snow scrolled their floors. Harper seemed a bit under the weather, so I left him in one of the cells and, setting out in search of Arctic Wings, found my way to Churchill's one and only beer parlor. In response to my query, a surly waiter pointed to a mountain of a man at a deal table presiding over a platoon of beer bottles.

Rotund and fiftyish, John Ingebritson looked like a kindly caricature of a Viking berserker. I introduced myself and stated my business. He drank most of a pint before replying.

"You came right place, wrong time, sonny. Goddamn son-of-a-bitch of a plane is broke. Gunnar take it south for a new goddamn engine. Sit down and have a beer...."

Several beers later I knew quite a lot about John Ingebritson. Born on an island off the northwest coast of Norway, he had emigrated as a young man to settle near Lake Winnipeg, where he expected to make a living fishing. However, the lake, though large, was fresh, and John did not feel at ease with fresh water.

"No goddamn *taste!*" he roared at me across a stockade of bottles. "Fish only fit to eat if they come out of *salt* water. I make up goddamn mind go back to sea."

The nearest sea was Hudson Bay, but when John inquired

about the fishing there he was told the Bay had no fishing industry, no fishing vessels, and probably no useable fish.

"Goddamn experts," John snorted. "Don't know nothin'! I
build me a goddamn Redningskoite, double-ender, forty feet
long, put her on goddamn flatcar and ship to Churchill. Then me
and wife and kids launch her and go fishin'. Pretty soon we fill our
nets so goddamn full can hardly haul 'em."

Indeed the fish were there, and John could catch them, but
there was no market for his catch. In the end he was forced to
give it up. Nevertheless, he and his growing family stayed on at
Churchill. During the war his eldest son, Gunnar, became enam-
ored of flying when some friendly RCAF types let him put in
time on a Link trainer and ride in the co-pilot's seat of a search-
and-rescue Norseman.

Gunnar fell in love with that rugged little plane. In 1945, having obtained his commercial pilot's license, he persuaded the
Roman Catholic Diocese of the Eastern Arctic to buy a
Norseman and let him fly it for them. So Arctic Wings was born.
When not ferrying missionaries around the diocese, Gunnar
flew commercial charters. Arctic Wings would gladly have flown
us to Nueltin had Gunnar and the plane been available.

"Too goddamn bad!" John bellowed as he ordered another
flock of beers. "He fly good, that boy.... Drink up, then we go my
house and drink some goddamn aquavit and try my sauna. Maybe
work something out."

I did as bidden and as Mrs. Ingebritson, a big-bosomed
Valkyrie of a woman, plied us with caribou steaks, her husband
brought the sun back into my life.

"Maybe you got some goddamn luck. Goddamn old Anson
blow in here couple days ago. Fly boy owns it is hungry for work.
Might take you into goddamn Nueltin."

John raised his bellow to a full-throated roar, addressing
another of his sons.

"LIEF! GET OFFEN THAT GODDAMN CHAIR. GO FIND

THAT GODDAMN ANSON JOCKEY. TELL HIM WE GOT ADMIRAL PEARY HERE WANTS TO GO TO GODDAMN POLE!"

Half an hour later a lean, lithe man of about my own age appeared in the doorway of the kitchen. He had the dark coloring and the features of a Metis, but was wearing a ratty old leather flying jacket of the kind affected by RAF types. In fact, Johnny Bourassa had spent three years overseas as a pilot of Lancaster bombers, then of Mosquitoes in a pathfinder squadron. Now he stood rather awkwardly before us until John shouted at him to sit in goddamn chair and have goddamn drink.

Soft-spoken and diffident, Bourassa bore little resemblance to the bush pilot of legend. In truth he had only been flying in the north since the previous summer, and his aircraft was not your typical bush plane.

Designed in the early thirties as a light bomber, the twin-engined Anson was already obsolete before the war began. Nevertheless it was mass-produced as a bomber-trainer. Most of those that survived to war's end were junked, but a few came on the market and Johnny bought one of the cumbersome, fabric-covered, yellow-painted planes. He flew it to his home in the northern Alberta bush and there, with the assistance of a taciturn mechanic called Gallagher (who seemed not to have any other name), fitted it with skis and went into business as Peace River Airlines.

In the style of tramp freighters of an earlier age, the flying banana, as her proud owner called her, rumbled her way about the arctic wherever a charter or a cargo offered. I asked Bourassa if he would fly us to Nueltin Lake and bring us back out again in October. And could he do it for four hundred dollars, which was all we had to spend on transportation.

He explained apologetically that he had never been to Nueltin and had heard its map location was inaccurate. Not that a map was of much use in winter, anyway, because the ice and snow which covered the tundra made land and water virtually indistinguishable from the air. Navigation over the barrengrounds in winter was, as Bourassa put it, "mostly by guess and by God." But, well, sure, he would give it a go.

First, however, the Anson had to ferry a load of freight to the Hudson's Bay Company post at Baker Lake, some four hundred miles to the northwestward. Johnny thought this might require three or four days, depending—as always—on the weather. He also thought that, with luck, enough time would still remain to fly us in to Nueltin before break-up, a six-week-long period of thaw during which planes can use neither skis nor floats.

No sooner had the Anson departed for Baker Lake than we were subjected to a series of blizzards, sleet storms, impenetrable ice fogs, and a howling northeast gale. After a full week without any word from Johnny, we finally heard he was weather-bound at Chesterfield Inlet, two hundred miles east of Baker, whither the Anson had been blown while attempting to return to Churchill. We awaited her eventual arrival in deepening gloom, for our window of opportunity was rapidly closing.

I spent much of the waiting time in the beer parlor listening to John Ingebritson and friends—men like Husky Harris, Windy Smith, and Hairy Joe Chamberlain, all of whom had spent time trapping along the southern verges of the barrengrounds. Harper did not join in these sessions, preferring to use the brief interludes of bearable weather to prowl around the townsite with his shotgun, potting early migrants such as horned larks and Lapland longspurs as they forlornly sought food and shelter. "Gathering population data" was how he characterized these excursions. He was not pleased that I chose to spend so much of my time with "wastrels" when I, too, could have been serving science.

PART ONE

THE
INCOMERS

CHAPTER ONE

THE INCOMERS

THE ONLY WORK FRED SCHWEDER WAS OFFERED in Churchill was helping unload boxcars at the government grain elevator down by the harbor. Complaining that this was beneath him, he spent much of his time in the beer parlor, where I learned something of his history.

Born in Prussia before the turn of the century, he emigrated to Canada while still in his late teens. When war broke out between his Fatherland and the Allies in 1914, he grew afraid he might be conscripted into the Canadian Army and have to fight against his own kith and kin, or be imprisoned as an enemy alien, so he fled from civilized parts in search of a hiding place.

He found one at Reindeer Lake, deep in the boreal forest five hundred miles to the north of Winnipeg. Here he encountered the Cree and with their help became a trapper of sorts, though not a good enough one to be able to make more than a subsistence living. In all likelihood he would not have survived without the support of the Cree, but he was by no means grateful. He considered them to be an inferior race and resented his dependence on them. When Armistice freed him from the threat of arrest, Schweder surfaced to take a job as general handyman at the Rabbit River outpost of the French-owned Revillon Frères trading company. He did not, however, entirely sever his connection with the Cree. In 1922, he took one of them, Rose Moiesty, to live with him.

Described by a government official in 1920 as "the most magnificent woman in the country," Rose had lost her parents and all her siblings to the post-war influenza epidemic which killed three-quarters of the native population of the region. And she and her children had been deserted by her "husband," a man named Fowler, the manager of the Hudson's Bay Company's South End post at Reindeer Lake. Transferred to a post in the high arctic, Fowler had done the customary thing by abandoning her. She was, after all, only a "country wife."

When Rose became pregnant by Fred, he offered to marry her *if* she would divest herself of her previous children. Heavily influenced by a Roman Catholic missionary, she let the children go to a "good home"—a church orphanage at The Pas. There is no record of what Rose thought or felt about all this.

The following year she bore a son called Charles, the first of six children to be fathered by Fred Schweder.

Charles remembered his childhood as a happy one. His playmates were of his mother's race and with them he enjoyed the freedom that characterized the early years of most aboriginal peoples, their lives unfettered by regular schooling. Nevertheless, Fred saw to it that his children learned to read and write.

Charles's childhood memories were mostly good, but he was afraid of his father. Proud of his Prussian heritage, Fred was a strict disciplinarian with a hair-trigger temper who was only at ease in the company of other German expatriates. Rose, on the other hand, was a warm-hearted if overburdened woman who was everybody's friend.

Fred worked for Revillon Frères in the Reindeer Lake district for a decade, then the Hudson's Bay Company offered him the job of manager at an outpost on Windy Lake, two weeks' travel by canoe to the north of Reindeer. He was not enthusiastic. However, those were Depression times, and promotion was hard to come by, so he gloomily accepted what he feared was banishment to the ends of the earth.

Windy Post had been established to trade with the Caribou Eskimos. It stood fifteen miles to the west of Nueltin Lake in a place the Chipewyans, whose country it was, knew as the Land of Little Sticks. On the verges of the barrenlands, its isolation was such that its first manager had fled before his initial year was out. By the time Fred Schweder was offered the post, it had been empty for several months.

Traveling in two canoes with all their personal belongings and the post's "outfit" (a year's supply of trade goods together with food and other essentials for the family), the Schweders arrived at their new home late in the summer—to find the log structure with all its contents had burned to the ground.

The family put in an exceedingly tough winter in a hastily constructed, windowless, earth-floored shanty. They cooked over a makeshift stove hammered out of a ten-gallon gas drum, which also provided the only heat. Bunks made of spruce saplings covered with caribou hides accommodated the two adults and their four young children. A wall tent pitched nearby served as the "store" or trading room.

Charles, who was then almost nine years of age, possessed his father's wiry strength. This was as well since, as winter drew down, he was required to play a man's role, catching fish, hunting meat, and even running his own trapline. His father preferred to stay in or near the cabin, but Charles roamed afield, establishing his first tentative connections with a land which would eventually claim him, heart and soul.

Once sled travel became possible, fur-clad Eskimos materialized out of the northern plains. *Ihalmiut* they called themselves, a name roughly translatable as *People from Beyond*. The visitors were delighted to find Windy Post re-occupied and restocked with rifles, ammunition, and even such luxuries as flour, tea, and tobacco.

Fred bought four sled dogs from them. Big, powerful animals, these became Charles's special responsibility and chief delight.

His rapport with them extended to the Ihalmiut, and before spring arrived he had acquired a rudimentary grasp of their language and was beginning to feel at home.

Not so his father. Fred actively disliked and was made uneasy by this sparsely wooded border country between the forest and the tundra. His antipathy toward the place extended to the Ihalmiut. Referring to them as "Huskies," he rated them even below the Chipewyans, whom he considered barely human.

Rose shared Fred's antipathy for the Land of Little Sticks. The naked fingers that the barrens thrust south into the thin taiga frightened her, and she longed for the protective forests in the land where she had been born.

The upshot of Fred's and Rose's mutual antipathy to the Windy Lake country was that, when summer again made water travel possible, Fred loaded his family, their scanty possessions, and the winter's take of furs into a large canoe and set off for the HBC post of Brochet at the northern end of Reindeer Lake three hundred miles distant. There he delivered the furs he had traded on the Company's behalf, together with a letter of resignation scrawled on a piece of wrapping paper. Having spent almost a year in what he described as "Siberian exile," he was now determined to rejoin the civilized world from which he had fled two decades earlier.

The family paddled on to The Pas, where they sold the canoe then boarded the Muskeg Special. Fred rented a decrepit frame house in Winnipeg in which the family spent the winter, enduring worse conditions than they had ever known in the north.

The Great Depression was at its nadir, and Fred could not find work. Forced to subsist on relief and unable to hunt wild meat or catch fish, the family often went hungry. Since wood for fuel could not be had just for the cutting, they also suffered from the bitter prairie cold. To make things worse, the white community rejected Fred because he had "gone native" and married a squaw. This rejection embraced all the members of his family since they *were* natives or, what was worse in the eyes of many, "half-breeds."

The children were deeply unhappy—Charles even more so than the others. He fiercely resented having been taken from a world where he had felt he belonged, to be thrown into one which, in his view, was hell on earth. In consequence he became surly, then openly rebellious. This brought his father's Prussian wrath down upon him. On several occasions he was severely beaten; nor was he the only member of the family to suffer so. In later times he would recall: "It was the worst winter Mother and us kids ever lived. Father went right wild."

While the Schweder family endured as best they could, the Company (as the Hudson's Bay Company was succinctly styled throughout the north) moved Windy Post to a new location, on an expansion of Windy River called Simmons Lake. The post opened at its new site in the autumn of 1936, but its manager was so distressed by the isolation and by the looming barrengrounds that, when he brought his furs south the following summer, he followed Fred Schweder's example and quit. He is on record as having said: "Windy Post is the end of the fucking world!"

The Company's Canadian headquarters was in Winnipeg, so news of its activities circulated freely in that city. Reports of what had happened at Windy Post soon reached Fred Schweder, who had undergone a change of heart. Visiting the Company's offices, he ate crow and pleaded for his old job back. After submitting to a stern lecture on the merits of loyalty to one's employer, he was rehired, though at a reduced salary, and was ordered to report to Brochet to pick up the Windy Post outfit.

Fred decided to take only his eldest son with him. Now eleven, Charles was overjoyed to be returning to a land and a way of life he loved. *His* exile was at an end. Fred Schweder's was beginning anew.

That winter fewer Ihalmiut hunters came to the new post at Simmons Lake. A fur ledger for 1936–37 gives their names as Hekwaw, Angakouk, Petow, Yaha, Hanna, Aveaduck, Angleyalik,

Mickey, Oley, Ohoto, Homogulik, Kakut, Engola, Anarow, Pommela, Halo, and Ilupalee. Eleven of these were heads of families, representing the eighty individuals who were all that remained of the nearly two thousand "Caribou Eskimos" Joseph Tyrrell had found in the region forty-two years earlier.[1]

Fred Schweder's meticulously kept ledgers illuminate the nature of the business. Most of the fur traded at Windy Post consisted of silver, cross, red, or white fox, with white predominating. Five hundred and forty-three pelts were brought in by the Ihalmiut during the 1936–37 season. Although the book value of these was shown as $6,171, this did not represent money paid to the trappers; it was a credit against the purchase of goods whose value had been doubled by transport charges and then marked up another hundred per cent or more above normal retail level. In practice, each family received on average about $175 worth of goods as payment for five or six months' labor on the trapline.

Most impoverished families on relief rolls in southern Canada at the time fared better than this.

One of the first things Fred Schweder did after returning to Windy Post was to equip Charles with a sled and team bought from an Ihalmio named Angleyalik. Fred intended Charles to run a full-scale trapline—whose production would not appear on the Company's books.

Charles was delighted to be a trapper, not alone for the pleasure he derived from it but also because of the contacts it gave him with the Ihalmiut, especially with Angleyalik and his family. Angleyalik, who was then about forty and at the peak of his abilities, was happy to take the white lad under his wing and teach him what he needed to know in order to live on and from the country.

[1] I have dealt with what is known of their history in earlier books, particularly *People of the Deer*, *The Desperate People*, and *Walking on the Land*.

Before long Charles was accompanying his mentor to the Ihalmiut camps on the Little Lakes just south of the Kazan River some eighty miles north of Windy Post. In due course the intervening stretch of tundra would become Charles's personal bailiwick, and Angleyalik's camp his second home.

In a number of ways it was a more important one for him than Windy Post. Angleyalik's family treated him as one of their own. Itkuk, the wife and mother, made winter clothing for him and gave him the full warmth of her affection. Her son, Engola, became Charles's close friend and companion in the hunt and on the trail. And Itkuk's daughter, Pama, became Charles's first love.

Charles was absorbed into the family in traditional Inuit fashion. During his visits he shared the communal bed and its concomitant physical intimacies. He may even have been initiated by Itkuk, with her husband Angleyalik's full knowledge and consent. For in that time and place it was both possible and acceptable for a youth to be a man while he was still a boy.

As Charles developed close relationships with the Eskimos, those with his father deteriorated. He took to staying away from Windy Post for longer and longer periods of time as his life became ever more centered in the Ihalmiut camps near the Kazan.

Because of Fred Schweder's aversion to "Huskies," Charles concealed the nature and extent of his friendship with them. It may also be that he concealed full awareness of its importance even from himself.

No record of Charles's fur catch was ever entered in the Windy Post ledgers. Fred was flouting the iron-bound regulations which forbade Company employees and their families from personally engaging in the fur trade.

In July of 1938 Fred and Charles canoed south to deliver the season's catch to the post at Brochet. They then continued on to South End, taking with them several bulky bundles supposedly containing caribou hides for Rose's relatives. However, when the canoe left South End bound for The Pas, the bundles were still aboard. They accompanied Fred and his son on the train to Winnipeg, where the fox furs they contained were sold for enough cash to enable Fred to buy a small chicken farm on the city's outskirts. Rose and the younger children were then installed to run this enterprise while Fred and Charles returned to Windy Post.

As father and son traveled north again, Fred had much to think about. Rearmament, the prelude to war, was stimulating a moribund economy, and the value of fur, particularly of silver and white fox, was rising. Although he dreaded the long months of isolation which stretched ahead, Fred anticipated a profitable season. However, he failed to consider the fact that white fox populations, like those of the lemmings which constitute their principal food, are cyclic. The winter ahead would see lemming and white fox populations crash. And a rare visitor to Windy Post would note that Charles succeeded in catching only seventy foxes and ten wolves, while the post's take was so small Fred Schweder was worried about his job.[2]

Fred had other problems as well. In 1939, for the first time, the Company planned to resupply its remote outposts in the Keewatin and northern Manitoba region by plane. Windy Post possessed a battery-powered short-wave radio receiver, and as spring passed and summer came, Fred could hear instructions being radioed to posts telling them when to expect the arrival of a float plane from Churchill, but no such message came for him. Sitting glued to the headphones night after night, listening for thin voices whispering in the ether, Fred grew more and more worried and short-tempered.

His mood was not improved by Charles's calm, almost contented acceptance of the possibility that the plane might not arrive at all, forcing them to spend the coming winter dependent on their own resources. If the worse came to the worst, Charles told his father, they could abandon the post and go live with the

[2] P.G. Downes in *Sleeping Island*, Coward-McCann, New York, 1943.

Eskimos. This suggestion so infuriated Fred Schweder that he ordered his son out of the cabin, screaming after him: "You want to live like a dog, go live with the *verdamit* Huskies!"

Fred was spared the dire possibility of having to become dependent on the Huskies when, in late August, a ragged roar overhead announced the arrival of a ponderous Junkers float plane carrying a load of supplies, together with orders for Fred to go on "furlough." The plane would return in a few days bringing a replacement manager, then fly the Schweders out to Churchill. Although Fred may have suspected that some of his shadier enterprises of the past few years were catching up with him, he was nevertheless enormously relieved to escape from Windy Post. Charles was not. He had no desire to go outside. War was looming, and his father had been fulminating about the likelihood of Charles being conscripted, a fate Fred claimed to have averted more than two decades earlier only by fleeing into the bush.

The two reached Churchill on September 3. On September 9 Canada joined in the war against Germany.

Fred had never concealed his sympathies with the German cause or his admiration for the Nazis, and he was afraid he might now be called to account. As he and Charles trundled south on the Muskeg Special, his aversion to life at Windy Post began to evaporate. He talked of returning there sooner, rather than later. On reaching the chicken farm, he found the business had literally gone belly up, which made him even more anxious about the future.

When Fred presented himself at the Company's headquarters, he hoped to be offered a new northern posting. Instead he was brusquely informed his services were no longer required. No explanation was forthcoming, and Fred probably needed none. Vast as the north may be, secrets are hard to keep there. He must always have known that someday the axe would fall.

That winter was one of the worst Charles ever experienced. Burgeoning wartime prices soon consumed the family's cash reserves. Stigmatized as natives, they could hardly find even menial work. Things became so unbearable for Charles, now fourteen, that at Christmas he announced he was going back to the barrengrounds to rejoin his friends the Eskimos and live the only kind of life that really appealed to him. When his father angrily forbade him even to think of it, antagonism between the two became so intense that serious violence seemed inevitable. Fred's Prussian will won out. Again rebellion was crushed, and Charles continued to shovel coal ten hours a day in the filth of a Winnipeg fuel company's yard.

By the early summer of 1940 the Schweder family's situation had worsened markedly. Never having applied for Canadian citizenship, Fred was still a German national, open to harassment if not imprisonment. At this juncture the moccasin telegraph (which operated as efficiently in Winnipeg's slums as in the bush) brought him the news that Jim Trafford, the man who had replaced him as manager of Windy Post, had been flown out suffering from bleeding ulcers, and the Company had closed the post, probably for good.

This news electrified the Schweder household. Fred saw a golden opportunity and seized it. Within the month he, Rose, fifteen-year-old Charles, thirteen-year-old Mary, eleven-year-old Else, nine-year-old Fred Junior, two-year-old Mike, and eight-month-old Norman were heading north.

Fred carried with him a freshly minted license authorizing him to operate a new trading post in Keewatin Territory. It was to bear the name Nueltin Post. Its specific location was remarkably (and uniquely) imprecise—"at Nueltin Lake"—which was equivalent to saying it was somewhere in a region comparable in size to the province of Prince Edward Island.

The vagueness surrounding the post's location was not accidental. It masked the fact that Schweder's new Nueltin Post was actually the Hudson's Bay Company's Windy Post which, with its contents, now stood unoccupied. Fred considered it comparable to a ship abandoned at sea—ripe for salvage by anyone bold enough to climb aboard. He was bold enough. Late in September of 1940, the post at Simmons Lake was reoccupied.

Thereafter, the Schweders virtually vanished from view until the Second World War was over; except that the federal Department of Mines and Natural Resources in Ottawa continued to receive handwritten applications for the renewal of the license issued to Fred Schweder to operate Nueltin Post.

During the war years the HBC forgot about Windy Post, both because the Company was too busy with larger affairs and because the war had made the trade in furs largely unprofitable. However, late in 1944 the Company began resuming peacetime operations and the question arose of what to do about Windy Post. Some directors were for simply writing it off on the grounds that the Eskimos it served were now so few in number as not to be worth the cost of refurbishing and maintaining the place. On the other hand, the Fur Trade Commissioner knew that Fred Schweder had become one of the despised "free-traders" and was not only daring to compete with the Company in southern Keewatin but was suspected of having occupied Company premises there.

One winter day a Metis trapper from Reindeer Lake showed up at Simmons Lake to trade pelts for tea and tobacco. From him Fred heard the rumor that the RCMP planned to send a patrol to Windy Post to check things out.

Schweder responded to the news by hurriedly building a log shanty ten miles downstream from Windy Post at the place where Windy River empties into a deep western bay of Nueltin Lake. Nueltin Post had finally became a physical reality, of sorts. However, Windy Post continued to serve as the Schweders' home and base of operations until early in 1944, when Rose Schweder died.

Nothing is known about the cause and nature of her death, which remained a subject her husband and children rigorously avoided. What *is* known is that she was buried in the sands of an esker on the north shore of Simmons Lake, and as soon as the ice left Windy River, Fred and his children abandoned the old HBC post and moved downstream to the new shanty.

By the summer of 1945 it had become evident that the Company did not intend to reclaim the Simmons Lake post, so the Schweders dismantled it and floated the logs and lumber to the mouth of the river, where the main building was re-erected. Now the notional Nueltin Post disappeared, and the relocated Windy Post became the undisputed home of the Schweder clan.

CHAPTER TWO

LIVING ON THE LAND

THE ANNUAL CYCLE OF LIFE AT WINDY POST WAS determined not by human wishes or even needs but by the age-old natural sequence. Modulations on it resulting from human actions were small in scale and in effect.

January and February plumbed the depths of winter. Tearing blizzards could all but obliterate the world for days on end. Sometimes they were succeeded by calms when the stillness became so intense that small explosions caused by sap freezing inside dwarf spruce trees at temperatures of fifty or sixty degrees below zero resounded like rifle shots.

Darkness prevailed. The sun was seen for only a few hours a day, and even then sometimes appeared as pallid and ghostly as a moon. Although the cold could be abyssal, it seldom caused severe discomfort to man or beast because heat-conducting moisture in the brittle air had mostly fallen out as snow crystals.

The stove inside the little log house burned only during waking hours. While people were asleep under their deerskin robes, the fire died to ashes and the chill without became the chill within. It was the task of one of the children to tumble out of bed when an old brass alarm clock signaled the beginning of a new day; stumble to the stove and stuff its firebox with spruce needles and twigs; add a few split pieces of dry wood; touch a match to the lot; and scamper back to bed while a soft crackle grew to a full-throated roar and the tin smoke pipe began to glow. This was the signal for someone to hurry over and close the dampers before the stove could erupt and turn the cabin into an inferno. Breakfast, cooked by Mary or Else, might include oatmeal porridge, sometimes thickened with the remains of ptarmigan or caribou stew; doughnuts, slabs of heavy bread, or bannock with jam; and pint mugs of strong tea.

Since the main room containing the stove (there was a lean-to storage room as well) served as kitchen, living, dining, and sleeping room, pandemonium tended to develop when all hands were getting up. Fred senior usually lay abed until the furor had been eased by the departure of those gone outside to relieve their bladders or to do early morning chores, including fetching armloads of wood and half a dozen pails of water to fill a barrel set behind the stove. The water came from a "well," a wooden crib set on the frozen river to protect a shaft chiseled and hacked through the ice to the flowing water beneath.

Of privacy there was virtually none at Windy Post.

Breakfast over, the family would disperse. The two young women had much to do. They cooked both for immediate consumption and to freeze for their elder brothers to carry with them on their journeys around the traplines. They repaired worn clothing and made new garments, especially inner parkas, gloves, and moccasins (outer parkas and deerskin boots were usually obtained from the Ihalmiut but, if need be, the girls could make them too). In general they saw to the minimum requirements of cleanliness and, prime requisite, kept the stove burning and a big iron tea kettle simmering.

When the two older lads returned from their traplines, the girls and younger boys helped thaw and skin fox and wolf carcasses, then stretched the pelts for drying. If the weather was suitable, some of the youngsters would take .22 rifles and go hunting chickens, as they called ptarmigan. Or they might spend an hour or so crouched over fishing holes jigging a naked hook on a length of line in hopes of snagging a lethargic trout.

If the two elder brothers were at home, they would feed their dogs, which were staked out behind the cabin. When they were away on the trail, those dogs not accompanying them—perhaps a bitch with pups, or sick or injured animals—would be fed by Else or Mary. During the winter, each dog might get as much as ten pounds of deer meat a day, but this could shrink to a pound or less when times were tough. Sometimes the dogs got nothing but bones and swatches of hide.

From November through March, Charles and Fred junior were more often absent than at home, running their traplines. During their brief stays at the post, they skinned their catches, repaired their gear, and made preparations for the next trip. The usually succinct entries in Charles's journals convey the nature of the daily round.

...Put mud on the runners of my husky sleigh. Froze it and planed it smooth ready for a trip...made a new camp stove out of a old five gallon coal oil can.... Tonight Fred made some new socks out of old sweaters. I fixed new fur pants and gloves because the girls busy cleaning fox skins.... Was hunting chickens most of the day for dog feed because not much meat in camp.... fixing a old .44.40 [rifle] the Eskimos had broke.... Made a coal [he meant "cold"] chisel by heating a trap spring in the stove. Father showed me how to put temper into it with ice water... fixed a new sleigh and drove almost to Windy Lake to find new poles for the big tent.... Fred and me built a stage high enough so dogs and wolverines can't get onto it to store what's left of our dry meat and deer fat... sewed a stove pipe piece onto one of the tents on my trap line.... We made a new table and two benches for the house...drove to Stoneman Hill to get a load of deer meat from a cache. In the afternoon brought home a load of firewood across Simmons Lake....

Evenings at Windy Post were generally easy-going. A roast of venison might be filling the cabin with a mouth-watering aroma, or perhaps Mary would be baking bread, or pies made with dried fruit or cranberries scratched from under the snow of a nearby bog. Sometimes the younger children made candy, though sugar was too scarce a commodity to be squandered.

Light came from two coal-oil lamps aided by candles or by dish-lamps burning caribou tallow. There was enough light to read by, although apart from a pile of tattered magazines, some of which dated back ten or fifteen years, there was not much reading matter.

Backing himself into a corner, Charles would carefully, almost surreptitiously, make his diary entries while the others played checkers, whist, or backgammon. Fred senior would usually be hunched over the battery radio "inherited" from the HBC. On a good clear night when the aurora was swishing its multicolored banners across the polar sky, the radio could receive as many as thirty stations from as far away as Europe, South America, even Australia.

The radio was Fred senior's greatest joy—and greatest trial. A primitive wind generator on the cabin roof charged the three acid-filled glass batteries which powered the set—*if* the wind had blown sufficiently hard and long during the preceding few days, and *if* the acid balance in the batteries was correct.

When the radio worked, Fred would spend long hours listening avidly to the war news. A German victory would delight him, whereas a Nazi defeat, especially one at the hands of the Russians, would pitch him into a state of furious despondency that might last for days or even weeks.

His children liked listening to music but were seldom allowed to do so for fear of draining the batteries. War took precedence over music.

"We heard some of what was happening," Charles recalled, "though it never meant much to us. Strange places and strange people. We never had no maps, so what they were doing away off there never made much sense. About the only time the war seemed real was a couple of times a year a plane might fly over, high up, then we used to bet each other whose army it belonged to."

If Charles and his siblings had difficulty understanding what the war was all about, the Ihalmiut were completely baffled by it. Charles remembered:

"I tried telling Pommela about it one time. He was interested about the guns, but the idea people were using them to kill each other instead of for hunting meat was hard for him to get.

"'Those white people kill lots of other people?' he asked me.

"'Yes,' I told him. 'Hundreds and hundreds.' He thought about that, then he wanted to know what they did with the ones they killed.

"'They eat 'em?' he asked, giving me a sour look. 'Or feed 'em to their dogs?'

"When I told him they never did nothing with the dead people except bury them, he was disgusted.

"'Wasting bullets is bad!' he says. I think he thought I was making the whole thing up. I guess it didn't seem real to him.

"It sure was real for Father though. More than anything around here. In the winter of 1943 one night the battery jars froze and bust. Then there was no more radio for about eight months, and he couldn't tell who was winning the war 'til him and me made our summer trip down to Brochet for next year's outfit and brought back some of them big dry cell batteries. Father could hardly live without that radio."

The family was not totally cut off from human contact. Two or three times a month during the winter, Ihalmiut hunters brought furs to be traded for ammunition, tea, and tobacco, which, by the time December ended, would be about all Fred had left to offer in exchange. He did not allow Eskimo visitors into the house, but dealt with them in an unheated trading cabin. When, on rare occasions, a Chipewyan hunter appeared, he might be invited into the house for a mug of tea. If a Metis trapper such as Joe Highway or Alphonse Cook arrived from Brochet, he would be welcomed into the Schweder home to be treated by Fred almost, though never fully, as an equal.

After Rose's death, Mary did her best to be a mother to the younger children. Else was more inclined to pattern her life on that of her elder brothers. Fred senior continued to play the heavy-handed paterfamilias, exercising his authority with severity, demanding rigid obedience and strict adherence to his beliefs and prejudices. None of his children dared test his will directly, though Charles was a secret backslider.

Even during his earliest years at Windy Post, he had tended to absent himself from home a good part of the time. After the death of his mother, which he took very hard, his absences became more prolonged. Not only had he become a hunter and trapper par excellence, he had also become a full-fledged "countryman" skilled at making his way over the barrenlands or through the forests. He was, in fact, leading a double life, doing his level best to conceal his real feelings toward and his close relationships with the Ihalmiut from his father and his siblings.

Angleyalik and Itkuk had had several children, but some had died, leaving them in 1942 with two sons—nineteen-year-old Engola and nine-year-old Anoteelik—together with Pama, their thirteen-year-old daughter, who was intended to become Charles's wife.

During the early summer of 1942 a girl child was born in Angleyalik's tent at the Little Lakes. She was called Kunee, which means something like River Sprite. I was never able to discover whether Kunee's mother was Itkuk or Pama. The baby's maternity was clouded, but then so was her paternity. Her father may have been Angleyalik, but could just as well have been Charles Schweder. This is a crucial matter, but readers will nevertheless have to come to their own conclusions about it. I myself cannot do so, nor am I sure that even Charles was ever certain of the truth.

By 1944 Charles and Fred were trapping so many foxes that, had the market been good, the family might have become well-to-do. But due to the war, furs were worth only a pittance, barely enough, in fact, to pay for the supplies that had to be brought from distant Brochet or Duck Lake. However, Fred senior was convinced that after the war the fur business would prosper again, and he intended to take advantage of the opportunity when it came. Not content with the fur production of his two eldest sons, he apprenticed his two daughters to the trade. Mary resisted, but Else acquiesced and did well at it. By 1944 she had her own team and was running a trapline along the valley of the Windy River. On occasion she even accompanied Charles or Fred on the extensive lines they had established all the way to the Kazan River and beyond.

In mid-March of 1946 she and Fred rendezvoused with Charles at a camp their older brother had built by the Kazan. Next day the three teams set off for home together.

Charles's team led the way, with Else bringing up the rear. When they were some thirty miles from Windy Post, a south wind sprang up and thick snow began to fall. Charles brought his sled to a halt and let the other teams close up.

"Looked like there was a pretty bad storm coming," he remembered, "but we was almost home so I figured we would get there before it got too bad. We tied Else's lead dog to the back of Fred's sled so she wouldn't get lost, then I drove ahead to find the trail. Turned out was the worst thing we could've done. Should've camped right there and waited it out, but we was real anxious to get home."

Within half an hour, the storm had erupted into a full-scale blizzard. Ground drift sweeping unchecked across the plain soon induced a whiteout in which the travelers lost sight of one another. When the trace between Else's lead dog and the second dog in her team parted, Fred, whose lead dog was following close on the tail of Charles's team, did not notice anything had gone amiss.

Bundled up on her sled with her back to the gale, Else also

failed to realize what had happened. Her team, composed of young and inexperienced animals, was now without a leader. The young dogs soon lost the trail.

Soon thereafter the furious wind began veering into the southeast. Charles sensed the change and kept his dogs headed for home. Fred's team followed close behind, but Else's leaderless dogs swung away into the teeth of the gale on a path that curved to the east.

Night had fallen before Charles and Fred stumbled into Windy Post. Only then did they realize that their sister was no longer with them.

"I told them at the cabin Fred and me was going back out and start looking, but Father wouldn't let us. Said we'd get lost in the blizzard. Said we had to wait 'til the storm blew over. He said Else would lay up somewhere 'til the worst was over, then she'd either find her way home or we'd find her."

Else did not lie up because at first she did not realize she was lost. Hours passed before her dogs, blinded by drifting snow and weary to the bone, brought the sled to a halt. When they failed to respond to Else's shouts, she stumbled forward, found the broken trace, and realized what had happened. She was alone—desperately alone in a darkling, roaring wilderness with no idea in which direction safety might lie.

She took the only steps she could to save herself. She turned the sled on its side, banked it with snow to make a windbreak, then burrowed into the drift which soon formed in its lee.

At dawn she emerged and prodded her dogs out of the caverns in the drifts where they had sheltered. The blizzard had ended, but the pallid sky flickering with northern lights presaged the onset of bitter cold sweeping in from the north. She fed the dogs most of the small amount of deer meat remaining on her sled, saving some fragments for herself, which she thawed under her parka before eating, there being no fuel with which to make a fire.

It was time to travel, but she could not decide which way to go. Prominent landmarks are rare enough on the barrens at any season, and in mid-winter land and water blend into anonymity beneath the snow. Else decided to travel south, hoping to gain the shelter of the forest's edge, where she might perhaps find a trapper's tilt.

Since the dogs could not be driven without a leader, she became their leader. After two days, the famished dogs began to fail and, after four, Else cut them loose to seek their own salvation. None was ever seen again.

Abandoning the sled, Else struggled on, carrying nothing but her sleeping robe. She was now suffering not only from starvation and raging thirst, but also—as a result of a spell of clear and warmer weather which had probably saved her from freezing to death—from the piercing agony of snow blindness.

On the eighth day of her travail, she collapsed on the ice of Nueltin Lake Narrows—and there she lay while snow devils swirled about her, building the drifts which would entomb her.

It was there that trapper Ragnor Jonsson, on a trip to his northernmost tilt, came upon her. Or rather his dogs did, nosing at her unconscious and almost invisible form beneath the drifting snow.

Jonsson put her on his toboggan and made for the nearest island. Here he built a fire, wrapped the girl in her robe and his, and placed her close to the heat. At first he gave her only hot tea, measured out by the spoonful. Later he pitched a tent in which Else dozed in and out of consciousness while the trapper nursed her back into the living world on a diet of pancakes and tea.

Long afterwards Else remembered, "Ragnor could maybe have used some cooking lessons, but he sure brought me back to life."

He also brought her back to Windy Post. There she found both her older brothers disabled by snow blindness after having spent almost two weeks scouring the barrengrounds in an increasingly despairing search for her.

"That finished Father at Windy," Charles recalled. "When we went south to Brochet that summer, he made up his mind him and the girls and little Norman would stay down there. But Fred and me and Mike wanted to come back to Windy...so that's just what we done."

CHAPTER THREE

BROTHERS

ONE LATE SUMMER DAY IN 1946 A DEEP-LADEN freighter canoe propelled by an antiquated outboard churned upstream through the rapids at the mouth of Windy River and ran ashore in front of Windy Post.

The crew, consisting of Charles, now twenty-one; fifteen-year-old Fred junior; and eight-year-old Mike, had spent two laborious weeks bringing their cargo north from Reindeer Lake, where their father, sisters, and younger brother would remain through the ensuing winter.

Although Charles carried his father's trading license folded between the pages of his notebook, it had become largely symbolic. The supplies the brothers had brought with them would barely suffice for their own needs during the long months ahead. They would have precious little to trade to the Eskimos, but this was of no great monetary significance since the Ihalmiut had dwindled to fewer than fifty people.

If the Ihalmiut were no longer of much economic value to the Schweders, the Schweders remained of paramount importance to the Ihalmiut. Less than a week after the brothers returned to Windy Post, three Eskimo men appeared there, having walked the eighty-odd miles from their camps close to the Kazan. They brought black news.

During the past summer the Ihalmiut had been ravaged by a

dreadful illness (probably diphtheria) which had killed fifteen of them and left many of the remainder badly weakened. To make matters worse, deer herds which normally summered along the upper Kazan had this year gone much farther north and out of reach. Fish were to be had, but northern freshwater fish do not make for a sustaining diet, especially for people recuperating from severe illness.

A fatal sickness, perhaps distemper, had also afflicted the dogs, those vital adjuncts to the maintenance of human life on the barrengrounds. Many dogs had died, including some which the Schweders had left to summer in the care of the Ihalmiut.

For Charles the worst news was that the epidemic had killed Angleyalik and Engola, who had been closer to him in some ways than his own father and brothers. The widowed Itkuk and her children Pama, Anoteelik, and Kunee had taken refuge with the family of Hekwaw, a good old man, but one who was hard put to provide for himself; his wife, Kala; and his grandson Belikari.

Seated cross-legged on the floor of the post that night, the visitors recounted what had happened, but did not dwell upon it. *Ayorama*. It can't be helped, they said, and turned the talk to problems of the moment.

Tuktu—the deer—would soon be flooding through their country in the great autumnal trek southward to the shelter of the forests where they would spend the winter months. It was imperative that the Ihalmiut kill enough animals during this migration to provide meat, fat, and skins to carry them through the long months ahead. The people had been apprehensive that they might not be able to do this because of the shortage of ammunition. It seemed that the brothers had returned to the land in the nick of time.

Secure in the belief that all would now be well, the visitors drank gallons of black tea while laughing softly and joking with one another and with the three young whites.

Charles did not join in the jokes or the laughter.

Desolated by the disaster to his adopted family, he was filled with apprehension for Itkuk and her children. And he was dreading the moment when he would have to tell his visitors he could satisfy only a fraction of their ammunition needs.

Next morning the three men in worn deerskin clothing made ready to rejoin their families and begin the all-important hunt. They stood silently at the door while Charles doled out four cartons of .30-30 ammunition, each carton containing twenty rounds. It was all he felt he could spare, even though he knew the lives of many people were hanging in the balance.

The recipients made no complaint, perhaps because they thought this was only an advance, and that more ammunition would be forthcoming when they had fur to trade. As they walked away over a tundra already flaming in saffron and gold from the bite of the first heavy frosts, they were content.

Charles went with them, a heavy pack on his back. Nominally he was going north to reclaim his and Fred's surviving dogs, but his deeper purpose was to visit Hekwaw's camp, there to assure himself that Pama and Kunee were safe. It was also in his mind that he might bring these two back with him to Windy Post. However, he was worried as to how his brother Fred might react. Fred shared his father's dislike and distrust of "Huskies." Charles was well aware that if his brother responded badly to the presence of two Eskimos in the home cabin, the delicate equilibrium necessary for the survival of all would be at risk.

As he plodded along beside his Ihalmiut companions, Charles reluctantly concluded it would be best to wait until he had further prepared the ground before bringing Pama and Kunee south.

Hekwaw was camped a little way to the east of the Big Bend of the Kazan, his conical deerskin topay firmly anchored by a ring of boulders heavy enough to resist the worst of the coming winter gales. A pair of stone pillars standing between tent and shore raised his skin-covered kayak out of the reach of hungry dogs.

Survivors of the brothers' two teams were staked out on the foreshore. These greeted Charles's arrival with a hullabaloo that brought the tent's occupants tumbling out.

There was grizzled Hekwaw; his crippled wife, Kala; and their beaming and somewhat simple-minded grandson Belikari; together with Itkuk, Pama, Anoteelik, and little Kunee. These greeted Charles ecstatically. Kunee swarmed all over him. That night, lying on the communal sleeping ledge, he held Pama in his arms.

Because there was so much to be done at home, he stayed only a night and a day at Hekwaw's camp. Before departing he gave the old man two cartons of .30-30 shells and the women fifteen pounds of flour, ten of sugar, some tea, and some tobacco. Then he set out for home, leading eight tethered dogs. His leader, Scamp, and one other privileged bitch ranged free, though staying close to their master. Dogs and man were cheered by small parties of deer which occasionally crossed their path, for these were the precursors of la Foule. Charles shot a fat young buck to feed himself and the dogs.

As October brought nighttime temperatures down to well below freezing, the exodus of the caribou began in earnest. Not before time, as far as the brothers were concerned, for they were anxious to prepare their traplines but could not do so until the deer arrived.

Because there was not yet enough snow to permit using their heavy, Eskimo-style sleds, they hitched the dogs to individual "summer sleds," another invention borrowed from the Ihalmiut. These were miniature travois which the dogs towed behind them. Each consisted of a pair of slim, eight-foot poles supporting a small platform that could carry about forty pounds. Having loaded eight summer sleds with travel gear and essential supplies (mainly ammunition), the brothers set off to the north.

They traveled about twenty miles each day, pausing often en route to shoot caribou. Carcasses intended for use as bait were left to lie where they fell. Others were gutted, quartered, and cached under piles of rocks to provide winter food for men and dogs. In all, about two hundred deer would be required.

This slaughter had to be completed before the first winter blizzards came rampaging across the barrens, sweeping the last of la Foule down into the forests. Time was short, so on this occasion Charles did not visit any of the Ihalmiut. Although well aware that they had precious little ammunition, Charles was not greatly concerned, for he expected them to obtain at least some of the meat they needed by spearing deer from kayaks at lake and river crossings.

By mid-November enough snow had fallen to permit sled travel, and it was time for trappers to make their sets. Two teams pulled away from Windy Post: Charles's with six dogs and Fred's with five, both pulling heavily laden sleds.

Fred's trapline ran the full eighty miles from Windy Post to Big Bend on the Kazan River. Charles's main line extended another eighty miles north and west from Big Bend to within sight of Little Dubawnt Lake (Kamilikuak, on current maps). Travel camps crouched at intervals of fifteen or twenty miles along the way. Most of these were simple canvas shelters just large enough to accommodate one person. Banked with snow, each had a mattress of twigs and moss and a small tin stove, and was stored with a few pounds of flour and some tea. However, at Big Bend Charles had built a proper cabin, ten feet square and five feet high, constructed of slender logs from the few tiny spruce copses to be found in protected nooks and crannies of the barrengrounds. This was Kazan Camp.

Fred and Mike slowly worked their way northward, digging out bait carcasses from beneath the drifts and making sets, each consisting of two to four steel traps concealed under the surrounding snow. Charles drove straight on to Big Bend to begin making sets along his own line, from which he would return to Kazan Camp to rendezvous with his brothers so that all three could travel home together.

Before returning to Big Bend, Charles visited Hekwaw's camp on the bank of the Kazan. Here he learned that, because of the early freeze-up, the kayak hunt had been an almost total failure. Forced to depend upon his .30-30 alone, Hekwaw had been able to kill only two dozen deer before exhausting his supply of ammunition. Some of these animals had already been consumed. Not nearly enough remained *en cache* to feed eight people, let alone the dogs, until the herds returned in spring.

Charles was appalled. Realization of the magnitude of the threat hanging over the Ihalmiut seems to have produced a kind of panic. He now gave all his remaining ammunition and food to the people at Hekwaw's camp—then fled the place.

Racing to the rendezvous at Kazan Camp, he found Fred and Mike preparing to enjoy a well-earned rest, but within the hour Charles had them on the road. He led the way back to Windy Post as if the hounds of hell were on his heels.

During the first weeks of December, Charles kept himself and his brothers busy dealing with their own needs. A large quantity of firewood had to be found, cut, and hauled back to the post, sometimes from fifteen or twenty miles away. Frozen deer carcasses had to be fetched from caches far out on the barrens and stockpiled near the post. Gaps between the cabin's logs had to be re-caulked with moss and the roof recovered with deer hides. Finally the running gear—harness, trail equipment, clothing, and weapons—had to be repaired and readied for the hard usage that lay ahead. And this year everything had to be done without the help of Mary, Else, or Fred Schweder senior.

Temperatures plunged to twenty, thirty, even forty below zero. The nights grew ever longer—the days shorter. A week before Christmas, Charles finally nerved himself to ask his brothers if they would consent to his bringing Hekwaw's family to live at Windy Post until the deer returned.

Mike, who seldom objected to anything his brothers thought or said, was agreeable. Fred offered no immediate reply. Charles pressed his case by pointing out that having a resident Eskimo family would ensure things would be looked after at home while the brothers were absent on the traplines. Eskimos could cut and haul wood, skin foxes and stretch the pelts, even fish through the ice for dog feed if need be.

Finally Fred responded. His answer was a resolute rejection. As Charles recalled it: "He said if one bunch of Huskies come and lived off of us pretty soon we'd have them all hanging around. Father wouldn't have put up with it and he wouldn't either."

Rather than argue the point, Charles quietly decided that when he returned from his next trip north, he would bring Pama and Kunee home with him anyway. His decision was reinforced a few days before Christmas when a man called Katelo, head of a family at the Little Lakes, stumbled wearily and hungrily into Windy Post with the news that the dogs were already dying of starvation. That night Charles wrote in his journal:

Some of the Eskimos have no meat at all and are eating deer skins...

Christmas would be a lean time for the Ihalmiut, but at Windy Post every effort was made to celebrate the festival appropriately.

I made pies, also made a jelly and a custard pudding, about half-gallon of each. Lit about 20 candles for Christmas at midnight. I put on stuffed chickens [ptarmigan] to roast for dinner tomorrow. Heard lots of Christmas songs over the radio tonight.... We sure had a good Christmas dinner, stuffed chickens, jelly pudding, custard pudding, 1 coconut custard pie and 2 dried apple pies and a big pot full of doughnuts and plenty of good bread.

On the morning of December 29 the fire in the cabin stove was allowed to burn out. As the last wraith of smoke trailed away from the rusty chimney pipe, the brothers set out to make the rounds of their traplines. The two teams remained in company for only the first few miles, then, urged on by anxiety for Pama and Kunee, Charles pulled away. Pausing just long enough to feed his dogs and brew a quick pot of tea, he reached Big Bend in the dark early morning of December 30. An hour later his weary

dogs dragged the sled up off the river ice at Hekwaw's camp...
only to find it deserted.

Not only had the big topay vanished but so had almost every
other indication of human occupancy except the skeleton of an
abandoned kayak from which starving dogs had stripped away
every vestige of skin covering.

Nothing remained to suggest where the people might have
gone, or in which direction they had traveled. There was no way
Charles could know that, when the camp had run out of food
and the dogs were already dead of starvation, Hekwaw had
determined to lead his little band to Dimma Lake, twenty miles
northward along the Kazan. During Hekwaw's younger days, this
lake had been a famous fishing place and not infrequently the
salvation of hungry folk. Hekwaw hoped it would prove to be
such again.

Hekwaw's little band had disappeared into such an immensity
of space that a random search would have been virtually hopeless. Charles decided he would first check his trapline then visit
the Ihalmiut at the Little Lakes hoping they might have news of
Hekwaw's whereabouts.

Returning to Kazan Camp, he fed his dogs chunks of frozen
meat then thawed a slab for himself. He slept only briefly. In mid-
afternoon he harnessed his team and drove westward into frigid
darkness. His leader, a calico-colored bitch called Scamp, found
her way unerringly from one bait carcass to the next. By the time
the sled reached the first travel shelter, it was carrying the rigid
corpses of three white foxes and a wolverine.

Charles spent New Year's night at his second shelter. It had
been ripped open by a wolf or wolverine and was full of drifted
snow. He had no thermometer, but guessed the temperature at
around forty below zero. He wrote in his diary:

*Very cold. Started early and arrive at 3rd camp at sundown. Got only one
white fox and lost four. Some was eaten up and some just gone, most likely
eat by the wolverine.*

The fate of a trapped fox was grim. On occasion one might free itself by chewing off its own foot. Others were killed and eaten by wolves or wolverines. The majority froze to death, but died excruciatingly slowly because of the superb insulating qualities of their long and silky fur.

It took Charles six days to complete the circuit of his line. Arriving back at Kazan Camp with the corpses of twenty-four foxes and a wolverine, he found Fred and Mike awaiting him impatiently. They had caught seven white foxes, but a rabid red had attacked their team and bitten two of Fred's dogs before it could be killed. Fear of rabies had impelled Fred to shoot both bitten dogs. The same fear made him exceedingly anxious to regain the relative security of Windy Post.

Fred's apprehension was shared by Charles, who well knew what the fate of a traveler on the winter barrens was likely to be if deprived of his dogs. And Charles had lost one of his own the previous day to some unidentified ailment which he now suspected might have been rabies.

The brothers' urgent desire to head south was frustrated by a fierce blizzard which pinned them inside the tiny cabin for two long days and nights. By the time they were able to emerge, another of Charles's dogs was dead. His plan to visit the Little Lakes camps in hopes of locating Hekwaw was wiped from his mind.

With only four dogs remaining in each team to haul thirty-one frozen foxes and a wolverine, progress south was slow. Only Mike could ride. The other two trudged along on foot.

Near the midway mark, they overtook a shambling figure of a man accompanied by two skeletal dogs. This was Pommela, an elderly but powerful shaman resembling a much-weathered gargoyle, who was usually capable of intimidating even Charles. On this occasion there was nothing intimidating about him. He explained that three destitute families, including his own, were walking toward Windy Post, hoping the *kablunait* would be able to supply them with food. Being stronger than the rest, Pommela had pushed on ahead.

When Charles asked for news of Hekwaw's whereabouts, Pommela at first claimed ignorance. Then he suggested that Hekwaw and his people might have gone to the HBC outpost of Padlei, 150 miles to the east. Certain that such a journey would have been beyond their strength, Charles concluded Pommela was simply trying to discourage him from spending time and food searching for the missing people—food that could be put to better use keeping Pommela and his clan alive.

If this is what the shaman had in mind, he was unwittingly abetted by Fred, who now declared that if Charles set off in search of Hekwaw's people he would not remain at Windy Post to be swamped by starving Huskies, but would take Mike and undertake the long sled journey south to Reindeer Lake to rejoin their father.

Charles made no response. The brothers reached the post late on the following day, and that night Charles wrote:

Sure wish someone would come up from Brochet like Joe Highway. He could take a message out. Haven't had any news of any kind from anywhere for six months now. We don't have much grub left. Maybe enough to the end of January. We have less meat here than we thought so the Eskimos won't be much better off than at their own camps.

On January 18 eleven emaciated men, women, and children from the Little Lakes straggled in to Windy Post. Not only did their arrival place a heavy strain on the scanty remaining food stocks, it foreshadowed the probable arrival of still more hungry refugees. And those remaining behind at the starvation camps would be driven by primal need to search out and consume the brothers' more distant meat caches, including even bait carcasses, without which trapping would be at an end.

Charles was faced with a terrible dilemma. Should he and his brothers remain at Windy Post and take their chances, or should they flee the country? If they fled, Charles would be able to warn the authorities that disaster was about to overwhelm the Ihalmiut. There would be a cost. To flee would mean abandoning the traplines from which the Schweder family derived most of its livelihood. It would also mean deserting Pama and Kunee.

On January 20 Charles wrote:

Almost finished skinning and stretching our foxes. Then we have to do something. Maybe Fred could go to Duck Lake for a load of grub. Or we could all go to Brochet. Somebody got to tell them outside the Eskimos are starving.

That night he reached a decision. In the morning, he instructed Fred and Mike to prepare for a trip to Duck Lake, a small HBC outpost 160 miles to the southeast. Duck Lake was equipped with a two-way radio by means of which Fred would be able to alert the RCMP in Churchill to the perilous situation of the Ihalmiut. That done, Fred could trade pelts for a sled-load of food and head back for Windy. If all went well, he and Mike would be home in less than three weeks. During their absence, Charles said, he would attempt to run *both* traplines and also collect meat from distant caches to feed the hungry Ihalmiut gathering around the post.

What Charles did not tell anyone was that when he went north, he intended first to find Hekwaw's camp.

A January journey from Windy to Duck Lake would be no light undertaking for the sixteen-year-old and the nine-year-old. The cold would be so intense as to make the lake ice contract until it cracked and boomed like the drums of doom. Even smoothly mudded sled runners would no longer slide easily but would drag as if running over sand. And there would be only four lean and hungry dogs to do the hauling.

There was also the problem of finding the way. Although Fred had made the trip once before accompanying Charles, this time he would be traveling without a guide, without a map, without even a compass. The chances of getting lost during a spell of bad weather (or even during good weather) in such a mighty sweep of country devoid of signposts, identifiable landmarks, inhabitants, roads, or tracks were fearfully high—as Else's brush with death had made abundantly clear.

Nevertheless, on January 22 Fred and Mike set out for Duck Lake. Charles left the cabin on the twenty-sixth to run both traplines and to search for Hekwaw's camp. If he found it, he intended to bring its occupants back to Windy Post.

I hope I make a quick trip. I could not make it in less than 12 days if there's no storm because the trapline is 140 miles long.

Charles was back at Windy Post much sooner than he had expected. The meat caches he had counted on to feed himself and his dogs had all been emptied. Some had been robbed by wolves or wolverines—but most by human beings, people who would not have taken food from another's cache had they not been in extremity.

Only two days after setting out, before even reaching the Kazan, Charles had to turn his team around.

I turned back because no grub of any kind but tea. I will go south down Nueltin Lake day after tomorrow hope to meet Fred. The Eskimo Angakouk [one of those currently camped at Windy Post] *will go with me.*

Unable now either to tend the traplines or to search for Hekwaw's camp, and with very little food remaining at Windy Post, Charles had little choice but to go south. If he was lucky enough to meet Fred and Mike coming from Duck Lake with fresh supplies, the three could then return to Windy Post together.

Charles and Angakouk left Windy Post on the last day of January, watched by a dozen haggard and silent Ihalmiut whose best hopes for survival were riding with the travelers. Although Charles's four dogs were emaciated, they were in far better shape than the two bone-bags hauling the half-sled Angakouk had contrived by taking an axe to his long sled. The going was good—mostly over glare ice—but still it took the emaciated teams two full days to drag the sleds to Ragnor Jonsson's cabin at the south end of Nueltin—only to find it cold and empty. A note on a table told them Jonsson had himself run out of meat and so had gone to Brochet to wait until the deer came north again. Glumly they lit a fire in the old iron stove and spent a warm, but hungry night.

They were awakened next morning by the snarling racket of excited dogs.

Fred and Mick arrived from Duck Lake with plenty of grub. Sure was happy to see them.

Luck had been with both parties. After losing their way while still outward-bound forty or fifty miles west of Duck Lake, Fred and Mike had come upon the faint track of a Chipewyan toboggan and had managed to follow it to the post, where the manager agreed to send a message to Churchill requesting help for the Ihalmiut. Fred traded pelts for a load of flour, sugar, lard, tea, and dried deer meat, but there was disagreement between him and the manager over the value of his furs, and he left the post seething with the silent rage which sometimes afflicted him, without awaiting a reply from Churchill.

He and Mike had intended to spend a day or two looking for deer at the south end of Nueltin Lake before heading north. Instead of deer they had found Charles and Angakouk.

The four now headed for home. A blinding snowstorm caught them on the ice of that great lake and the three teams soon became separated.

I arrived home at sundown. Fred and Mick half an hour before I did. Angakouk arrived in the dark. Each of us got lost coming up Windy Bay. The cabin was almost covered up with snow when I got there.

Fred's team had been able to haul only two hundred pounds of food from Duck Lake. This was not enough to sustain the brothers and the dependent Ihalmiut (whose numbers had been increased by the arrival of yet another family) for many days. And it would do nothing for those still in their home camps. However, Charles believed a relief plane would soon appear. It might even have enough fuel aboard to enable it to fly on to the Little Lakes and search for Hekwaw's camp.

Such were Charles's hopes, but when a week of good flying weather slipped by without sight or sound of any plane, hope faded. Concluding either that Fred's message had never reached Churchill or had been ignored, he felt he no longer had any choice but to undertake the long journey to Brochet to seek help.

He decided to take Pommela with him.

February 8th, Saturday. No wind. Must be forty below. Start out late. My sled and Pommela loaded with [the pelts of] 200 foxes, 2 minks and 20 weasels. I and Pommela can't take any more so we have to leave the wolfs and wolverines behind....

On reaching the south end of Nueltin, the travelers exchanged their long sleds for toboggans that Charles had cached there the previous year. Sleds were ideal for traveling over the open barrengrounds, but toboggans were better in the deep snow of the forests.

From Nueltin the route followed the frozen course of Kasmere's River west to the height of land, then south by way of the Cochrane River to Reindeer Lake. The journey was made on very short rations and was slowed by a series of winter gales. The land was appallingly empty: no human beings; no caribou; nothing moving except for an occasional raven, a black mote high in an empty sky.

February 12th. Going very tough. The hardest I ever seen on any trip. Sure wish to see some deer but so far none. Did not travel far today because we got lost....

February 15th. South wind and snow. We are out of meat and flour and only grub left is a little salt and tea. We been on the road 8 days so far. Pommela's dogs about played out. I wonder if he will get to Brochet with them. Haven't seen a soul so far. Looks like no one traveling at all but us.

Pressing grimly on, they finally reached Brochet's scattering of log cabins. Although any of the inhabitants, Cree, Chipewyan, or Metis, would have welcomed the exhausted travelers with food and warmth, Charles chose not to halt his dogs until he reached the Hudson's Bay Company store. It was fortunate he did so. The Company clerk, one-legged Frank Henderson, came out of the building to warn the newcomers that an epidemic was sweeping the country and had already killed several natives in the village.

Charles took the warning to heart. He and Pommela pushed on, driving a further twenty miles across the ice of Reindeer Lake to a fish camp owned by a merchant in The Pas, but managed by Fred Schweder Senior.

The camp consisted of a log bunkhouse, a cookhouse, and a shack for the "boss." Charles turned his cargo of furs over to his father and briefly told his story, after which he and Pommela stumbled into the bunkhouse to sleep for a day and night.

While Charles slept, Fred Schweder drove into Brochet, where he and the HBC post manager between them drafted a radio message to the authorities in The Pas warning of famine in the Kazan country and asking for immediate help.

The fish camp employed five men to work long nets set under as much as four feet of ice to catch lake trout and whitefish. Freezing quickly in the frigid air, the captured fish were stacked like cordwood to await transport on a tractor-drawn train of sleighs over an iceroad to the railhead at The Pas.

Charles and Pommela shared the fishermen's spartan quarters for five days while they and the dogs recuperated. On the fifth day, a red Norseman on skis roared overhead, circled, and landed. From it descended Dr. Robert Yule, a functionary of the federal Department of Health and Welfare sent to investigate the radio message.

After interviewing Charles, he reported to his superiors that "the Kazan people appear to be in need of assistance," and requested permission to send a relief flight to them. But he added a caution:

These people are pagans. The only God they know is this young chap Charles Schweder.... I do not consider it advisable to supply these Eskimos with food regularly as it would result in a tendency for them to sit around and wait for handouts.

A relief flight was authorized to be flown by Tom Lamb, owner and chief pilot of Lamb Airways, based at The Pas. The plane would be the same red Norseman that had brought Dr. Yule to the fish camp.

Charles volunteered to act as guide, but was told the plane's departure might be delayed a few days and that he should go on ahead with his sled-load of supplies. If a guide was needed, Fred Schweder Senior would be available. Charles was also told to remain close to Windy Post after his arrival there, in case he was needed to help Tom Lamb locate the more distant Eskimo camps.

Charles and Pommela set off on their journey home, confident that the worst was over and that the Ihalmiut would soon receive the help they desperately required.

CHAPTER   FOUR

A SPRING TO REMEMBER

ON FEBRUARY 24 CHARLES AND POMMELA DROVE to Brochet, remaining there just long enough to load their toboggans with as much food as the dogs could haul. Brochet was no place to linger, for it was now in the grip of a devastating epidemic, which, although never officially diagnosed, was probably influenza. Charles noted in his journal: *Lots of people dying around here from sickness.* A tractor belonging to the Roman Catholic mission was being used to dig mass graves.

The two men were in good spirits as they drove north up the ice highway provided by the frozen Cochrane. The weather was cold, but windless and brilliantly clear. The toboggans were piled high with supplies, and more would soon be arriving at Windy by air. Soon, too, la Foule would come surging up out of the taiga, bringing a renewal of life to the barrengrounds.

With well-fed dogs the travelers made good time, camping late each evening to cook bannock soaked in bacon fat and eaten with jam or honey, while the dogs wolfed down frozen fish brought from the fish camp.

Several Chipewyan toboggans were seen in the distance at Misty Lake. Pommela thought their owners might have deer meat to spare and suggested going to meet them; however, Charles feared they might be carrying the disease so the two men steered clear.

Near Fort Hall Lake they encountered trapper Joe Highway and one of his sons. Opportunities for social intercourse being so rare, Joe elected to accompany Charles and Pommela as far as Nueltin Lake. Joe was not a cheerful traveling companion. Having gloomily confirmed that a lethal epidemic was raging throughout the country, he predicted that spring would be very late and in consequence the deer migration would be delayed.

There were no signs of caribou beyond Kasmere Lake. Taking this as confirmation of his fears, Joe Highway and his son turned back.

"You going to be pretty hungry up there before you see them deer," was his farewell prediction.

At the south end of Nueltin Charles and Pommela exchanged their toboggans for sleds and pushed on. They made fast time on the last lap of their journey, arriving at Windy Post on March 7.

Got home at two oclock in the morning. Fred had arrived from the north two days ago. He caught 2 wolfs and 18 white foxes…he shot nine deer.

However, Fred had seen none of the Ihalmiut at the outcamps, nor had he made any attempt to contact them. He and Mike had set out with only enough dog feed for two or three days. On the third day they had met a small group of caribou bucks who, impelled by some extraordinary urgency, had come north far in advance of their fellows. Fred killed most of them. He loaded his sled with meat and cached the balance, taking every precaution to ensure it would not be found by scavengers, human or otherwise. Now well provisioned, he and Mike had been able to follow their line almost to the Kazan and to bring home a load of meat as well as a load of frozen foxes.

Charles had been sure the Norseman would have preceded him to Windy Post, but it had not done so. Nor, as the days following his return slipped by, did the plane appear. He was in a mounting state of uncertainty as to what he should do. If he trekked north with food for the people at the Little Lakes and the plane arrived during his absence, who would guide it to the distant camps? None of the Ihalmiut at Windy had ever flown before, and they were not likely to be of much use as aerial guides. And Fred did not know the whereabouts of most of the camps.

March 9th. Sunday. North wind cloudy and snow. I haul wood. Fred go to haul some meat and find one of two bucks he brought back eaten by Eskimos...

March 11th. I haul the last of our meat... could not make up my mind to go north or not.

March 12th. Don't know what to do, to go north or to stay at home.

March 13th. Fred, Mick and I with a Eskimo went up to Simmons Lake to try to fish.

March 14th. Start to fix the net and heard a plane. I start for home right away with the best dogs. Just got there in time before they start off again. It was father and doctor. They only stay long enough to say they be back tomorrow. They brought some grub for the Eskimos but left it at Putahow River [at the south end of Nueltin] yesterday.

Exactly what had happened remains unclear. According to Dr. Yule's report, he chartered Lamb's Norseman to fly a load of food to the Kazan River Eskimos on March 2. Eleven days later the plane, guided by Fred Schweder Senior, flew, *not to the Kazan* or even to Windy Post but to the mouth of the Putahow River 140 air miles south of the Kazan camps. There the supplies were unloaded on a frozen beach and the Norseman returned to Brochet. Next morning it once more headed north carrying Lamb, Yule, and Schweder, a thirty-pound canister of powdered milk, and three forty-five-gallon drums of aviation fuel. Passing over Putahow, it flew on to land at Windy Post, remaining just long enough to unload the milk and gas and to tell Charles the plane would return the following day after picking up the relief supplies left at Putahow.

"Tomorrow you'll guide us to the Eskimo camps," Dr. Yule instructed Charles.

Although flying weather remained good, the plane did not

return next day. Nor the day after...nor the day after that. On March 16 Charles wrote:

I sure hope the plane will come tomorrow as we have no more dog feed.... The dogs will starve most likely and so will the Eskimos unless the plane will come soon.

By March 20 he would wait no longer. Leaving Fred and Mike to deal with the Norseman if it should appear, he set out for the Kazan carrying as much of the brothers' own scanty supply of flour, oatmeal, and lard as his dogs could haul. As Fred made clear, this was food the brothers could ill afford to part with. "What'll happen when the Huskies here eat everything we got?" Fred asked. "Mick might starve."

Charles had no reply.

He had gone about fifteen miles on his way when he heard the distant whine of an aircraft engine. Enormously relieved, he turned the dogs and drove full tilt for home expecting to find the Norseman parked on the river ice.

It was not there.

The Eskimos living near the post had also heard a plane, but it had passed high overhead—perhaps an American military aircraft engaged on some inscrutable mission.

Grimly, Charles headed north again. A cutting wind and driven snow made progress painfully slow. It was not until nearly midnight of the second day's travel that he reached Kazan Camp. Here he fed his dogs a little dry oatmeal in lieu of meat before crawling under his sleeping robes.

It was savagely cold the next morning as he hitched up his dogs and went looking for the camps. By late afternoon he had still found no sign of human life, when Scamp suddenly halted the team beside a faint set of footprints. Charles urged her to follow them and a short time later came in sight of a snow-banked caribou-skin tent.

Inside he found Katelo with his wife, Oquinuk, and their son and daughter—four living skeletons huddled on the sleeping ledge under their sole remaining deerskin robe. They had eaten the other robes. Oquinuk was barely conscious. Katelo, however, was able to tell Charles where to find Hekwaw's camp.

Eskimos very hungry. Katelo say three die in Hekwaw's camp so I only stay at Katelos long enough to give them grub and make tea then went on to another camp but could not find it in the dark so camped out for the night.

March 25th. Found the Eskimo camp gave them some grub then went on to last camp [Hekwaw's] *where I found all the women died. The others were living on a deer skeleton they killed last summer which is nothing but bones and maggots....*

Itkuk was dead. So was Hekwaw's wife, Kala, and their grandson Belikari. And so was Pama.

Kunee and Anoteelik were alive, but reduced to grotesque travesties of children with sunken eyes and arms and legs like sticks.

Hekwaw had somehow managed to keep everyone alive through the terrible January and February on occasional fish jigged through a hole in the ice of Dimma Lake. When the fish disappeared, he had led his little clan back to their old camp by the Kazan...and there the dying had begun.

Charles's journal contains no details of what he found in Hekwaw's camp. When he could be induced to speak about it at all, he was almost as reticent as his journal. He did add that the survivors were so hungry they choked down chunks of frozen flour before he could thaw it out, let alone cook it for them. But as to what they might have thought and felt—and as to what *he* thought and felt—there is no record.

Loading the survivors on his sled he drove back to Kazan Camp, pausing on the way to lend Katelo two dogs so the Inuk could make his way to the other camps, give survivors something to eat, and tell them to gather at Kazan Camp, where Charles would distribute food.

By March 28 twenty-six of the Ihalmiut had gathered there. They came on foot, for all their dogs were dead. They patched together remnants of deer skins to make themselves shelters which they banked with snow. Little fires were lit with handfuls of twigs gathered by the strongest amongst them. Then they cooked a kind of soup made with rolled oats or flour, lard, and water. They ate sparingly of this, for to have done otherwise would have brought the excruciating stomach pains which afflict starving people when they first eat again.

Soon Charles's stock of food had shrunk to only a few pounds. Hoping that some of the deer meat he had cached along his trapline in the autumn might have escaped scavengers, he made a fast trip toward Little Dubawnt, but found barely meat enough to keep his dogs going for another few days, and very little extra with which the Ihalmiut could strengthen their gruel.

Although he may no longer have believed it himself, Charles told the people that *tingmeaktuk*—a plane—was on its way, bringing food enough to sustain them until the deer returned. So every day thereafter, and all day, twenty-six human beings strained their hearing for the distant drone that would mean salvation.

They heard only the keening of the wind.

On March 30 Charles visited the meager little shelters surrounding the Kazan cabin. At each he left a pint of flour or oatmeal and instructed the huddled inhabitants to stay where they were (most could not have done otherwise) while he returned to Windy Post to fetch another sled-load of food.

Before departing he made this journal entry in his usual neat handwriting.

I start for home early. I take two Eskimo kids [Kunee and Anoteelik] *with me to stay for a while.*

There is an additional sentence, uncharacteristically scrawled across the top of the page:

I am going to take her tomorrow or they starve.

During the journey south the girl-child acquired a new name—Rita—a private name Charles had formerly bestowed upon Pama. A *white* man's name which Charles may have believed, or at least hoped, would narrow the gulf between white and Eskimo, the gulf his father considered unbridgeable.

Charles and the two youngsters reached Windy Post to find food stocks so diminished as to leave precious little for the Schweders, let alone the dependent Ihalmiut families there.

For a time Charles hardly appeared to care. Brooding over what had happened at the Kazan, he seems to have withdrawn into an opaque world of his own. Even Fred's unconcealed hostility to his having brought Rita and Anoteelik to Windy Post did not affect him. Nothing did, until Fred began making preparations to visit his trapline, whereupon Charles demanded that his brother drive first to Kazan Camp and deliver a load of food to the Ihalmiut there. "I was pretty well played out," Charles remembered. "I thought I better stay home a while and get some rest."

Grudgingly Fred agreed to do as asked, but with a proviso. If, upon his return to Windy, he found the "Husky kids" still living in the cabin, he would not remain there. Charles responded by promising to convert a small log outhouse into a temporary home for Rita and Anoteelik until, he said, he could return them to their own people.

Fred took the trail on April 3. Reaching Kazan Camp, he unloaded about a hundred pounds of food, mostly flour and lard, which he left for Katelo to distribute. He learned from Katelo that four more people had perished since Charles's visit.

Fred turned back to service his trapline. Four days later he arrived at Windy Post with seventeen foxes, one wolf, and two hind-quarters of deer meat on his sled. He and his dogs were in excellent shape, having fed well on the carcasses of some of the deer Fred had killed during his previous trip and had cached so skilfully that the hungry inhabitants of the barrengrounds had not found them.

By mid-April Charles had no further hopes of ever seeing the promised plane. Supplies were now almost exhausted. Although nets had been set under the river ice, the spring fish run had not begun, so the nets yielded little. The only country food available was ptarmigan, and the birds were scarce and wary.

I am tired of living on flour and [dried] milk...all of us might have to go down the lake to meet the deer. They must be close to Nueltin now....

A move had to be made while the dogs still had the strength to travel. More feed for them could be obtained only by going south. If the brothers found the deer at south Nueltin they would be able to bring the relief supplies Lamb had left at Putahow north to the Ihalmiut camps.

Departing from Windy on April 17, the Schweders and the two Ihalmiut children sledged to Jonsson's Island without encountering any trace of deer. Nor had Ragnor Jonsson returned to his cabin. Charles left the others there while he continued on alone up the Kasmere River in search of anything with which to feed the emaciated dogs. He met no living deer but did locate a couple of well-rotted carcasses someone had cached the previous autumn. Charles let his dogs gorge to repletion then gathered up what remained and hauled it back to Jonsson's cabin.

The small space within was crowded. Too much so for Fred. Tensions between him and Charles were now almost tangible, so Fred took to vanishing through most of the daylight hours. Nominally he was looking for deer, but actually he was tucked away beside a small tea fire on the far side of the island.

When a week had slipped by without any deer appearing, Charles decided to make a dash for Duck Lake and radio another request for help to the outside world.

April 26th. I start with 5 dogs and a toboggan. Fred is going to move camp to Putahow River while I am away. I make first camp at Hook Lake where I tried to get a porcupine who eat the bark of about 20 trees but could not find him....

Charles saw no deer on the way to Duck Lake, and on arrival

there the local Chipewyans told him none had yet appeared. He noted gloomily:

Looks like the deer won't get onto the barrengrounds til May if they ever come.

There was more bad news at the trading post. The radio was out of order.

Charles did not linger. Spring was exploding, and he was in danger of being marooned by a sudden thaw. He exchanged some fur for two hundred pounds of store grub and a new toboggan.

April 30th. Start back heavy loaded. Had to walk all day behind the dogs. Snow so wet they can hardly pull the load. Only traveled five miles. It is thawing and lots of snowbirds around. Have to wait until dark and freezing before I can travel....

May 3rd. Arrived at Putahow River early in the morning. Nobody here so I guess they got stuck in the thaw. Cooked up some oatmeal for the dogs who are very hungry. Start out for Jonssons Island and meet them all on the ice already covered with water.... Will stay here [at Putahow] for a while to rest my dogs which are almost falling over then I am taking another load of grub to the Eskimos. What a trip to Duck Lake with starving dogs.

The exhaustion of his team combined with the drastic deterioration in travel conditions resulting from the thaw forced Charles to remain at Putahow through the next five days. During this time he became aware of a remarkable change in Fred's attitude toward the Eskimo youngsters, and especially toward Rita.

Instead of avoiding her, Fred now seemed to court her, and Rita responded with a warmth and vivacity which was second nature to her. At first Charles was delighted, if a little puzzled.

"I never see Fred act so happy for a long time," he remembered. "It sure seemed like things was going to be a lot better for us, except Mick. It used to be wherever Fred went Mick went along. At Putahow Fred was going out pretty near every day looking for deer, but it was Rita went with him riding on his sled and Mick got left home."

A sharp frost during the night of May 8 restored Charles's mobility. Two hours before dawn on the ninth, his sled swished out onto the ice of Nueltin. Although half-famished, his five dogs put their shoulders to the traces, tucked their heads down, curled up their tails, and pulled, as pleased to be on the trail again as was Charles himself.

Things went well at first, but by mid-morning the snow cover remaining on the lake ice had mostly turned to slush. Fortunately, it froze again during the night, producing a surface over which the sled's mud-coated iron runners whispered with the sound of gigantic razors being stropped. The sled went so swiftly it required only half a day and a night to reach Windy Post.

Charles stopped here only long enough to distribute flour to the families camped nearby and to fry up a stack of bannocks for use on the trail ahead. He was desperate to get on.

"I was so tired but I was scared they'd all be dead at the Kazan because the deer still hadn't come north, so I kept on going. Traveled mostly at night and sometimes didn't even know where I was. The dogs sure knew. Scamp led the way to every meat cache. Only the foxes, wolverines, and wolves hadn't left enough to bother with. I fed the dogs oatmeal. They could hardly work on that but it was all I had."

He reached Kazan Camp late on May 12. The dogs had made a remarkable run—close on 150 miles in four days. Charles was too tired to enter details in his journal, but he recalled:

"The Eskimos was asleep when I came. Most of them too weak to get around, so they was spending their time sleeping. Katelo heard my dogs and came out to tell me Oquinuk was dead. I had some wood on the sled, so we got a fire going and cooked up flour soup and bannocks for everybody. Then I fell asleep and never woke up until a day later."

Charles was back at Windy Post by the sixteenth. He had intended pressing on to Putahow next day but things were catching up to him. The dog harness was in shreds. His clothing was so torn and ragged as to verge on being useless. He was so lean that, as he later said, "my ribs stuck out like a deer been dead a year." An old hernia was plaguing him, and he was so physically drained he could hardly remain awake. And yet:

"I couldn't sleep much. Just kept dreaming about all what had happened."

He spent two days at the cabin repairing his gear and sewing up the worst rents in his clothing before traveling on to Putahow, which he reached on May 19. He had been absent just ten days, during which he had traveled at least three hundred miles.

He found the Putahow camp deserted except for Mike, who was so glad to see his eldest brother that he cried. He told Charles deer tracks had been seen on the lake that very morning and everyone except himself had gone hunting. Charles would have joined in, but he and his dogs were exhausted. He lay down in a tent, where Mike brought him a mug of tea and a piece of the only fish they had caught at Putahow.

Anoteelik returned alone that evening to report having seen several deer. He was ashamed to add he had not been able to kill any with the rusty .22 rifle Fred had loaned him. Nevertheless, the mood in camp was one of inexpressible relief. Printed large across a page in Charles's diary were the words:

So the deer come at last after we been waiting for them for a month.

Indeed the outriders of the great herds had arrived at south Nueltin. However, as everyone was well aware, they might not reach the Ihalmiut country for several days. So Charles decided to take another load of food north... just in case.

May 25th. Sunday. Lots of deer passing now. I shot three. Fred [and Rita] came home. He shot two. He went as far as Jonsson's cabin, saw Chips [Chipewyans] camping there on their way up to their summer fish camp at Putahow. Also saw lots of geese and ducks on a patch of open water at the rapids.

Before starting north, Charles noted:

Baby or Rita wanted to come with me but I thought it would be too cold for her.

Had he realized what was happening, he would assuredly have taken the girl-child with him, but he was not thinking clearly. The problems of past and present had converged to create a complexity he could hardly handle. Although he rarely exposed his inner feelings on the pages of his journal, now he could not contain himself.

May 27th. Arrive home at sundown yesterday. One dog all played out. House snowed right in. Looks as if it hardly thawed up here yet. Spent the day digging out the windows and door and carrying in wood.... God I am tired. I sure wish I could have a weeks rest and I am sure is lonely. Rita my own little child but a Eskimo instead of white, why are you down the lake instead of being with me. I know you wanted to come but I thought it was to cold. So I see that since I brought you down there is nothing but trouble between Fred and I. So I guess I have to take you back, but where. I know no one wants you back. God I'm so tired, so tired that I can sleep for a week. It is still a long way to Kazan.

After what amounted to a three-day hiatus—one he could not, or would not, afterwards recall in any detail—he roused himself to continue the journey north. North, into the land he dearly loved, but which was now so darkly shadowed for him.

May 29th. I got ready to start at noon. Sure wish I could have some more rest. I am still feeling awful as if I have no rest all winter. Its now the 29th of May and hardly no thaw up here. It looks as if its going to be one of the latest springs I ever seen.

He reached Kazan Camp at noon on the thirty-first.

Just before I reached it met Hekwaw and Angakouk on the Kazan River. They were after some deer, the first deer they seen this spring. They sure looked hungry for meat. All the Eskimos but Katelo and his son have left here now the deer is coming.

Charles's final journey had not really been necessary. However, if the arrival of la Foule *had* been further delayed it is virtually certain that the horrors visited upon Hekwaw's camp and those of almost all the other Ihalmiut would have been repeated yet again. And, if this had come to pass, I do not believe Charles Schweder would have been able to endure.

Late in the evening of June 1 he started for Windy Post, promising himself that when he reached the cabin he would indeed sleep for a week. Perhaps he hoped that when he awoke there would be some surcease from memories. Perhaps he did not much care whether he awoke or not.

PART TWO

WINDY POST

C H A P T E R   F I V E

WINDY POST

JOHNNY BOURASSA'S ANSON RETURNED TO Churchill on May 27, buzzing the settlement almost at rooftop level before touching down on the ice of Landing Lake three miles out of town.

John Ingebritson and I drove out in his decrepit truck to fetch the crew. They had had a tough trip.

En route to Baker Lake, the weather had closed in, forcing the plane lower and lower. Since she was equipped to fly only VFR (visual flying rules), she could not climb over it. Her vintage radio receiver was not working properly so Bourassa could not determine what the weather was like at Baker Lake. Short of fuel and uncertain about his location, he held on and hoped for the best. By the time his Baker Lake ETA rolled around, the plane was nearly at deck level and visibility was almost zero. However, the trader had rallied all the Eskimos in the little settlement and lined them up on the lake ice to mark out a nonexistent runway, at each end of which he had set fire to barrels of oil-soaked rags.

"A piece of cake," Johnny told us modestly as we sipped aquavit in the Ingebritsons' warm kitchen. "I saw one of the fire pots and banked the old girl over on her side and there was a strip marked out by about fifty Eskimos. Trouble was, they were lined up *crosswise* to the wind. I made a couple of low passes trying to chase them off but they wouldn't budge. We were flying on empty by then, so I just plunked her down. Didn't hit anybody, but some of them may still be running for the hills."

When Bourassa and Gallagher tried to return to Churchill, a spring blizzard forced them two hundred miles eastward to an emergency landing at Chesterfield Inlet. Here they were storm-bound for three days during which time the hydraulics in the starboard landing strut developed a leak, causing the Anson to heel over to one side like an elderly drunk.

"One more day and the wingtip would have been touching the ice," Bourassa told us. "It was take off right then or settle down in Chesterfield and take up sealing for a living. We got off all right, but it was a bit dicey landing here on one leg."

Fort Churchill's meteorologists promised us better weather for the morrow, but instead we got a southeast gale with blinding snow squalls. There would be no flying that day, so I spent it repacking our gear and trying to reduce its bulk and weight to manageable terms. There were forty-one crates, boxes, and cartons, including an entire case—144 big bars—of Fels-Naptha soap with which Harper hoped to keep the dirt devils at bay. His personal outfit included two huge steamer trunks of 1914 vintage filled with scientific equipment; a telescope; and a four-by-five-inch studio camera with an enormous tripod. He also had a witch's brew of chemicals, including enough arsenic, strychnine, and potassium cyanide to have eliminated most of the population of Keewatin. These deadly substances were intended for killing specimens ranging from insects to wolves, which would then be preserved in other potent chemicals such as formaldehyde, of which he had two gallons. He had also brought along six large wooden butter tubs (sans butter) as containers for fish preserved in alcohol.

I had brought the alcohol—five gallons of 97 per cent triple-distilled grain spirits procured for me by the Royal Ontario Museum under special license and clearly labeled: TO BE USED ONLY FOR THE PRESERVATION OF SPECIMENS.

That night it snowed as if it would never stop. When I awakened on the morning of May 30, the sky was still overcast and the temperature had soared from several degrees below freezing to well above. A major thaw was under way. Without waiting for breakfast, we all climbed into Ingebritson's truck and headed for Landing Lake only to find the way blocked by six-foot drifts. Although the army came to our rescue with a bulldozer, it was late in the afternoon before we reached the Anson. We found her sitting in a pool of melt water with her right wing drooping like that of a wounded bird. The hydraulics had failed again.

Bourassa raced off to the air force base to plead for the loan of a compressor to pump up our hydraulics, only to be told none would be available until the following morning. In his absence, I sat on a snowbank watching a cock ptarmigan who seemed to think I had designs on his mate.

"Go-beck.... Go-BECK.... GO-BECK!" he chanted at me, stomping his feet for emphasis.

I flung a snowball at him, for I was not in a forbearing mood.

Johnny returned and, for the first time, seemed dispirited.

"If we don't make it tomorrow, I'm afraid the show is off. A couple more days of thaw like this and I'll have to shift the old girl back onto wheels. And no, Farley me lad, we can't shift her onto floats. No Anson's ever done that yet, and this bamboo bomber of mine ain't likely to be the first.

May 31st. Met Johnny for breakfast at 0600 and got a thumbs-up even though the forecast was a bitch. Snow flurries and a nor'wester at 30 knots, right on our nose. Followed the compressor tractor from the base out to Landing Lake. Pumped up the strut with difficulty. Gallagher thought it might hold till they get back to Churchill.

At 1130 Gallagher started the engines, turning the propellers by hand because the starters have quit. Skis frozen into the slush so we all got out and rocked her loose. Our stuff piled up to the cabin roof leaving the four of us jammed into the nose tight as baby birds in a nest. Had to leave the reserve

45-gallon drum of avgas behind because take-off conditions were so bad—
six inches of water on top of the lake ice—we might not have got off. During
take-off couldn't see a bloody thing for spray but we must have cleared the
stunted trees at the end of the lake by no more than ten or twenty feet.

Flying at less than 1000 feet we were rubbing the underside of a heavy
overcast. Enormous problem telling land from water...everything down
there looked like a dirty rice pudding with occasional clumps of bushes stuck
into it like raisins.

According to the map a north-northwest compass course would take us to
Nueltin Lake, about 250 miles out from Churchill. After that we'd have
to find Windy River on our own.

I was sweating it out but Harper was happily enjoying his first airplane
ride. Had an old-fashioned 16mm movie camera big as a suitcase stuck out
the side window to film caribou. What caribou? There was nothing to be
seen; absolutely nothing except snow.

After a while Gallagher pointed to the fuel gauges. They registered half
empty. It was then 3:00 p.m. and we could see nothing that looked like a lake.
Johnny held course for another ten minutes then shook his head and began
a turn ready to head back.... We were down to 500 feet when a big rocky
ridge loomed up ahead. Johnny climbed to clear it and, off to the right, I
glimpsed what looked like a little black cabin. Johnny saw it too and stood
the Anson on one wingtip. He leveled off and we landed on rough ice, taking
some hellish jolts. But nothing broke, and we were down.

We had found Windy Post, and it was living up to its name.
Half a gale whipped torrents of snow over the crest of a bleak
ridge to the south of us as we heaved our mountain of bags,
boxes, and crates out of the aircraft onto wind-burnished ice.
Leaving the plane with both engines turning over, we slipped and
slid across the bay ice for half a mile to reach the cabin.

Sited a few hundred yards from the mouth of frozen Windy
River and tucked tightly under the lee of a low hill for shelter
from the north, it was buried to its roofline in drifted snow. Two
small windows peered out at us through tunnels cut in the drifts.
The door, at the end of a twenty-foot trench, was not locked.

Pushing past it, we found ourselves in a dank, chilly, and foul-smelling cavern. The flickering flame of my lighter revealed a drapery of wolf and fox pelts hanging from walls and rafters—partial source of the pungent odor. The main room was about ten feet wide and fifteen long with two little cubbyholes attached at the back. The walls were of skinny logs which had originally been floated down Windy River from the nearest stand of "big" timber fifty miles away. The low roof was made of two-inch saplings covered with sod, over which tar paper and uncured caribou hides had been stretched. Light was mainly provided by candles and kerosene lanterns; heat by a massive cast-iron cook stove brought north in sections by dog team and reassembled here as the heart of the Schweder home.

On a rough-hewn table lay a page torn from a pocket note-book on which someone had written in a round and careful script:

May 29th. Just in case you come back before I do lots of deer last two days but couldn't get any could not go on last two days dogs all in. Hope to get some meat before I get out of the deer. One dog played out and they couldn't pull the load. Am all ready to start north in the morning.

There was no signature, but the message told us the Schweder boys were alive and, evidently, not far away. I was glad to know this because, on reaching the cabin, Harper had collapsed on one of the two bunk beds, ashen-faced and breathing heavily. Johnny pulled me to the door and murmured:

"Maybe he should go back to Churchill with me?"

What to do?

There was no time for prolonged discussion. The Anson's right wing was drooping, and the day was almost spent. Somewhat diffidently, I suggested to my partner that perhaps we both ought to go back with Bourassa. Maybe, I said, we would be able to arrange another sortie into the interior later on.

Harper would have none of this. Sitting up, he shook his head vehemently.

"No, sir," he said stoutly. "I am here, and here I stay."

Gallagher, Bourassa, and I slogged back to the plane, where I opened a can of orange juice and, having poured out some of the contents, refilled the can with grain alcohol. Gallagher gulped his portion in an effort to ease the pain resulting from an old rupture reopened while starting the Anson's engines by hand. I downed mine just as swiftly in order to bolster my fading courage.

There were no prolonged farewells. "See you in October," I shouted. Johnny waved. The Anson bumped out onto Windy Bay. Her engines roared, and she lifted off to vanish into low cloud.

I packed sleeping bags and some food to the cabin, where I opened a tin of cooked bacon and some biscuits for my companion, who was in urgent need of food. Whoever had last used the place had left no fuel except a few handfuls of green spruce twigs. With difficulty I got a fire going and eventually managed to boil the kettle and make tea. By then the place had warmed enough that we could no longer see our breath.

Food and hot tea seemed to improve Harper's condition, so I tucked him into one of two bunk beds set against the side walls. There being little else I could do until morning, I climbed into the other bunk, where I lay awake for a long time, listening intently to my companion's breathing and wondering just what the devil I had let myself in for.

The first of June brought freezing temperatures under a leaden sky. Harper spent most of the day in his sleeping bag keeping warm, for I was too busy with other chores to go searching for fuel. A storm threatened, and it was imperative to get our perishable supplies into shelter.

I made trip after trip between the cabin and our landing place on the bay ice, toting a heavy backpack and constantly breaking through drifts knee- and thigh-deep. It was grueling work, but I was not lonely. Scores of ptarmigan gathered out of nowhere to watch with interest as I floundered past. Still mostly in their white winter plumage, they were like ghostly chickens possessed of a perverse sense of humor, cackling with manic glee every time I stumbled. When their sniggering became too much to bear, I downed my load, went for my shotgun, and killed a pair of them for supper.

In late afternoon I took a break from coolie labor, climbed the snow-free ridge behind the cabin, and was astounded to find the whole of Windy Bay alive with caribou. Hastening northward in strings and gaggles of from fifty to a hundred animals, they disappeared into an immensity of rolling tundra stretching to a northern horizon so distant it blended with the slate-colored sky. It was a world bereft of vivid colors except for a thin dark green ribbon stretched in niggardly fashion along the twisting course of the Windy River valley.

The green was a scanty fringe of dwarf spruce, the sole local source of fuel. I spent the next several hours hacking off enough twigs and branches to cook supper, sometimes almost swimming on my belly to avoid sinking into drifts.

Next day, instead of trying to gather wood from the denuded little copses in the vicinity of the cabin, I hiked a couple of miles upstream on the ice to a slightly less devastated grove from which I was able to collect a pile of sticks, which I then hauled home on a broken toboggan.

Cheered by this achievement, I took time off to climb the ridge and admire the spectacle of la Foule. During the next quarter-hour, perhaps a thousand animals passed within a few hundred yards of me—close enough so I could smell them, and hear their grumbling bellies and the castanet-like clicking of their ankle bones.

Then I heard howling! *Wolves*, I thought and spun around to see five huskies hauling a long sled down the ridge toward the river.

The sled halted in the cabin yard. Through binoculars I watched the driver cautiously survey the welter of tracks I had made and scan the crates and boxes I had not had time to stow away inside. Even from a distance his anxiety was apparent. He seemed of two minds—whether to investigate, or whether to retreat. Finally, as warily as a dog investigating an alien presence, he walked to my miserable excuse for a woodpile and picked up my shiny new axe to examine it as gingerly, as if it were an artifact from outer space.

Returning to the sled, he stood in indecision for several minutes before unsheathing his rifle and approaching the cabin door, which he slowly pushed open with one foot.

This is how I saw it. In his journal Charles Schweder described things somewhat differently:

June 2nd. Monday. No wind. Cloudy and cold. Went right home from Sandhills without a stop. Two whites were there, of all things. I never knew who they were. I never expect anybody unless it was Fred and I be surprised if he be back from Putahow yet. I sure was surprised. They told me they came to collect birds and mammals for specimens and that they seen my Father in Churchill. In Churchill of all places! I thought he was at Brochet or in The Pas. Got two letters which the gentlemen brought from my father telling me to come out. But they came in 31st of May and the plane they came in left the same day.

They sure were glad to see me. They had stuff packed almost up to the roof and from end to end of the house, but all the same I am glad to see them. One is a young fellow and his name is Farley Mowat and he was in the Canadian Army four years and been over nearly half the world. The other was a old man his name is Doctor F. Harper and is up from the States. Had my first drink of whiskey tonight and is not bad at all. Lots of deer passing here now, mostly does and going north like mad.

Charles was of medium height and build, lanky and loose-jointed. Dark skinned, he had deep-set dark eyes; broad, mobile lips; and an ice-breaker of a nose. He was wearing a scruffy aviator's-type helmet over black, uncombed hair that hung lank to his shoulders. Under his deerskin parka, he wore ragged woolen trousers, high-laced rubber boots, and a torn and tattered sweater.

His smile was guarded and fleeting. So soft-spoken as to sometimes be inaudible, he had the engaging habit of shaking himself every now and again, the way a dog does before it lies down.

Whatever he may have felt about this totally unexpected invasion of his life and premises, he accepted it without demur. He hauled the remainder of our freight off the ice with his sled and team and stowed it inside the cabin. Later he would tell me that, from the size of our outfit, he concluded we must be planning to stay a year at least. Such a prospect might reasonably have distressed him, yet he showed no disquiet. He was a true product of a world where there is never any question about sharing with one's neighbors. What he had was ours, as need might dictate. It probably never occurred to him that we might not feel the same way.

A few days later, after his younger brothers Fred and Mike and the Eskimo children had returned from south Nueltin, Harper made it clear how *he* felt. After acknowledging that the Schweder clan was short of almost everything, he warned me more or less in these words: We only have supplies to last until October. Though we may be tempted to be generous, we have to remember our commitment is to science. We are obliged to keep the bulk of our supplies for our own needs.

That he did not entirely trust me to do this soon became apparent as he began squirreling away yeast, canned butter, baking powder, dried fruit, vegetables, and chocolate bars.

The other members of the clan had arrived home on June 5.

Fred Schweder showed up at 0500 having driven 60 miles on the ice of Nueltin Lake through a six-hour rain storm at freezing point, over slush and wet snow, with three kids and a hundred pounds of freight on a beat-up toboggan pulled by only four dogs. He didn't wake anybody till he had breakfast cooked for everybody—fried caribou steaks. Not even Charles was on deck to greet him. What he thought about the mounds of weird paraphernalia filling the cabin will forever remain his secret because Fred does not talk.

At almost 17, he is small for his age, very dark, a pocket-sized edition of Charles but nearly voiceless. His silence is so total it has body to it. It unnerves me and when I am with him I find myself whistling in an apologetic way. His vocabulary seems limited to hy-um-um. This, in a low whisper, is his answer to all questions, if he answers at all.

Little Mike Schweder, usually called Mick, is nine, and garrulous compared to Fred. Although most of his communicating is done with shrugs of his narrow shoulders or bobbing of the head, he sometimes says "yes," or "no," or "maybe."

The Eskimo boy, Ano-teel-ik, is about 13, a squat, compact youngster with an enormous grin and a pleasant, if flattened face. He wears what may once have been a pair of Charles's dungarees, a canvas jacket, and a crumpled peaked cap. He smokes a stone pipe; is very amiable and willing; and worships the ground Charles walks upon.

Ano-teel-ik's sister, Kunee, or Rita as Charles calls her, is five or six but looks younger—tiny as a midge and just as active. She has stringy black hair hanging all over her face which hides an engaging wink. She likes practical jokes and is deadly accurate with a slingshot, particularly when the target is a white man's ass. She also smokes a stone pipe, but cigarettes too. It is quite a sight to see this minute creature trotting over the hills with a huge pipe clenched between her jaws. If it goes out she relights it by striking a match on her front teeth. Harper, a rabid non-smoker, is horrified. Rita is wary of him, and Charles says she thinks he is an angeokok, a shaman or witch doctor.

Although Charles insisted there was room for all of us in the cabin, Harper and I concluded life would be simpler, if not sweeter, if we pitched our two small tents independently on the gravel ridge behind the cabin. This move ensured privacy, but had its drawbacks. There is no real darkness at Windy River in June. The stars do not shine and only Mars and Venus are bright enough to be visible. Although the sun goes down at 9:00 p.m., it does not go far down, and twilight lasts until shortly after midnight. By 1:30 a.m. the light is strengthening again and by 3:00 a.m. dawn is breaking.

My tent is as translucent as oiled silk so it seems as if someone left the light on all night. Furthermore, the damn fool birds never stop singing. On June 4 mobs of migrants began arriving: robins, gray-cheeked thrushes, horned larks, and a horde of others. By 0400 sleep is impossible for the *bloody noise. If I ever come back up here again I'll damned well bring ear plugs and eye shades.*

The arrival of the birds (and better weather) seemed to fully restore Harper, and he vigorously began collecting anything and everything that came within range of his shotgun. Nothing that walked or flew was secure against his enthusiastic pursuit of specimens. On one occasion he mistook a dog that had got loose for a wolf, and let fly both barrels. Fortunately, the range was extreme and the animal was not seriously damaged.

The spring thaw now came upon us with a vengeance.

Windy River has melted holes through its ice at the rapids and snow-drifts on the ground are melting at a rate of 8" a day. There is going to be one hell of a lot of water running around here soon.

The disappearance of the snow brings problems. The area around the cabin has been staked out all winter with dogs belonging to the Schweders and visiting Eskimos. Neither dogs nor Eskimos share our concept of sanitation. The place is also strewn with the naked corpses of several wolves, scores of foxes, various other cadavers, and small mountains of caribou bones. As the snow melts, the size of this charnel yard spreads. It looks like an abandoned abattoir. The thought of what it is going to smell like when the weather warms up is too awful to contemplate. Meanwhile, the unsanitary implications are driving Harper wild. He spends all his spare time dragging carcasses out onto the river ice to be carried away when it melts, but hardly makes a dint in the corpse population.

Herring gulls circle the site in hundreds, but turn up their noses at this banquet. They want fresh meat. The same kind of birds we see scavenging at the seashore down south sit around up here waiting for someone to set off with a rifle hunting caribou. The sound of a shot hardly has time to die away before they are swarming overhead. A deer carcass left unguarded will be devoured by them in a day or two. But at camp they only sit around and complain about the mess.

This morning [June 9] Harper and I breakfasted alone as we usually do since the rest of the mob seldom stirs until noon; but then they mostly stay up all night. This behavior greatly irritates Harper, who believes in regular activities. He goes to bed in broad daylight at 9:00 p.m. because that's the time he's always gone to bed, and gets up at 7:00 a.m. though by then the sun is pretty nearly overhead. He believes everyone should follow the same routine, especially me. He likes his meals on the dot, and I am expected to provide them because his time is entirely taken up with science.

He has been goading me to do more scientific work, so yesterday I laid out a trapline, 47 mouse traps set in runways under the snow and in a little swamp. Mike and the Eskimo kids watched from a respectful distance. Even Fred and Charles seemed baffled until somebody suggested I was trying to catch mice for the pot. At first all hands thought this was hilarious. But Rita is now suspicious of anything I put on the table.

Went the rounds of my mouse trapline this p.m. and got three per-omyscus (deer mice), a phenacomys (a kind of blond field mouse), four red-backed mice, and a cinereous shrew. The shrew caused a sensation back at camp. Nobody had ever noticed such an animal before. At less than two inches long including the tail, this is about as small as a mammal gets. Mike and Rita watched me skinning it with absolute incredulity. Even Charles had trouble trying to comprehend what possible use could be found for a pelt smaller than his little finger.

Skinning a shrew is almost as demanding as engraving the Lord's Prayer on the head of a pin. Charles admitted he would sooner skin a hundred foxes than one shrew; then he wanted to know how I proposed to "stretch" the finished skin and, finally, what trading company would take it, and for what price? Fred only said, "hy-umm-umm" and disappeared. We haven't seen him since but Charles says he will come back if and when he has made some sense out of what Harper and I do.

I cooked dinner for everybody tonight. Thick, rare sirloin steaks. Breaded ptarmigan breasts. Homemade bread.

Although they seemed to like my cooking, the brothers and the young Eskimos found many of Harper's and my activities incomprehensible, even sinister. We had engrossed most of the communal cabin space to our own purposes, with Harper pre-empting the large kitchen table while I made do with a small corner one. Each tabletop displayed a row of vials, jars, and bottles, most of which displayed skull-and-crossbones poison warnings and contained a sorcerer's array of chemicals.

There was also an intimidating array of scalpels, surgical shears, scissors, forceps, brain spoons, bone saws, and dentist's drills, which were employed one way or another in skinning and preparing specimens ranging in size from shrews to foxes; from sparrows to loons; from fleas to beetles; from maggots to tape-worms.

Loosely stuffed bird and mammal skins with labels attached to their hind limbs were laid out to dry on all the shelves around the cabin walls. Insects (which had been poisoned in cyanide bottles) were skewered with long and evil-looking pins to strips of cardboard in the bottoms of cigar boxes. Fishes were pickled in alcohol-filled wooden tubs. Small, soft-bodied animals and assorted internal organs of larger creatures went into jars of formalin solution also ranged along the shelves. Botanical specimens were dried between layers of blotting paper in suitcase-sized plant presses.

With our armory of assorted shotguns, rifles, traps, nets, and poison baits (including cyanide "wolf getters"), Harper and I could, and did, deal lethally with most forms of life in the vicinity of Windy Post. In retrospect, I can understand why some of our companions might have begun to wonder just where we would draw the line.

Our first days at Windy River witnessed a kaleidoscope of events and impressions.

...Most of the spring birds except flycatchers and warblers have arrived. They sing bravely and loudly enough but look pretty miserable because though it thaws during the day it still freezes hard at night. God alone knows what they are getting to eat.

...Last night Harper cornered the Schweders in the cabin. Claiming they were lousy, which I don't believe, he browbeat them into submitting to U.S. Marine-style haircuts which made them look like candidates for a *concentration camp. He tried to trim the Eskimo kids too, but they smartly vamoosed, which annoys him very much. He is peeved at me because I am growing a beard, which, he says, is a dirty habit. His concern about hygiene is getting out of hand. Dishes have to be washed and then rinsed in boiling water and there is an uproar if he finds a caribou hair in the tea. One compensation: he does the dishes himself because he doesn't trust the rest of us. And he won't use the backhouse, a little log shanty with a peeled pole for a seat, because all the rest of us use it. We do so for a damn good reason. Half the dogs are running loose now and they have peculiar tastes. If you don't use the crapper you'd better take along a good big stick. I hope poor old Sanitary Ike, as I privately call the good doctor, gets wise in time.*

…Charles shot two deer right behind our ridge and Harper insisted we skin them out for specimens. We were engrossed in this task when a herd of 50 more came along the river ice below us. Charles stepped out the door and shot 3 for dog feed. All were pregnant. When, perhaps foolishly, I made some cautionary comment about that he simply shook himself and said, "Does's all there is right now."

…Ensuring a winter supply of dry firewood isn't easy on the edge of the barrens. The way you do it is you choose a windy day in the driest part of summer, then set fires in the scanty bits of bush along the river valleys. If there's enough wind "top" fires roar through what woods there are and kill the trees but don't consume them because they are too green. A year later the dead standing wood is dry enough to cut for firewood. Last year Charles had prepared a good stand this way a few miles west of the cabin but a band of starving Eskimos that descended on him in the winter used most of it trying to keep warm in their skin tents, so we are burning twigs.…

CHAPTER SIX

MAN AND LEMMINGS

WE HUMAN RESIDENTS OF WINDY POST began to behave as if we belonged to two different subspecies, one mainly diurnal and the other partly nocturnal. Harper and I had pre-empted so much of the cabin for work and storage space, and he spent so many of his waking hours there, that the Schweder clan felt free to use it only after he had gone to bed. During daylight they catnapped in the woods or somewhere out on the tundra plain. Like flying squirrels, they became active at night, and I found myself falling into their rhythm.

One evening Charles, Rita, Mike, and I set off down Windy Bay for a deer hunt. Thousands of does had gone through, and the big herds of bucks following them were thinning out. Since the Schweders would not be able to set fish nets for at least another three weeks, they needed to lay in a supply of meat for the dogs, who were still in poor shape after a tough winter. Charles was particularly worried about two pregnant bitches upon whose pups the boys depended for future transportation.

We left the cabin at 8:00 p.m., Charles's five dogs hauling a heavy Eskimo sled with Rita perched behind. I drove Fred's team of four, pulling a smaller and much lighter toboggan with Mike as my passenger.

The run down the bay was sheer delight. The snow on the surface was almost gone and the ice so slick we went like skaters. The moon rose high and almost full and the luminescence of a lingering sunset softened the silhouettes of the hills around the shores.

The dogs soon scented deer and speeded up until the toboggan seemed almost airborne. It was far more exhilarating than a ride in a fast car, more like skimming close to the ground in a glider.

We went ashore on the north side of the bay opposite the cliffs of the Caribou Hills where, according to Charles, peregrine falcons would nest later in the season. After tethering the dogs in a clump of dwarf willows, we three men climbed the height of land to scan the countryside for deer. Rita remained behind to light her pipe and gather willow twigs for a fire on which she boiled the tea billy and baked bannock dough wrapped around sticks leaned over the coals. When we returned, breakfast was ready. As she served it up in the half-light, I thought she resembled one of the Little People of the fairy kind.

Not far below us lay a strip of open water—the first to appear on Windy Bay that spring. It was like an avian subway station at rush hour, jam-packed with yellow-billed, red-throated, and common loons; old squaw ducks; red-breasted mergansers; surf scoters; Canada geese; and one lone white-fronted goose. They were all pushing the open-water season, which was singularly late this year.

Ptarmigan were playing mating games all around us, whooping and hollering like zanies. Three or four cocks—snow-white up to the shoulders but with dark red heads and necks—would come whistling past; glide down stiff-winged; then, cackling wildly, chase each other over the drifts until exhausted. They would stand and glare at one another for a while before flying back to their waiting ladies to do a little bragging. The visual effect was uncanny: seemingly bodiless heads and necks scuttling about in the dusk.

We sat drinking tea, nibbling hot bannock, and waiting for the deer while gray-cheeked thrushes, robins, and Lapland longspurs sang their hearts out in a nearby patch of scrubby spruce. We waited, but no deer appeared. At 1:30 a.m. I went for a walk up the long slope behind us and came upon two white wolves trotting along the crest of the esker. Either they failed to see or wind me or they chose to ignore me and passed quite close, white wraiths drifting along an opalescent skyline.

When I got back to the bivouac fire, Rita was blowing up the embers to bring the tea billy back to a boil. Mike was asleep on a patch of moss, curled up like a puppy. Charles had vanished. Dawn was breaking in the north and a livid moon was setting in the east. The heavens seemed all topsy-turvy and full of wonders.

At about 3:00 a.m. Charles returned with a brace of ptarmigan, which Rita expertly skinned and in a minute had them frying. Then Charles touched my arm and pointed south, where he claimed he could see seven deer on the crest of the Caribou Hills two or three miles distant. Even with the help of my binoculars I could see nothing. Eventually Charles lost sight of them and proposed we go look for a wolf's den he knew about.

An esker near the mouth of Smith House Bay had produced a conical mount of yellow sand a hundred feet high where wolves had denned for generations. The current den, on the west side of the knoll, was a hole about the diameter of a forty-five-gallon oil drum, slanted into the hill at the foot of a gnarled little spruce tree. The sand near the entrances was dotted with splintered deer bones and criss-crossed with wolf tracks, some bigger than the span of my hand.

Full of bravado, I crawled into the holes but darkness and the possibility of meeting the owner quickly drained my resolve and sent me hurriedly backing out.

From Wolf Knoll we could trace the course of the esker running out of sight across the tundra to the north and crossing the bay to the south as a string of sandy islands.

Eskers are amongst the most fascinating phenomena in the north. Essentially, they are the beds of rivers that once tunneled through the mile-thick glaciers which covered most of the north twelve thousand years ago. When the glaciers eventually melted, the accumulated detritus of the river beds slumped onto the land below to become sand and gravel ridges, some a hundred feet high, running cross-country for miles and miles like giant railroad embankments.

The sun was already high as we trudged back to the bivouac, drank more tea, and sprawled out for a nap. I was awakened by a subdued whoop from Mike and started up to find ten bucks crossing the bay ice a mile to the east. Charles was nowhere to be seen, so I grabbed my rifle and sprinted toward a ridge from which I hoped to be able to intercept the herd.

Feeding leisurely up the slope toward me, the deer were almost within range when we heard a barrage of rifle fire from Charles farther up the bay. The deer stopped, sniffed the wind, then loped back the way they had come. In desperation I fired a shot, which missed but turned them so they started up the slope again. When they were close enough, I dropped the lead animal. I could have shot several, but the sight of this one struggling to get to its feet with bloody froth ballooning obscenely from its mouth distracted me and I let the others go.

Then I discovered I had left my knife back at the fire. I ran the mile back to get it. When I told the kids I had made a kill, it was as if I had passed some kind of test. Mike smiled and actually spoke directly to me. Rita rubbed her hands together gleefully. I told Mike to hitch up our team and join me, then hiked back up the hill.

By the time I reached the deer, at least twenty gulls were at work on it. I chased them off, but they hovered overhead, screaming and cursing while I began awkwardly skinning the animal. Mike and Rita soon joined me, and I was glad to assume the role of dog-minder while the two of them pounced on the carcass and, with a speed and dexterity the gulls must surely have envied, reduced it to a hide and a stack of meat on the one hand, and a head and a pile of steaming guts on the other.

Back at the bivouac we were joined by Charles, who had ambushed a herd of fifty bucks and killed five. His long sled was loaded with meat and was red with blood.

Gathered around the little fire, we stuffed ourselves with broiled kidneys and thick slices of liver, then curled up like a pack of satiated wolves and snoozed until the sun was going down and the melt water on the bay had frozen over sufficiently to let us head for home.

Spring did not really establish its grip until mid-June, by which time severe nighttime frosts had ended and noontime temperatures were in the fifties. The deep drifts of winter literally shrank away before our eyes. Little River, a minor stream a mile and a half east of the cabin, suddenly went berserk and burst its bounds to fling hundreds of tons of shattered ice out upon the still-frozen surface of the bay.

The long-imprisoned waters of Windy River were no longer to be contained. At dawn on June 16 I was awakened by Charles shaking my little tent.

"She's going!" he yelled.

I scrambled out to join him just as the river took charge with a rumbling roar like the opening salvos of an artillery barrage. Below us an ice pan as large as a small house slowly reared up on its side to topple over with an almighty crash, sending a spout of water almost as high as the ridge we were standing on. Then the whole surface of the river splintered into a mosaic of great pans as much as six feet thick that went charging ponderously downstream, filling the gray dawn with sound and fury.

The still-solid ice on the bay resisted the onslaught, and a cloud of glittering ice crystals billowed above the battlefield. The river pans began piling up atop one another until before long they had built themselves a dam forty feet high across the river's mouth.

The water behind this dam rose so rapidly it reached the

cabin before Charles and I could hurry down from the ridge. A barrier of brash ice saved the cabin from destruction—though not from being flooded.

Fred and Anoteelik now appeared, and the four of us began frantically piling gear on bunks, tables, shelves, even atop the stove. Still the water rose until it was up to our knees. We were about to start moving everything to safety on the ridge when a grumbling roar shook the ground, and the dam gave way, spewing a mighty deluge out over the bay ice.

It had been a near thing. Had the dam held for another hour, the cabin could well have been smashed and carried off. In the event, the flood did us some good service by washing away the charnel house debris.

However, as I noted in my journal, it also precipitated a major social crisis.

Sanitary Ike is on the warpath. While we were rescuing things in the cabin, including Harper's kit and specimens, Charles put on a pair of the old boy's high rubber boots. He had none of his own and the water was paralyzingly cold. When the panic was over he took them off and put them on the roof to dry.

There Harper, who had stayed on the ridge out of harm's way during the flood, found them. When he learned that Charles had been wearing them he gave him a sergeant major's dressing-down in front of everybody. According to Harper there were a great many horrible diseases one could get from wearing someone else's footgear; the pretty clear implication being that Charles probably had them all.

Then Harper doused the boots with formalin to disinfect them. This was a bad mistake because the chemical rotted the rubber, turning the boots into a semi-liquid mess.

Charles said nothing during this imbroglio but that night as we walked together to the mouth of Little River (normally a mere freshet but now a raging torrent) he surprised me with the news that he, his brothers, and the Eskimo youngsters were all going north up Little River the next day by canoe. Why now? His reply was that he had to skin some wolves trapped during the winter, which he had cached in a snowbank near the Kazan.

"But the Kazan is eighty miles away," I remonstrated. "With Little River ripping down like this you'll have to carry the canoe. Your wolves will be thawed out and rotten long before you get there."

"Don't matter. Sooner be up there than down here." He paused before suggesting, "You could come too...meet the Eskimos at the Kazan?"

As I chewed this over, he continued, "Something else I got to do. We're real short of grub and just about everything else, but I guess you fellows need all the stuff you brought in for yourselves, so soon as the ice on Nueltin melts Fred and me'll have to take the big canoe down to Brochet for a load of stuff."

This shook me. "Surely you aren't going to leave Mike and the Eskimo kids here for us to look after while you're gone? I don't think I could take that on, and I'm pretty sure Harper won't."

Charles's sly grin appeared. "I guess Rita and Ano wouldn't take to it either, so I got another idea. What if you and me went south 'stead of Fred? He could stay and look after the dogs and the kids and help the Doctor. It'd be a dandy trip...good rivers... nice country. Meet the Chips along the way. Kinda hard on the portages, but I'd sure be glad if you come along...."

He gave me scant time to consider this before continuing. "I been pushing my trapline farther north every year far as Little Dubawnt Lake. This summer I was going to paddle right north to Thelon River and the muskox country, then go east to Baker Lake and back south up the Kazan. Now, though, I could go from Baker right out to Hudson Bay and along the coast to Churchill and fly back to Windy with a winter outfit in the plane coming to pick up you and Dr. Harper...."

It was a long speech for Charles. He paused and gave me a sidewise look before concluding with a hesitant "Would be a big trip...we could make it together."

"It would be the *hell* of a trip, Charles! And I'd love to go, only Harper is my partner and I can't just up and leave him here. I *might* be able to go to Brochet with you if Fred stayed to look after things. As for the Thelon trip…I'll have to think about that."

Next evening the Schweder clan set off for the Kazan. Even with all five of them paddling they were hardly able to move their eighteen-foot freighter canoe upstream against the roaring current. I did not envy them their Sisyphean labors, but it seemed clear they would rather be battling Little River than enduring the situation at Windy Post.

After waving them on their way, I returned to the cabin to continue serving my time as a scientist. My journal gives the flavor of it.

The cabin is in a hell of a mess and I am at least two days behind in skinning the birds and small mammals that have been piling up. My heart isn't in it. I ask myself whether the whole collecting thing isn't a snare and a delusion. How much value to science or anybody else can all these mummified little beasties really have? Harper and I might be more usefully employed selling newspapers, or peddling booze.

…Came out of my tent this morning rubbing my eyes to find two of the dogs had swum the river. When I looked again they were two dandy big wolves, mostly white with grayish ruffs. I thought about going for my rifle then thought again and just watched as they sniffed along the shore. They must have seen me but figured I meant them no harm. One cocked his leg in my direction then they trotted up the hill and vanished. Harper wasn't pleased with me. Says they would have made a great pair of specimens.

…Found a lemming in my mouse traps this afternoon. First we've caught. A cockeyed little beast as broad as he is long with rich orange-colored fur, a black stripe along the back, huge paws, and a snub nose. He was only caught by a leg so I tried to keep him alive but when I looked in his tin-can cage an hour later he had given up the ghost. Some of these little critters probably die of fright when trapped; must be a hellish shock to them.

…Did a wash this evening. My socks were getting brittle. While thus engaged I cogitated on my work, on Man and Lemmings, and where we all

fit in. Do I really want to spend the rest of my life amongst dusty specimens and dusty scientists? Wouldn't that be an early kind of death?

…Most of this rainy day I have done little but sit at my skinning table figuratively thumbing my nose at mouse traps and my small-bore shotgun which is designed for shooting little birds. As always when confused, I whistle to myself. H. asked me to stop doing this because it bothers his concentration. He has not yet asked me to quit breathing, but who knows? I've been reading Anna Karenina and I thought to get him interested but he told me he doesn't read Tolstoy "and all those other sordid Russians."

…Spent all afternoon on the ridge behind camp under a crystal sky with a brisk and laughing wind blowing through my hair, cleaning a dirty, stinking caribou hide that is destined to become a museum specimen. Among the memories of this afternoon I shall not cherish is cutting 186 warble fly maggots out of the skin. The highlight of this occupation came when one of the maggots—each about the size of my little finger—burst and squirted juice in my eye. At the same time a multitude of blowflies buzzed around laying their eggs on flesh and fur, both the deer's and mine.

After a couple of hours of this I said the hell with it and took off over the tundra plains to the north. Rough-legged hawks were patroling the high, blue sky; cock ptarmigan proclaiming their territorial imperatives; snow buntings singing above already completed nests in the moss; and a least weasel—not much larger than a mouse itself—popped out of a rock pile at my feet and bravely chittered at me, warning me not to trespass.

I climbed a ridge six or seven miles from camp and was sprawled behind a boulder on its crest smoking my pipe when five big bucks climbed the other side and ambled to within twenty feet of where I sat before catching the tobacco smell.

Clearly puzzled, they stopped to stare then began edging closer. I kept still until we were almost eyeball to eyeball. Every now and then one of them would toss his head and burp, which seemed so silly that I got the giggles. They still didn't spook until I got to my feet and took a step toward them. Then—poof!—they were gone, scattering like partridge and within seconds fading out of sight on the open barrens. Caribou have this uncanny ability to appear as if out of nowhere, and disappear just as suddenly. The antlers of this lot were only half grown and in velvet but already formidable. Damn good thing they weren't looking for trouble.

...H. thinks I am slacking on the job, which I surely am, so I try to keep out of his way. He doesn't like the dogs so I spend a lot of time with them. They are good company, though feeding them can be something of a chore. The meat is now runny rotten, which doesn't bother the dogs but spoils my appetite. The nine of them eat the hell of a lot and I worry about running out of meat. Meantime they seem to have accepted me into the pack. I am allowed, even encouraged, to scratch ears and pat heads. When they get loose, which some of them do every day, they meekly allow me to haul them back to their stakes by the scruff of the neck, or even by the tail. Killer dogs, they ain't.

Harper and I are the real killers around here.

...I'm curiouser and curiouser about the Eskimo kids Rita and Anoteelik and how they fit into the scene. The little girl spins around Charles like he's her mother and her father, which isn't surprising if, as I gather, Charles saved her life. Charles responds, but Fred sometimes seems to want her gone and at other times seems to wish she'd spin around him. Perhaps he's jealous. Anoteelik doesn't appear to be a problem. He knocks himself out trying to be a help to everyone. Then there's little Mike, so silent and unobtrusive as to be virtually invisible to everyone except the Eskimo kids, who make much of him. It's a weird little family under a lot of stress. And I guess Harper's and my presence isn't making things any easier.

CHAPTER SEVEN

SCIENCE LOSES ONE

T HE MOOD AND QUALITY OF THE TIME I SPENT
alone with Harper is perhaps best delineated in my journal, to which I confided both my sometimes maddening
frustrations and my not infrequent moments of delight.

*This fine spring morning I decided to practice my skills as a dog musher by
making a trip to the mouth of Windy Bay to see if the ice on Nueltin Lake
has begun to melt. I took Charles's team, hauling his big Eskimo komatik.*

*Fifteen feet long, it is constructed of two huge, hand-hewn runners with
crossbars tied between them every fourteen inches, and shod with strips of iron.
On it I lashed my bedroll, a grub box (which also holds a few cooking and eating utensils), and a gunny sack filled with stinking deer meat for the dogs.*

*My route was overland the first few miles, which meant the dogs had to
pull across patches of gravel, rock, and frozen moss with me walking alongside pushing when they got stuck. Then we crossed a small lake with a foot
of slush on top of ice and the dogs and I and most of the gear got soaked.*

*The dogs haven't yet recovered from their winter ordeal and it made me
feel guilty to make them work this hard. Ill-assorted as to shape and size, they
range from a big white malemute to a cocky little runt not much bigger than
a coyote. They answer to "hew" and "chaw" for left and right, and "whoa"
and "hi" for stop and start. They also answer very quickly to a little affection.*

*I gave the leader, a pregnant bitch called Scamp, freedom to pick her own
trail. When we got out on the bay ice, Scamp showed a preference for slush*

and water and I had to perch on top of the load to keep from being drowned. She knew her stuff though, because there were a lot of sinkholes and current melts where the whole kit and caboodle of us could easily have gone under. Yet she managed to skirt them all.

As Windy Bay widened out, the ice got drier and by the time we were in sight of the big lake you'd never have known spring had come. Solid ice as far as the eye could reach. Not a crack, or lead of open water. It was going to be a while before anyone went canoeing on Nueltin Lake. I turned for home and got there just at dawn.

...Today I walked north to Spruce Camp following Charles and Fred's winter trapping route to the Kazan.

The ridges along the way have little pillars of stones on them—inuksuak—or "stone men" as Charles calls them. Built by the Eskimos to guide travelers when the snow obliterates most other landmarks, they also make the land seem alive—give it a human presence. Some of them may have been here even before the Eskimos.

Made a fire at the boys' little lean-to trapping shelter at Spruce Camp, so-called for a tiny grove of three-foot-high spruce "bushes," where I boiled tea and took a rest before starting the long hike back to the cabin. From my perch I looked out over the true barrens: endless rocky ridges, rolling grassy swales, a scatter of small ponds and lakes, and the twisted course of Little River running through muskeg bogs that seemed like cauldrons of dark chocolate.

There were maybe fifty buck deer to be seen if you looked hard enough; the tail end of the migration, they were scattered all over the landscape, blending into it so well as to be almost invisible. The birds were mostly Smith's longspurs—confiding little beings with a song like that of the western meadowlark. On the way back I stopped by a tundra pond to watch the mating gyrations of a pair of Old Squaw ducks and discovered the icy water was swarming with life. Countless little freshwater shrimp less than half an inch long were copulating like mad in company with hordes of brilliantly crimson relatives not much bigger than a pin head, details of whose private lives were, alas, invisible to me.

Late in the afternoon the almost-always-present wind dropped right out, leaving a sudden silence that was tangible and oppressive. Then I heard *what sounded like a squadron of Heinkel bombers droning toward me. Though I could see nothing, the sound quickly rose to an enveloping roar and suddenly I was being buffeted by a hurricane. Bits of moss and twigs whipped my face; the world vanished under a flail of driving rain and I was actually forced to my knees. Though it only lasted a minute or two it was quite terrifying. Then the sun blazed out again and I started for home at a trot; not without an occasional apprehensive glance over my shoulder. I felt as if the spirit of the barrengrounds was breathing down my neck.*

…Harper bitching again about doing camp chores. Says he is too busy with his real work to do any himself. Grinding my teeth, I went at it and collected enough wood to fire the cook stove for a week. In exchange, I demanded he feed the dogs. Poor bugger couldn't very well refuse, though the very idea probably gave him the grippe. But he fooled me. He simply dragged a rotten quarter of meat around the dog lines on the end of a rope—letting each one help itself. Touché. But he lost points this afternoon when he shot a wood frog with his 12-gauge shotgun! Wasn't enough left of the poor thing to put on a postage stamp but he scraped up the bits and stuck them in a bottle of formaldehyde to establish a new northern record for the species.

…A very good day. Walked around the bay to the wolf den this morning. Found nobody home and the lack of tracks suggested the family had moved off to summer quarters. While I was sitting on the crest of Wolf Knoll three bucks came along the esker. They were curious about me, stopping ten paces away to stare and burp. I mustered my resources and burped back. This seemed to surprise them but one with a crooked antler took up the challenge and let fly a good belch in return. I replied, and we kept up the exchange for several minutes. The other two stood and listened to this battle of champions until I had to quit, exhausted. Ernest Thompson Seton says in one of his books that caribou grunt as a form of communication. The hell they do. They burp!

When the deer had moseyed off I heard a raven's "bell" note. Much searching with binoculars revealed him, all alone, perhaps half a mile high in the immensity of faded sky, doing aerobatics. After a short burst of level flight at full speed he would flip over on his back for a few strokes, then slip off sideways into a barrel roll. At intervals he executed masterful loops, or did the falling-leaf trick. Sometimes he folded his wings and dived like a falcon, finishing with a loop-the-loop. During the whole show, which lasted half an hour, he talked sotto voce, congratulating himself with a bell-like peal of sound after completing each maneuver.

On the way home I met a wolf in a willow swale—a big, white fellow who looked twice the size of a German shepherd. He ignored me and went on about his business, whatever that may have been. I went on about mine too, and pretty swiftly for I was not carrying a gun.

Not far from Little River I flushed a least sandpiper from her outsized eggs in a nest tucked into a big tussock. Although she herself was only as big as a sparrow, her four eggs were pigeon-sized. She ran off through the grass squeaking like a mouse, dragging one wing in an attempt to get me to follow her. But it was suppertime, so I went home.

It was 9:30 p.m. by then and H. had gone to bed. I fried a huge and well-hung steak and gorged on it and bread I made yesterday. Then I sat up by candlelight until the wee small hours, sipping grog—part grain alcohol and part cold tea—and reading "Endymion." The last line of that epic poem has to contain the greatest anticlimax in English literature—the line where Peona is left alone by the immortal lovers and "goes home in wonderment." In wonderment? That's it? After what she's been through?

…Nearly had a showdown with H. today. I was cooking lunch in the cabin when he called me outside and pointed to a ruddy turnstone—a gaudily colored shorebird—huddling on a bit of beach beside the river. By rights it should have been with a flock of its fellows migrating north along the coast of Hudson Bay, but somehow it had gone astray. Harper was ecstatic because its presence in the interior constituted an "unusual record"—one that had to be confirmed by killing the bird and preserving its skin. He had left his shotgun in his tent so I was ordered to do the job.

Resisting the impulse to refuse, I did as I was told. However, when I picked up the little bundle of bloodied feathers I felt like a thug. Although this is by no means the first time recently I have felt this way, it pretty well decided me to give over being a butcher in the service of science. So I have brought home most of my mouse traps and have no intention of setting them again.

Tension between Harper and me continues to mount. In an attempt to ease the situation I cooked a bang-up dinner for us tonight, but we had a real row anyway. Might have been comic as a scene from a domestic play, but there is nothing funny about it when it's happening up here. He accused me of being a renegade to science, which I guess I am, then demanded I pay half the bill for the Anson, whose charter fee was covered by a travel grant from the Arctic Institute. When I declined he stomped off to bed looking as if he had lockjaw.

In calmer moments I can feel for him. He is a professional, and science is his life. This expedition is his dream, and his hopes and reputation hang on it. He thinks my unscientific attitude is lousing it up. Well, as Archie the Cockroach used to say to Mehitabel the Cat: Life's like that, so wotthehell!

...There was only one more day's feed of dog meat left in the fast-melting snowdrift that serves as an "icebox" so I knew I had to go shoot another deer today, something I really did not want to do. Fortunately it rained, or rather it snowed and sleeted, so I had an excuse to stick close to home. All the small birds in the region seem to congregate around the cabin. Pipits; juncos; tree, Harris, and white-crowned sparrows; spotted sandpipers; gray-cheeked thrushes; and blackpoll warblers all mingled in one wet and forlorn flock. The cold of the last few days seems to have killed most of the insects so the birds are scrabbling for whatever grub they can find amongst the debris in the yard.

H. thought this would be a good opportunity to blitz a bunch of them, but I turned mean and stomped on the idea. Now he won't talk to me, except to grunt in passing. He takes his profession so damn seriously—like the high priest of some half-baked cult. Science is his holy grail.

...Out of meat for two days, and still it rains and snows. Filthy weather! I wonder how Charles and the gang are making out. Sure hope they have some shelter. Between snow flurries after lunch I went for a walk and spotted eight bucks near Bear Slough. I hadn't brought a gun so I crawled half a mile on my belly in order to avoid spooking them then ran a mile to the cabin, grabbed a rifle, and ran back. And, of course, they had vamoosed.

I climbed the nearest ridge and from the crest could see them loping off to the northwest. I ran like hell to outflank them, then had to crawl through a sodden, half-frozen muskeg. By then they were at least 250 yards away, but the dog-meat situation was so serious I took a long shot and dropped one. As I was gutting the carcass it dawned on me I'd have to carry the meat two miles back to camp over rocky ridges and through muskeg. Never mind; the dogs will love me.

...As I was coming back from a walk up Little River a bird flushed right under foot. I soon found the nest pouched between rocks under a clump of dwarf willows. It was unfamiliar and so were the five heavily speckled eggs, so I got out my binos and chased after the owner, who was flitting anxiously through the shrubbery. She turned out to be a Harris sparrow! Well, this is the way rarities are found—by accident. So far as I know only two Harris sparrow nests have ever been discovered, this being the second.

I thought about leaving it alone, but thought again and carefully picked up nest and eggs and brought them back to Harper as a peace offering. He was really pleased, and grateful. He blew the eggs, treating them as if they were Dresden china, then spent an hour searching the nest for bird lice, which he caught with forceps and carefully preserved in a vial of alcohol.

...Today is July 1st and I was wakened by a fusillade of rifle shots. Leapt out of my tent to find Fred blazing away at some deer across the river. He had arrived home all alone at about 2:00 a.m. in a fifteen-foot canoe that Charles had stored at the Kazan with an Eskimo called Pommela. Fred told me the others were following in the big canoe.

Trying to get the story of the trip out of him was like pulling teeth from a ptarmigan. I gathered it took them eleven days to fight their way up Little River. Fred wouldn't say why he'd come home alone, but I sense trouble between him and Charles.

I fed him a huge breakfast then at his suggestion we took the little canoe out to some islands in the mouth of Windy River hoping to find duck eggs to replenish our larder. Found 8 merganser, 7 old squaw, and 3 herring gull eggs. Decided to eat the gull's eggs as a snack then and there so Fred boiled them in my tea billy while I squatted by the shore watching sticklebacks frolic in the shallows. I caught one of these tiny fishes in my hand and showed it to Fred, pointing out the row of sharp spines along its back with which, I told him, it defends its nest and eggs. He gave me a look as if I was right off my rocker. Fish building nests like birds? It's likely he'll never again believe anything I tell him. We went home with the wherewithal for a bloody big omelette for supper—and bloody it was because some of the eggs were pretty well incubated.

...Today H. asked me to take him across to South Bay where he wanted to botanize. He took along two big packsacks full of cameras and collecting gear, a landing net, a casting rod, a gaff, a butterfly net, tripods, a shotgun, and a rifle. Enough stuff to damn near sink the canoe and to make for hard paddling, which he left to me. It isn't that he is lazy or physically incapable. He seems to be strong as a moose and thinks nothing of slogging for miles across the tundra after specimens. I guess he just wants to conserve his energy for science.

Leaving him on the shore at South Bay, I climbed to the crest of the Caribou Hills. An appalling vista stretched to the south—a maze of totally barren hills so thickly encrusted with frost-shattered boulders I swear not even a caribou could cross it without breaking a leg.

The contrasts in this country are astounding. A quarter mile farther along I came to a gully with a stream at its bottom nurturing a stand of relatively giant spruce trees. Some were two feet in diameter at the butt, but their trunks, held down by the wind, were so truncated as to be almost pyramidal. The tallest was no more than fifteen feet high. Amongst them waved luxuriant stands of cotton grass and a scattering of purple saxifrage in bloom. It was a beautiful and totally unexpected hidden garden.

I continued east as far as the cliff facing Wolf Knoll across the bay, and found it in the possession of a pair of peregrine falcons. They took a dim view of my presence, dive-bombing so ferociously that I retreated. But I was not to be let off so easily and was enveloped by a cloud of mosquitoes, the first I've met this season. They descended like a biblical plague: tiny, voracious, speedy, indefatigable, and without warning. I pulled my sweater up over my head and fled back to the canoe, but the plague was there before me and had already driven poor Harper half wild. He was trying to fight off the attackers by flailing at them with a canoe paddle.

We were both enormously relieved to get out on the water though the hungry hordes pursued us even there. Where they came from so suddenly

I do not know, but there is an Eskimo legend that inner earth is swarming with the little demons and only an ice plug keeps them in their place. When it melts...watch out!

...July 3rd. This evening the big canoe appeared at last bearing Charles and the rest of the gang. I almost literally fell on their necks. Charles and I stayed up most of the night eating, drinking, and yarning. He described a hell of a trip north bucking ice and high water, sometimes making good only a mile or two in a day's hard travel. They visited some Eskimo camps and found the people there had speared lots of deer and were doing well, though still emaciated from last winter's starvation, which is something Charles does not yet seem ready to talk about at any length.

Fred didn't join us tonight. Something is very wrong between him and Charles. Charles is not talking about that either, but I'm sure it has to do with Kunee/Rita. Maybe Fred expected Charles to leave her and Anoteelik behind at the Kazan with the other Eskimos? Well, now they are back at Windy Cabin and when Charles and I go south Fred will have to look after them. He's going to have his hands full with three kids, nine dogs, and Harper.

The Schweders are just about out of everything except what can be got from the country. Windy Bay is supposed to be fish heaven so now that the big canoe is back nets can be set; but you can't catch tea, sugar, flour, and lard in fish nets. The store at Brochet is 300 miles away, and might as well be 3,000 so long as the main body of Nueltin is still chock-a-block with ice.

...Staggered out this morning to find Charles in such a sweat to start for Brochet he had not gone to bed at all. We corralled the kids to help get the big canoe ready for the trip. Five of us (Fred was notable by his absence) spent the morning scraping her weatherbeaten bottom using axe heads, butcher knives, and chunks of broken glass. When the old paint came off a lot of canvas came with it. I had to patch plus-sixty holes left by our too-enthusiastic shipwrights, and the carpenter's glue, which is the only glue we have, won't dry despite the application of a red-hot frying pan.

In the evening Charles and I set a lightweight, two-inch mesh net in the bay. When we hauled it at midnight it contained some suckers and a thirty-pound lake trout who had wrapped himself up in it. We cut him into steaks and fried and ate until everybody's belly was bulging. Wonderful feed!

Charles wouldn't go back to the cabin. Says it is poisoning him. I don't know if he means the chemicals or the feud between me and Harper. He suggested since we can't head south yet because of the ice on Nueltin, why don't we take the little canoe up to Windy Lake. Sort of a test run. Just him and me.

Pushed off at dawn. Windy River was running a six-knot current and the rapids were roaring. We had to track the canoe up them, and couldn't make much headway even in the quieter stretches, except we hauled ourselves along by clutching at the willows on the banks.

The sunset this evening looked as if the gods were pouring molten metal into a mighty crystal bowl. Or maybe I've been reading too much Keats. To top it, a fireball shot overhead. I thought it looked frighteningly like a tracer shell, but C. saw it as a good omen for our big trip south.

Traveled on through the half-light until, at 0200, we reached Simmons Lake and an old trading post. It is twice the size of Windy Post, and built of big, beautifully squared logs fitted so tightly they hardly needed caulking. Doors and windows were gone and the roof was pretty well rotted out, but the walls were still sound.

Charles told me what he knew of its history. Del Simmons was an old-time barrenlands trapper-turned-independent-trader who in 1927 built a shanty of skins and saplings at Poorfish Lake out on the edge of the barrens. A little later a Chipewyan medicine man told him about an island on Windy Lake with a spectacular stand of spruce trees on it. Fox fur was worth a fortune then, so Del went south and hired a Swede carpenter fresh from the old country and took him to the island. There the two of them and a crowd of Indians built the finest log house ever seen in the country.

No sooner was it up than Revillon Frères, a French trading outfit, came in and built a competing post almost next door. Revillon was a big outfit, determined to squeeze Simmons out. However, instead of quitting he took his house apart, numbered all the logs, and floated them down Windy River to Simmons Lake, where he could intercept the Eskimo trade coming from the north. In the end Revillon was forced to quit.

Simmons went outside one summer in the thirties and never came back. Nobody knows why—maybe he went to war and got killed—but the walls of his house will stand for a long time yet.

The place is supposed to be haunted, and that it is—by mosquitoes in such numbers I had to sleep with my head inside my bag, choosing between suffocating or getting sucked dry. I fled the place before dawn leaving C. buried inside his bag, whose surface, crawling with mosquitoes, looked like a thing alive. The house sounded like a busy factory, so loud and penetrating was the hum. Outside, the mosquitoes formed a cloud around one's head that was visible thirty feet away. A smudge fire gave some protection but not much. Fortunately the bites didn't itch or bring up lumps so after a while you could get used to them. Sort of.

We took our time returning to Windy Post. I think Charles was relieved to find I could pull my weight, though it took me a while to get the feel of his way of paddling, Chipewyan-style. You paddle three strokes on one side, toss your paddle into the air, catch it with your hands in the opposite positions, and paddle three strokes on the other side. Then repeat the procedure. No need for steering strokes, and you never get tired; but if you miss grabbing the paddle while you're switching sides on a rapid, you can be in bad trouble.

We weren't alone on Windy River. It was thick with fish running upstream to spawn. In one shallow pool below a rapid I watched a three-foot lake trout, an even bigger northern pike, and a couple of grayling (a pink-fleshed arctic trout of salmon size) going through what looked like some sort of convoluted dance. We were out of grub so Charles shot one of the grayling with a .22. A neat trick if you can do it! The grayling's immense dorsal fin, shaped like that of a shark, was ablaze with iridescent color but the shimmer faded fast to a gray slick as the fish died.

The rapids intimidated me but Charles is a superb steersman and we shot through quick as an otter. We hauled out at Soapstone Point, at the river mouth not far below the cabin, and there encountered a good omen. A golden eagle was sitting on shore within a stone's throw of our landing place. He gave us the eye, but never budged.

We pushed off again to haul the two-inch net and found it so full of holes it looked as if a fleet of torpedoes had gone through it. One big trout was still in it though, so we took him ashore and cooked him on the beach for supper. We put the guts, tail, and head on the rocks for the eagle. He did not accept *the offering immediately, but it was gone by morning and so was he. Satisfied, I hope.*

…July 7th. Cooked breakfast for the gang (rolled oats with jaundice-yellow milk made from rancid milk powder), after which we painted the big canoe. Then we set and, in due course, hauled a five-inch-mesh net. Eureka! It was literally full to bursting with trout, grayling, pike, and some smaller species. H. was on hand when we came in and was ecstatic. Although he will collect any creature he can get his hands on, fish are his greatest passion. With this bonanza in view he announced he was taking over the entire stock of grain alcohol so he could fill every available receptacle with pickled fishes.

I saw red and mutinied. I reminded him pretty forcefully that I had bought the five gallons of alcohol. I said I was fully prepared to share it with him, but was damn well keeping part for my own use. At that he stalked off in high dudgeon.

Half an hour later he sent Mike to me with a letter informing me I was no longer a member of the Keewatin Zoological Expedition and he was taking possession of all the remaining supplies (though willing to reimburse me for my share at some later date). Furthermore, I was instructed not to mention him nor use the expedition's name in anything I might do, or write, in future. He concluded by billing me for half the cost of the air charter.

Ripping a page from my field notebook I scrawled a reply in which I told him just where to put his expedition; that he could keep our jointly purchased food and I hoped it would choke him; that rather than pay a nickel for air transport I would walk home; that he could rest assured neither his name nor that of his expedition would cross my lips so long as he walked the earth; and, finally, that I hoped the Great Collector in the sky would find a suitable wall in his celestial museum upon which to display Harper's pelt. All very childish of me…but very satisfying.

So ends my official connection with the Keewatin Zoological Expedition. From now on I am a free soul.

After that incident I hurried to tell Charles I would now be happy to accompany him to the North Pole if that was his fancy. The pair of us then withdrew to his private sanctuary—

Soapstone Point—where we grilled some trout, drank a little toddy, and gave ourselves over to the pleasure of making plans.

We decided that as soon as we had completed the obligatory trip to Brochet we would, with the help of Charles's dogs, pack our gear and the little canoe north to his Kazan Camp. There we would leave all but the two best dogs in the care of the Eskimos. Using the chosen pair as pack animals we would haul, paddle, and portage west across the height of land to the upper reaches of a river the Eskimos called River of Graves, then follow it north to Dubawnt Lake and so down the Dubawnt River to the Thelon.

Time and circumstances permitting, we would then paddle west up the Thelon to the fabled Thelon Oasis which, with its muskox and grizzly bears, lies in the very heart of the barren-grounds. Having visited it, we would turn about and descend the Thelon to the Hudson's Bay Company post on Baker Lake. There we would resupply and decide whether to return to Windy Post up the Kazan, or follow the coast of Hudson Bay to Churchill, where Charles could purchase his winter outfit before flying back to Windy in the Anson when Bourassa went in to retrieve Harper.

It promised to be an epic journey—if we could accomplish it. We planned on traveling very light, living off the land Eskimo fashion. Should we lose our canoe or be caught by an early freeze-up, we would walk out with the aid of our two pack dogs. Charles foresaw no insurmountable difficulties, and who was I to argue with him?

It was in high good humor that I went off to ready the bulk of my gear for shipment out in the Anson in October, then I returned to the shore to finish painting the big canoe. When Charles joined me, his look was dark and his manner strained. Harper had cornered him in the cabin then spent a long time try-ing to persuade him to abandon *both* the proposed journeys. Harper had instead proposed that Charles take him on a tour of Nueltin Lake to obtain specimens of freshwater seals which, it was rumored, were to be found at its northern end. If Charles was willing to do this, Harper would undertake to share the expedition's remaining rations and other supplies with the Schweder clan.

When Charles failed to accept the offer Harper warned him that, should he continue to associate with and "be guided by" me, he would be in trouble with the "authorities."

I could see that Charles was shaken by the possibility his trading and trapping license might be in jeopardy. Although holding my tongue is something I don't easily do, I had the sense to keep quiet and let him make up his own mind as to which course to follow, though I was very much afraid he might buckle under the pressure being brought to bear upon him.

PART THREE

IDTHEN
ELDELI

CHAPTER EIGHT

SOUTHBOUND

THE UNEASE CHARLES AND I FELT THIS NIGHT WAS SO *pervasive neither of us could sleep. It was drizzling so we holed up in the cabin until 2:00 a.m., when by unspoken agreement we reached a decision. Nueltin was probably still frozen over. Well, the hell with that; we were going anyway. And right away.*

The canoe was at Pipestone Point. The three kids appeared out of nowhere and gloomily helped move our gear down to it. The pre-dawn had a sepulchral quality, and a cold easterly breeze was blowing wisps of fog across the bay. The omens hardly seemed propitious, but we were bound to go.

Getting away wasn't that easy.

Although Harper had had more than enough time to write any letters he wanted to send out, he hadn't produced them. I was for pushing off anyway, but Charles insisted we give him a last chance, so we waited.

We put in the time by making a minute search for fuel for the old Lockwood outboard, the kicker, as they are called in this country. Charles had saved and cached ten gallons from his previous summer's trip for use this year. But when we went to get it we found the drum on its side with its stopper unscrewed and barely a quart left in it. Neither of us really believed this was just an accident, but all we could do was scour the camp for anything the kicker might burn. Old gas drums, a gasoline lantern, even a half-empty can of lighter fluid yielded their mites. By noontime when Harper finally produced his letters, we had about half a gallon of a fluid that at least smelled like gasoline.

*By now the east wind was blowing right on the nose and rising. Rita was
bawling. Anoteelik was trying to smile but making a hash of it. Mike got
hold of Charles's hand and wouldn't let go. Fred appeared briefly, then without a word stalked off into the barrens. Harper remained incommunicado in
the cabin.*

Time to go.

*We launched the canoe and climbed aboard. The kicker spluttered into
life though it sounded as if it were gagging on what it had in its tank. It's a
Lockwood, built in the late 1920s, but despite age, hard usage, and the soup
we've given it, all five horses kept on kicking until they took us across the
upper reaches of the bay and into the lee of the Caribou Hills. There the tank
went dry. But what the hell? We were on our way!*

From here on we had to paddle the canoe, a slab-sided brute with
a squared-off stern to take an outboard, made (not built) in
Winnipeg, apparently of cottonwood covered with cheesecloth.
Dry, she might have weighed 150 pounds. Water-logged, which
was her normal state, she weighed closer to 200. Lightly loaded,
as she was on this trip, she sat so high out of the water that I, as
bowman, had to reach down to wet the blade of my paddle.

Her cargo consisted of our bedrolls; my army-surplus pup
tent (designed for one man but capable of sheltering two); an
orange crate serving as grub-box-cum-kitchen; and a bag of mis-
cellaneous camp gear. As a gesture of goodwill toward Harper, we
also took along one of his butter tubs filled with formalin solution in which to preserve fish specimens from farther south.

Because of the shortages at Windy, we took very little food:
a few pounds of flour for making the ubiquitous bannocks; a
three-pound can of fatty bacon; a little tea; and a small tin of jam.

With the arrival of Europeans, bannock soon became the staple food of arctic travelers. To make it, one need only untie the
mouth of a sack of flour; sprinkle a teaspoonful of baking powder on the exposed surface; mix the baking powder into the top
inch or so of flour; make a depression about the size of one's fist;

then slowly pour cold water into this hollow, stirring as one pours. When the resultant ball of dough is thick enough *not* to stick to your flesh, pat it (a knee makes an adequate working surface) until it is a little smaller than the diameter of your frying pan and about half an inch thick. Put a chunk of lard or other fat into the pan and heat till it starts spitting. Slip in the bannock dough and cook, flipping at intervals until both sides are golden brown. *Voilà!* Here is breakfast, lunch, dinner, and snacks in between.

Having hauled the now-useless Lockwood aboard, we paddled on to Windy Point. The gale whistling around it challenged us to a duel, but we declined. Although the cabin lay a mere six miles astern, it was distant enough to give us peace of mind, so we went ashore, pitched the little tent on a thick bed of sphagnum moss, and celebrated the beginning of our voyage with a feed of whitefish.

I thought to have had a good sleep this night, but Charles was in a mood to unburden himself. Although his fragmentary talk was full of allusions to people and events about which I as yet knew very little, it centered on the terrible disaster which had overwhelmed "his" Eskimos during the past winter.

He also talked obliquely and opaquely about little Rita as if she belonged to him, though in just what way was not at all clear to me. Was she his daughter? Or adopted? He did not say. However, one thing was clear: Charles's relations with his brothers was suffering from the little girl's presence, and this weighed heavily upon him.

Around 2:00 a.m., he crawled out of the tent and went walking in the icy fog blowing in from the frozen lake. I pretended to be asleep when he returned but heard him mutter:

"Not *going* to send her back...she's *mine*."

Next day I wrote in my journal:

Something inside Charles is eating him up. It might be he has picked up an Eskimo custom of becoming engaged to a child and playing a father's role until she is old enough to be his wife. Apparently there was something between him and a girl called Pama who died this past winter on the Kazan. I gather that had she not died he intended to bring her to Windy Post, whether as mistress or wife I haven't a clue.

He seems to believe he could never get a white woman and for some reason rejects the idea of taking up with an Indian, though this is what his father did. The only thing left would seem to be the Eskimo connection.

Does this explain Rita? Certainly he is lavishing all he has of affection and care upon her and she responds. But how can I know what is really going on?

Fred is surely part of the equation. He and Charles are virile young males leading a hard and lonely life and, I would think, desperately in need of sex. To complicate matters, there are apparently few young women left alive in the Ihalmiut tribe, and presumably none to spare for outsiders.

Part of Charles's inner conflict may stem from the fact that he feels he is categorized as a half-breed but sees himself as a white, yet one who cannot truly belong to white society; does not choose to belong to Indian society; lives apart from those of mixed blood; and therefore has no option but to turn to the Eskimos. Yet he doesn't want me or any other white to think he is going native, as the saying has it.

I wonder what he'll do. If he goes outside he'll have to try to become a white man. If he stays in this remote corner of the north he'll have only a handful of Eskimos to populate his world. I suspect this guy is in one hell of a bind.

At the moment I'm not doing so well myself. I'm shaken by the hostility I feel toward Harper. It is scary to realize how much enmity can be generated so quickly with so little real cause between two men, both of whom ought to know better. The departure from Windy Post should have brought me the same kind of relief I used to feel on getting leave after a battle. Instead of which I feel distressed, confused, and apprehensive.

Next morning brought a windless, cloudless sky and what felt like a real summer sun. It was too good to be true. Scarcely had we launched on the main arm of Windy Bay than a nor'easter came howling over the hills.

We bucked it for a couple of miles before deciding to cross to the opposite shore and seek a lee. Pack ice, which had previously been hidden by a veil of fog, caught us in mid-channel. It looked to be impenetrable until we spotted a narrow lead into which we paddled, hoping to get through it before the pack could trap us.

Now a vicious squall of wind and sleet struck us, and by the time the storm scud had cleared away the lead had vanished. There was no alternative but to wrestle with the pack itself.

This was a scary business. Minor leads opened and closed unpredictably as we paddled, poled, and pushed. Ice grating against the canoe's fragile flanks seemed to grate against my very bones. The wind increased, and soon a heavy swell was making the thick floes rise and fall ponderously. Cold and frightened, we had no option but to persevere, tracing a tortuous path through a grinding maze, often forced backwards, sometimes traveling in circles. It was late in the afternoon before we escaped into a narrow strip of open water sheltered by a chain of islands.

We went ashore on one of these apparently barren rocks to rest and flushed a white-winged scoter off her nest. Knowing the eggs would be well incubated, we took them anyway. At the rate we were going, we expected to run out of grub long before reaching any place where we could renew our supplies.

Eventually we clawed our way to the mouth of Windy Bay and there found mighty Nueltin, eighty miles in length and up to twenty broad, *solidly frozen over from shore to distant shore.*

We put in to the western headland of the bay and pitched camp with man-high snowbanks behind us and stranded pans of lake ice in front of our little tent. It was hardly a summery scene.

The sour aftertaste of our departure from Windy Cabin dissipated during the night. To further improve our mood, we found that a west wind had opened a narrow shore-lead. Only about fifty feet in width, and barred off at every projecting point of land, it nevertheless offered a passage to the south.

Or so we hoped. The hopes proved ephemeral. The lead

forced us to follow the most minute indentations in the coast and to portage over innumerable out-thrust points. Because the shore water was shoal, we often had to walk or wade, towing the canoe behind us. This proved so tedious we were eventually tempted to try hauling the canoe across the unbroken pack.

Although the ice was several feet thick, it had been "candled" by the hot sun into long crystals none-too-securely held together by friction. These tended to disintegrate when stepped upon, plunging us into frigid water. When this happened, we had to grab the gunwales of the canoe and hoist ourselves back aboard, dripping and cursing. I soon lost track of the number of times the ice crumbled, dunking me to the waist.

After some fifteen hours in this icy purgatory, we reached the entrance to a cove leading to a place Charles called Hidden Valley. He described it to me in glowing terms as a sort of linear oasis extending ten or more miles into the barren, broken hills to the west.

"Sure is some pretty in there. Lots of deer and birds and fur. Anybody lived in there'd be king of the country. Nobody'd *ever* find him." This last was said with wistful emphasis.

I was entranced by what little I could see of it: golden eskers winding their serpentine ways through rolling, lichen-carpeted parkland dotted with fine, big spruces; clear lakes with sandy shores; and a placid stream winding through a green willow swale. I was for camping, but Charles insisted we push on. Perhaps he did not wish to share his secret valley.

Crossing the bay, we made short portages between three ponds to avoid going around Big Point, a hulking, almost insular, mound of rock four or five miles long and two or three broad jutting far out into the ice-bound lake.

Reaching an almost landlocked and marvelously sheltered cove behind this point, we went ashore below a level, mossy terrace strewn with what in the half light I at first took to be a carpet of bones, but which proved to be a tangle of weathered poles that had once supported a score or more conical skin- or bark-covered tents. The tents themselves had long since vanished, leaving only shallow, circular depressions over which a few standing poles leaned at crazy angles. These poles and their fallen companions had been transformed by time from limber saplings into a substance almost as brittle as glass and as hard as iron.

I asked Charles whose camp it was.

"Likely Chips. Denikazi, he's the oldest Chip I ever met, said his people used to camp here hundreds of years ago on their way north after the deer. Then one time something bad happened here. Sickness maybe. Anyhow, a lot of them died and nobody never camped here after."

This sheltered place behind Big Point may have last been used by people the early arctic explorer Samuel Hearne knew as the "Northern Indians." Later travelers called them Chipewyans, but they knew themselves to be *Idthen Eldeli*—People of the Deer. Hearne wrote that on January 1, 1771, he and his Idthen Eldeli companions crossed on the ice of the large lake *Nuelthintua* to reach a camp on the western shore where some twenty women and scores of children were awaiting the return of their menfolk, who had gone to Fort Prince of Wales (now Churchill) to obtain guns, powder, and shot.

Ten years later smallpox raged through the entire Idthen Eldeli country, which in those times reached north to the Thelon River and west to Great Slave Lake. According to Hearne this deadly scourge destroyed nine-tenths of the Northern Indians. The year 1791 may well have been when the camp behind Big Point became a village of the dead. I expected we would pitch camp here; instead, Charles began collecting armfuls of the weathered poles and loading them aboard the canoe.

"What's up?" I asked.

"Not going to stay here, that's what. Find us a better place. But this old wood burns good, so we'll take some along."

While he busied himself gathering fuel, I mooched about to

see what I could find. Weathered wooden splints two feet long, sharpened at both ends, were scattered around old firepits. Charles identified these as skewers upon which the Idthen Eldeli had roasted their meat. There were also fragments of hand sleds, canoe ribs, and even crumbling pieces of birchbark.

All the wooden objects were of the same silvery-gray color and bore the same silken sheen, a patina resulting from innumerable seasons of exposure to the aseptic arctic atmosphere.

A thick lump of moss within one of the tent circles drew my attention, and I nudged it with my foot, uncovering part of a yellowed human skull. I hurried back to the canoe to tell Charles.

"Yes," he said softly. "So now you see why nobody camps here."

We paddled on in silence until Charles steered us to another strip of beach terrace nearly identical in appearance to the one we had rejected. Here we pitched camp and should have gone to bed, but I was restless. Although I could sense Charles's disapproval, I took advantage of the early dawn light to walk back to the ancient Idthen Eldeli camp. At its near end a pair of boulders sat like two stools in a circular patch of sand flecked by glittering shards of flint—detritus left by generations of hunters who had used the boulders as seats, or as anvils, while chipping flint tools and weapons.

In a nearby firepit I found a strangely shaped elliptical wooden blade with serrated edges, about a foot long and a quarter inch thick. When I brought this back to Charles, he took it from me, tied a length of fishing line to a hole in one end, then stood up and began whirling it around his head. The blade spun rapidly at the end of the line, filling the dawn with a sonorous throbbing that was felt as well as heard. It was such an extraordinarily eerie sound that I was glad when Charles let the blade sink to the ground. He handed it back to me and said, without a smile:

"Don't know what it's called. Eskimos make them to chase away bad spirits."

Not bothering to set up our tent, we catnapped on the beach

for a few short hours. When Charles shook me awake, the new day had broken, calm and sunny—too good to waste, especially since the easterly wind might return and drive back the ice, trapping us against the shore.

Before setting out, we made a reconnaissance on foot. From the summit of Big Point we could see much of Nueltin, although the profusion of islands, capes, and inlets made it impossible to determine its true shape.

To the north and to the east it presented an unbroken expanse of ice. However, some five or six miles to the south of us was a band of mist that Charles thought might indicate open water.

Though in a hurry to get underway, we had first to repair several tears in the canoe's canvas covering. While Charles did this, I examined three nearby tent sites ringed with boulders, which Charles told me was the usual Eskimo method of anchoring skin tents.

Eskimos this far south? Yes, said Charles. Some time after the Idthen Eldeli abandoned the big campsite, and until fairly recently, Kazan Eskimos had occasionally come this far south for wood with which to make tools and equipment and, later, to trade with outposts from Reindeer Lake.

A southeasterly breeze sprang up as soon as we pushed off, driving the local ice and us to the western shore of the cove under the lee of a four-hundred-foot rock face alive with cliff swallows, a species I had not expected to find so far north. Their mud nests clung to the rock everywhere. Well, *almost* everywhere. Screaming voices and the tearing sound of diving wings signaled the presence of a pair of peregrines who were also nesting on the cliff. Then two ravens stormed off *their* nest, a huge, ramshackle pile of sticks, and dived upon us. All this avian action attracted a posse of gulls, who cheered and jeered as we departed.

The ice now forced us into a dead-end from which there was no escape except overland. So overland we went, portaging canoe and gear from one pond to another until we could regain the main body of the lake, where, to our delight, we found the ice field breaking up. Thereupon we became brazen and instead of coast-crawling made for an open lead about a mile offshore.

This entailed a nightmarish struggle as we forced the canoe between pans or hauled her over rotten ice between potholes and slender leads, frequently falling in and constantly cursing the foul honeycomb underfoot, which was neither good solid ice nor ice-free water. Eventually we reached the big lead and found a postage stamp of an islet. We landed on it and devoted the rest of our wood supply to building a fire big enough to dry us out a little, and to cook some bannocks.

We had intended to return to the mainland to spend the night, but a great black squall looming up in the east gave us cause to pitch the tent where we were. Though we anchored it with a wall of rocks, it looked singularly fragile and insecure against a background of rising sea and darkening sky.

A full gale howled in from the southeast, and a deluge of rain and sleet tried to beat the tent to the ground. Though the floor proved water repellent, the roof was not. The upshot was that we spent the night in a subarctic approximation of a child's wading pool.

By the time I got to sleep I knew my decision to set aside some of the grain alcohol for the preservation of the living rather than dedicating it all to the preservation of scientific specimens had been the right one.

Charles may have thought so too. In his journal he wrote:

Mowat and I had a nice little talk tonight. Wish I could talk a little more to people and then I may forget what have happen in the past few years.... I am worrying again tonight but whats the use, it would not help anyway. I feel as if something has been taken from me that I can never get back.

CHAPTER NINE

MANY ISLANDS LAKE

A T DAWN CHARLES POKED HIS HEAD OUT THE doorway and reported fog too thick for us to travel in, so I went back to sleep. Some time later I woke to the heartening sound of a crackling fire. No fuel was to be had on the islet, but Charles (using some sixth sense of his own) had paddled through the murk to an invisible mainland to gather an armful of driftwood deposited by rivers running into Nueltin from the forest country.

Hot tea did much to dispel the gloom of our refuge, which we now found we were sharing with a pair of arctic terns. These wailed so plaintively around us we concluded they must have young. Charles wondered why anything that could fly would choose to nest on this benighted scrap of rock. He was incredulous when I told him the terns had probably flown a round trip of thirty thousand miles in order to have this dubious pleasure.

These ethereal little beings—with a pigeon's wingspan and a weight of only a few ounces—annually travel from their arctic nesting grounds across the Atlantic to Europe, on to Africa, then all the way south to antarctic waters, where they winter, returning north via South America the following spring. They make the longest known migration of any bird.

"How you know all that?" Charles asked skeptically.

I told him that, in the spring of 1935, I had helped place

aluminum bands on the legs of young arctic terns at Churchill, and a year later one of the bands had been returned from a military station on the Congo, where the tern which bore it had been shot.

"Since then lots of terns have been banded and returns have come in from all along their migration route. There can't be any doubt about it. They fly like long-distance angels, but don't ask me why they go so far."

Having nothing better to do for the moment, we searched the islet and turned up one fuzzy and bedraggled ternlet crouched under a stone. Its parents screamed at it to take to the water, which it did, a tiny bundle of wet down swimming off into the murk, muttering to itself. Charles watched it go and shook his head.

"That little thing going to go to Africa and back? Don't seem likely."

Eventually we paddled on into a vortex of swirling vapor, a sinister obscurity where the only sounds were those made by the dip and drip of our paddles. Toward midday the fog began to burn off, revealing a maze of channels and islands at Nueltin Narrows. A fringe of spruce and tamarack on the larger islands showed we were crossing the ephemeral boundary known to geographers as timberline.

Charles piloted us to a cache made by Fred during his return to Windy Post by dog sled in early June. The site was marked by a lob-stick, so we had no difficulty finding it. We went ashore in high anticipation since, according to what Fred had told us, the cache contained tea, a twenty-five-pound bag of flour, and some sugar. Alas, we were to be disappointed. We found only some mildewed moccasins, a case of Gillett's Lye (used by the Schweders in making soap from deer fat), a box of candles, and some iron sled runners.

This was a serious blow because in outfitting for the trip we had counted on this cache. With almost nothing left to eat, we now had to pin our hopes on finding a second cache, supposedly containing flour, lard, sugar, and tea, which Fred claimed to have made at the south end of the lake.

Before proceeding we had to do something about the canoe. Leaking, waterlogged, and badly roughed-up by ice, she did not slip easily through the water but lumbered along like a coal barge. We concluded that if we were ever going to reach Brochet we would have to speed her up. Charles thought it might be worthwhile to melt down the candles and smooth her lacerated canvas with a coating of hot wax. I opted to investigate ways and means of putting her under sail.

Here I should note that I have been shipmates with small craft most of my life, and all have borne names, usually ones with affectionate overtones. But so unlovable was Charles's freighter that nobody had ever christened her—or at least not with a name fit for mixed company.

Could she be induced to sail? This *was* a challenge! Eventually I worked out a bastard lateen rig somewhat similar to that employed on Arab dhows, using the tent as a mainsail. Though Charles (who had never sailed) was politely skeptical, he nevertheless helped cut, peel, and trim a mast, boom, and gaff, then stood dubiously by to watch me rig our ship.

When she was ready for sea trials, I took the stern seat and assumed command. Charles gingerly settled himself amidship, where he clutched at the gunwales apprehensively as we set off on our maiden cruise.

A fresh northwesterly breeze was blowing, and the canoe responded surprisingly well at first, proceeding ponderously across an east-trending section of the narrows at a speed of three or four knots. I was delighted with her—until the wind changed direction, coming at us over the port bow, whereupon the canoe heeled over and began skittering sideways like a crab.

This so alarmed Charles that he ordered me to run her ashore. But I was captain now. After a lot of shouting, I managed to persuade him to hold his paddle vertically over the side so it would function as a keel and give the canoe some grip on the water. This primitive leeboard worked well enough to enable me to steer a course the rest of the way through the narrows—a distance of about twelve miles.

Emerging into what Charles called the Big Opening, we went ashore to adjust the rig. Charles was now generous with his praise, and my chest swelled. For the first time in our relationship, I had stepped out of the apprentice's role. In an attempt to reinforce my tenuous advantage, I offered a somewhat pompous discourse on the theory of sail.

Charles cut me short. "Never mind about that. We got a long way to go, so you just make her sail till we can find some gas. Should be able to borrow some from Ragnor Jonsson, then we'll get to Brochet pretty quick."

Humbled, I did as bidden.

The Chipewyan name *Nuelthintua* means Many Islands Lake, and it certainly does contain a lot of them, especially in the southern portion, where it is little more than a maze of channels. Big Opening is the exception. Stretching twenty miles south from the narrows to the mouth of Putahow River, it is divided into broad lanes by parallel rows of low and barren islands, roughly oval in shape, and somewhat resembling ships of a battle fleet sleeping at anchor.

It was a superb evening as we set sail down the opening, crystal-clear and very warm. Sunset was producing a torrent of fluctuating flame that seemed almost too gaudy to be real. At about 8:00 p.m. we landed on one of the stone battleships for a mug-up.

The wind dropped out while we were ashore. When we pushed off, under paddle again, the blood drained out of the sky, giving way to a dazzling stellar display the likes of which I could not recall ever having seen before. We paddled wordlessly as if in a trance, eyes raised to a sky that had truly become a window on infinity.

It must have been past midnight before we closed with the heavily wooded shore of Jonsson's Island. We were still a hundred yards off when I became aware of a sullen and sinister sound, as of German bombers droning over the English coast en route to London. It was the only warning we had of the reception awaiting us.

The air above the beach was almost viscous with mosquitoes. As the canoe nosed up on the sand, wave after wave dive-bombed us kamikaze-style. Dropping our paddles, we burrowed into our packsacks for canvas parkas, the hoods of which provided some protection but could not keep suicide squads from plunging into eyes and mouths.

Abandoning the canoe, we fled at a dead run along the beach looking for trapper Ragnor Jonsson's cabin. The sound made by mosquitoes flinging themselves against my parka hood was like the rattle of hail. I had snatched a bottle of fly dope out of the canoe and this we poured over hands and faces, but it only served to trap the attackers in sticky masses. Although the distance to the cabin was no more than half a mile, I was close to panic by the time we reached it.

The cabin upon which we had pinned our hope of refuge turned out to be a log shack about twelve feet square with one tiny window. The door was barricaded from the outside to keep out animal intruders, but we tore it open and plunged inside—to find ourselves in a truly nightmarish den thickly hung with dozens of raw wolf pelts. The stench was indescribable. To make matters worse, the place was as dark as a cave.

Fortunately Charles had the stub of a candle in his parka pocket. By its flickering light we were able to heave out enough stinking hides to make room for ourselves, only to discover that the walls were so full of chinks that the mosquitoes could—and did—flood in from all sides. Frantically searching the place, we came upon an old Flit gun, filled it with lamp oil, and pumped furiously until the air became almost unbreathable. In desperation I even turned the sprayer on my face, thereby temporarily blinding myself.

Ragnor Jonsson had left a note pinned over the stove saying he had started for Brochet a month earlier, his canoe heavy-laden with wolf pelts, but had smashed his outboard on a rapid and been forced to carry everything back to his cabin before undertaking the horrendously difficult trek on foot to Duck Lake, well over a hundred miles to the east.

"Stayed here, he'd be eat to death!" Charles muttered as he slathered over his face and neck some rancid bear grease he had found in a cupboard.

A further search of the cabin and its environs produced six gallons of gas, a one-pound tin of butter, and some dried figs. We fled back to our canoe, gassed up the motor, and roared away into the midnight dusk. The relief we felt when we shook off the last of our pursuers was indescribable.

We cruised about for a long time, seeking a safe haven and giving all well-wooded islands a wide berth. Eventually (and suspiciously) we approached a rocky reef in the middle of Big Opening. Finding it mercifully free of bugs, we pitched our little tent, fried some addled and incubated tern eggs in Ragnor's butter, and went to bed as the sun rose—only to be awakened a short time later by the dreadful sound of thousands of little feet pattering on the canvas roof.

Thank heaven it was only rain!

A roaring westerly kept us pinned to the reef for most of the next day. The gale washed up the corpse of a caribou fawn so well preserved by the icy water it looked edible. Charles was willing to cook it, but I was not yet hungry enough to eat carrion. Instead we munched some stale bits of bannock, dried our clothing and bedrolls in the wind, and greased the engine while Charles told me a little about Ragnor Jonsson.

"He's a nice man but not too careful the way he lives. Got a Cree girlfriend at Brochet he'd like to marry, only she says she can't live with him. Well, I guess you seen yourself how he lives. We stayed around his cabin a while last winter when we had to come south 'cause we was out of grub. I pitched a tent outside 'cause I couldn't sleep in there. Rita and Anoteelik wouldn't sleep in there. Said it made them sick to their stomachs. I guess if Ragnor ever does get himself a wife it'll have to be a wolverine."

Born in Sweden around 1900, Ragnor came to Canada with his immigrant parents just after the First World War. By 1926 he had drifted to South Reindeer Lake, where, like Fred Schweder before him, he was befriended by the Cree community. Amongst them was Joe Highway, doyen of local Cree trappers. When Ragnor wondered where he might stake out a trapline, Joe suggested the northern end of Nueltin Lake, but Ragnor rejected the idea of living north of the timberline.

"Said he would go crazy out there," Charles explained. "Had to have trees around him. One time he did come north as far as Windy Post but only stayed a couple days before he run back south again like the wolfs was going to catch him."

The wolf was Jonsson's *bête noir*. He claimed that during his early years as a trapper he had lost a dog team to wolves and in consequence had nearly perished. Thereafter he became a dedicated "wolfer," killing wolves with the passion and persistence other men bring to making love. Such was the strength of his vendetta it was said he would walk right past a silver fox for the chance to kill a wolf.

Like most trappers of his ilk (and most wolf hunters even today), Ragnor was not particular how he got his prey. Steel traps worked well but were heavy and expensive. Poison— either arsenic or strychnine—was cheap, light, and easy to use, so it was Jonsson's preference. During our search of Jonsson's cabin, I had come across a pint jar filled with white powder and marked with a skull and crossbones. When I asked Charles what it was, he appeared embarrassed and did not offer a straight reply.

"'Taint sugar anyhow," was all he said as he took the jar from me and shoved it to the back of a cupboard.

Joe Highway eventually took Jonsson to south Nueltin, a gateway region for caribou migrating between the winter woodlands and the summer barrenlands. Setting himself up at the south end as a kind of gatekeeper, Jonsson did his best to kill every wolf that came his way. He boasted that by so doing he had saved the lives of countless caribou, but he never spoke of the many hundreds or thousands of deer he himself had butchered to serve as bait for his sets and to feed himself and his dogs.

The barrenland caribou has fired the curiosity of western man since explorers first encountered it. Unlike the prairie buffalo whose life was largely open to the scrutiny of the new invaders, the barrenland caribou long remained shrouded in mystery.

Numerous almost beyond belief—some observers estimate that as late as the nineteenth century ten million caribou still inhabited the Canadian north—la Foule could appear in such numbers as to literally blanket the landscape, yet in a few days might be gone again. Where did they go? To what destinations and for what reasons?

We know that la Foule mostly summers on the open tundra and seeks the protection of the boreal forests in winter, though its peregrinations are much more complex than this.

In the spring of 1947 the first deer to appear at Windy River were bands of pregnant does, flowing and melding, separating and reuniting, but maintaining a single massive presence as they hurried north. For two weeks they dominated the world, then they were gone except for a trickle of stragglers, mostly old, sick, or sterile does. Before the last of these had vanished they were overtaken by herds of bucks in such numbers they seemed like a veritable avalanche of life. They were not, however, as compulsively driven as the does, and the last of them did not disappear into the tundra plains until the end of June.

Those passing before me in the spring of 1947 were hardly things of beauty. They were molting, and the passage through the forests had rubbed much of their hair away, revealing unsightly patches of black skin. The distended bellies of the pregnant does and the oddly angular shape of both sexes did not accord well with the elegant image conjured up by the word "deer." Certainly they bore little resemblance to the pretty reindeer of Disney fancy. Nevertheless, their long and knobbly legs and huge splayed feet carried them over the roughest terrain with speed and certainty.

By the end of June the deer were gone from Windy River, but a record of their passage remained vividly imprinted on the land, where hundreds of acres of bogs had been churned to chocolate-colored puddings by innumerable hooves, and the homely stench of barnyard lingered for weeks. Even bald ridges paved with frost-shattered stone had been scored by their innumerable feet. So many trails criss-crossed hills and valleys alike that it was difficult to find a patch of open ground in all that wide array that did not bear the deep impress of the passing multitudes. In some defiles these paths had actually been incised into the living rock.

In July of 1948 I would meet la Foule again near Dubawnt Lake on the southern edge of a vast fawning ground extending northward to Back River. The does there had already given birth (mostly within a week of one another), and the precocious fawns could already outrun a man and even a wolf. I watched them coughing and grunting as they milled around their restless mothers, and it was impossible to count them. From the crest of a low hill I looked across the tundra plains for miles, and everywhere beheld an ever-shifting frieze of does and fawns that may have numbered well into the tens of thousands. Moreover, the frieze was not static. It drifted steadily from east to west as new contingents came into view and others departed.

Once fawning is over, the great aggregations break up into smaller herds that remain forever on the move. Caribou have no home. In the course of an average year, they may travel a direct-line distance of seven or eight hundred miles north and south, while actually walking many times that distance.

Late in July small herds start drifting southward. They carry other herds along with them, and momentum builds until by early August it has become a flood. Then la Foule, the lifeblood of the barrens, pours south led by does and fawns, soon followed by the bucks, now carrying enormous racks of velvet-covered antlers.

Surprisingly, when the flood reaches the edge of forested country, the herds often come to a halt, mill about, and turn back in apparent disorder. The disorder is, however, only apparent. The deer know what they are about, and soon the whole mighty assemblage is on its way north again.

Many attempts have been made to explain this late-summer "reverse" migration. Some think it an attempt to escape the plague of biting flies. Others believe it is part of an ancient legacy dating back to the last glaciation. I think it is probably a matter of economics. Tundra vegetation grows very slowly and does not accumulate in significant quantities. At best it can offer only sparse and scattered pasturage. Vast as the arctic prairies are, they can provide only so much bounty. Utterly dependent on that bounty, the caribou must forever be on the move. It is not for nothing that the Idthen Eldeli call them children of the wind.

By mid-September the eddying herds may be well to the north when a new mood comes upon them. The rut is drawing near.

Now they are fat. By late summer, a prime buck will have accumulated a layer of suet two or three inches thick across his back. The glistening new coats of all the animals gleam with rich shades of ocher. Having recovered from the ordeal of bearing and nursing their young, the does are sleek again and, if not eager, at least passively ready for the October days when the rut will take place. Velvet streamers peel from the bucks' antlers, which have become so massive they seem to rake the skies. The does, too, are sporting antlers. Though these are mere spikes compared to the spreads of the bucks, they are a considerable curiosity because caribou does are the only female North American deer to bear antlers at all.

The rut is a time of fantastic sights and sounds. Companies of bucks engage in almost constant, if mostly symbolic duels. Struggles for dominance continue day and night, and at times the crash of antlers against antlers becomes so loud and continuous it is hard for anyone camped near the rutting herds to sleep.

The rut continues to swirl across the barrens until the first heavy snow arrives. This is clear warning that winter is about to come roaring down out of the high arctic, and the deer heed it. Something akin to frenzy seizes them as they come surging south, intent on gaining the shelter of the forests, not because they fear the cold—they are so well insulated that cold is seldom their enemy—but because wind-packed drifts encase the tundra plains in winter and make finding food difficult.

Once the forests have been reached, the panic subsides. Again the Throng dissolves into individual herds, some of which may wander as far south as the Churchill River. At least, they used to go so far in the days before we laid our doom upon them.

One of the greatest winter concentrations is around Reindeer Lake, which explains the origin of the name.

In November of 1948 Peter Moiestie, a seventy-year-old Metis, took me by dog sled to a once-famous caribou river crossing not far north of Reindeer Lake. Although the ice was already several inches thick, it was still crystal clear, and through it I could plainly see a chaotic tangle of bones and antlers reaching close to the frozen surface.

That night we camped in an abandoned cabin nearby, and Peter told me something of the story behind that enormous submarine cemetery.

In his grandfather's time the deer arriving from the north entered a natural defile between two adjacent eskers, which funneled them to this crossing place. In those days, they were so numerous it was as if a river of deer intersected the river of water. The living flow would continue for two or three weeks and, so Peter claimed, number as many individuals as there were stars in the night sky. Doubtless he exaggerated, for an old man's memories may be greener than events. And yet...there were all those bones underneath the ice.

How did they come to be there?

When the buffalo on the western prairies had been butchered close to extermination, the great trading companies began experiencing a shortage of pemmican, the staple food which fueled a fur-trade transportation system stretching all the way east to Montreal. In this extremity the traders turned upon la Foule and coerced and bribed the Idthen Eldeli into becoming the new suppliers of pemmican.

The methods by which the Idthen Eldeli were recruited are instructive. Generous "debt" was extended to them, and they were strongly encouraged to buy anything and everything that met their fancy, especially new repeating rifles and virtually limitless quantities of ammunition with which they would be able to slaughter deer and so redeem their debts.

By the time Peter Moiestie's grandfather was a youth, the great blood-letting of la Foule had begun. Every winter thereafter the ice at the narrows Peter showed me groaned under the weight of butchery. In the course of time the deep channel became so clogged with caribou bones a canoe could no longer navigate it. And in the course of time the river of living creatures that had once flowed between the esker ridges to the crossing place dwindled and faded, became a trickle, and all but ceased.

Pemmican eventually lost its importance, but the wholesale slaughter of the deer continued as other ways were found to profit from it. White trappers, who were dedicated killers, invaded the caribou country. The aboriginals themselves, inculcated with new appetites for manufactured goods and equipped with the means of destroying far more animals than they had ever been able to kill before, contributed to the massacre.

In 1948 the residents of Brochet, where as late as 1920 as many as fifty thousand deer had wintered within a day's sled travel of the settlement, were hard put to it to find and kill enough caribou to feed themselves and their dogs.

The deer were not the only living things to suffer decimation. In 1900, according to records kept at the Brochet mission station, the Idthen Eldeli numbered some twelve hundred men, women, and children. By 1948 they numbered fewer than three hundred.

I had a conversation about their plight with a Brochet trader that year.

"It's mostly their own fault," he told me. "They killed the deer like there was no end to them. Well, there *was* an end. Now the natives and some of the white trappers has pretty near cleaned out the herds. Maybe when those fellows are all gone the deer will come back."

Maybe so ... and maybe not.

CHAPTER TEN

TELEQUOISIE

OUR FAILURE TO FIND FOOD AT FRED'S FIRST cache, or to find any useful amount at Jonsson's cabin, was a major disappointment, so as soon as wind and waves permitted we set off in search of Fred's second cache. For several hours we scoured labyrinthine passages between innumerable islands, without success, while depleting our small supply of gas. When we abandoned the search, we were left with the prospect of having to travel two hundred miles or more on two pounds of bacon, seven of flour, a pound of butter, some sugar and tea, and a handful of figs.

Fred had let us down, and I grumbled aloud, blaming sibling rivalry or some such problem for having made Fred less than candid about the contents and locations of his caches. My speculations evoked a cool reaction from Charles, so I changed the subject to the mysterious disappearance of the Keewatin Zoological Expedition's hand-fishing gear, some of which could have been of invaluable aid in feeding us. When I expressed my suspicions that Harper might have been to blame, Charles nodded but refused comment. It was characteristic of him that he was unwilling to discuss the alleged shortcomings of others.

Our futile search for the second cache ended in Nueltin's southernmost bay, embedded in a full-fledged forest of spruce, tamarack, Jack pine, and white birch. This was true boreal forest, and we did not have to penetrate very far into it before encountering some of its aboriginal inhabitants.

The bay concealed the broad mouth of the principal river flowing into Nueltin. Called Thlewiaza (Great Fish) River by the Chipewyans, it was known to the Cree and to white trappers and traders as Kasmere's River, after a man who until the late 1930s had been predominant amongst the Idthen Eldeli, and the real power in the land.

Shortly after entering the Kasmere we came upon an encampment of five wall tents perched in the shelter of a high riverside esker. The Lockwood's raucous cough brought nine men, ten women, and fifteen or twenty youngsters out of the tents to scramble up the esker and watch our approach.

These people were amongst the last survivors of the Idthen Eldeli, who, by 1947, had been reduced to three small bands: one at and about Wollaston Lake; a second at Misty Lake; and a third—the Barrenlands Band—south and east of Nueltin.

As we eased onto a beach where three canoes were drawn up, the watchers on the ridge remained silent and immobile. They appeared neither welcoming nor hostile; neither curious nor indifferent. Small, dark-skinned people, they could, despite being clad in black overalls or skirts, smoke-stained sweaters or jackets, visored caps or tattered head scarves, have been models for a frieze of mourners on a funerary urn from ancient times. I felt myself in the presence of a people truly alien to my kind and culture.

To my surprise Charles reacted as if he were experiencing the same feelings. Making no move to get out of the canoe, he did not even look in the direction of the watchers on the esker. Instead, he lowered his head and muttered diffidently, "Can't speak Chip."

Seeing nothing else for it, I began assuming the role of the White Explorer Encountering Natives by making friendly gestures.

There was no response until I produced my tobacco pouch and held it out at arm's length. Slow smiles greeted this venerable offer, then people broke ranks and began straggling down the sandy slope toward us. Almost everyone—man, woman, and child—either filled a pipe or rolled a cigarette and in no time we were all amicably engulfed in tobacco smoke.

A lean, sardonic-looking man with a Fu Manchu mustache, who introduced himself as Louis, now spoke to Charles in Cree, at which my companion's shyness melted. When some of the other men also admitted to speaking a little Cree, Charles was able to communicate fairly freely. I, on the other hand, had to rely on gestures, grins, and homemade sign language.

The women built us a fire on the beach, and when we had brewed up we invited all hands to be our guests. They accepted with alacrity as the camp had been out of tea for several weeks. Men, women, and even very young children produced mugs and tin cans, and soon we were all squatting chummily around the fire.

I suggested to Charles (not entirely disinterestedly, considering his warnings of many portages ahead) that we find someone to accompany us to Brochet. Charles put the question to Madees, a rotund fellow who looked strong enough to carry a moose. Madees suggested his younger brother, Telequoisie, who, he said, spoke a little English. Charles and Telequoisie withdrew to talk it over, leaving me to host the multitude. My task was made easier when someone produced a three-gallon galvanized pail in which I could make enough tea at one go to overflow the mugs of all comers.

Mosquitoes, blackflies, and sandflies were also present. The dogs, staked out on the beach, had dug themselves holes in which to hide their bleeding noses and ears. I was denied such protection, and my discomfort was so apparent that several young women went off and gathered armfuls of spruce boughs with which they made a smudge. This, if it did not keep the flies at bay, at least made the torment they caused seem almost the lesser of two evils.

Charles came back with the news that Telequoisie spoke only about ten words of English but had agreed to come with us. Charles chose this moment to tell me more about a terrible flu epidemic which had swept through the country early in the spring, killing about a hundred people, mostly Chipewyans. Every family had lost someone, he said, and several families had been virtually wiped out. To make matters worse, deer had been scarce during the winter. Because of the epidemic and the shortage of meat, trapping had been greatly curtailed and even the few pelts taken had been of little value due to a collapse of the fur market.

In consequence, the people we were amongst were enduring considerable hardship. They had only a few pounds of flour left and were heavily dependent on fish, which were in short supply.

Although their situation looked bleak to me, none of them seemed downhearted. To the contrary, they were in high good humor. When I tried to pitch our little tent and could not get the pegs to hold in the soft sand, a crowd of women and girls surrounding me found my efforts hysterically amusing. The men were somewhat more inhibited, but when I undertook to prove to Madees, by means of a drawing in the sand, that a canoe could be made to sail to windward, his incredulity set him laughing so hard he choked on a mouthful of tea.

Charles and Louis went off in our canoe to pick up a few gallons of gas someone had cached farther upstream. In their absence I set about dealing with a particularly vexatious personal problem. The seat of my old army trousers had worn so thin and been ripped so often it no longer gave any useful protection against blood-sucking insects. I had tried to patch it, but my efforts had not held. Now I tried again and was making a botch of the job when an old woman took pity and by means of signs offered to be my seamstress.

This posed a difficulty—not so much one of modesty as of

how to protect myself from the flies while I was parted from my pants. A middle-aged man named Nahzee saw the problem and had the solution. He beckoned me to follow him.

Nahzee did not seem to own a tent. He and his family apparently lived outdoors, sleeping under a somewhat tattered mosquito net—which I was now invited to use as a changing room.

So there I sat for nearly an hour, the cynosure of all eyes, while my trousers were being repaired. Many people, especially children, gathered close around my cage to stare—giggling a lot and now and then bursting into outright laughter. I believe I now know how a baboon in a zoo must feel.

It was a delight to be able to spend the night in a camp possessing such an aura of goodwill. In his journal for the day Charles wrote:

I think very nice to hear childrens voices again even though they are not like once [sic] I used to hear.

Although I would have been happy to have spent some days with these people, they clearly had insufficient food for themselves. We were offered a whitefish, but refused it because we had seen the fishermen come in from their nets and knew they had caught only three fish with which to feed the entire community, including the dogs. When we cooked a bannock (a very small one), we ate it almost guiltily in the privacy of our tent. This was a hunger camp, and no place for us to linger.

We left as we had come, without any demonstrative display on either side. As we pulled away, I saw a small boy tentatively wave a hand; but perhaps he was merely bidding farewell to Telequoisie.

Our new companion was around twenty, short of stature but burly of build. His smooth, moon face suggested an unflappable good nature. Though he spoke little, he chuckled a lot.

Soon we came to Nileen, a cluster of decrepit Idthen Eldeli winter cabins where the river roared over a fourteen-foot falls, forcing us to make a half-mile portage before we were properly launched upon the Kasmere, the Idthen Eldeli's principal summer route to and from the barrenlands. We would ascend for ninety miles or so to the height of land then cross to the Cochrane River, which we would follow south to Reindeer Lake.

Soon after portaging around the falls, we found ourselves facing four miles of ferocious whitewater. Appalled by this thunderous spectacle, I asked Telequoisie what it was called. He bobbed his head and murmured something that sounded like "*Nilee-deesee.*"

"What the devil does *that* mean?" I asked Charles, who grinned and replied, "I think Bad Bitch rapid."

And so it was. Wide, shallow, and unbridled, the river flung itself over a tumult of boulders such as a fish might have been hard-pressed to find its way through.

Charles thought we might be able to ascend it by poling, so we went ashore and each of us cut and peeled a pole eight feet long and about an inch and a half in diameter. Being freshly cut, they were at once slippery with sap and sticky with pitch and the very devil to control. Or so I found mine to be, but then I was the veriest beginner at the arcane art of poling a canoe through whitewater.

With Telee (his full name was too unwieldy for constant use) standing in the bow, myself in the middle, and Charles in the stern, we began inching our way upstream.

All of us poled on the same side, keeping the canoe slightly diagonal to the current. The trick was for the center man to maintain a hold on the bottom while the other two whipped their poles up, then thrust them forward and down, forcing the canoe a few feet upstream as the center man repositioned his anchor pole.

This was a procedure for which I had no natural aptitude. It was so easy to jam one's pole into an unseen crevice, which either meant abandoning it or clinging hopelessly to it while the canoe inexorably slipped away from under. We had not gone a hundred yards before I was parted from my pole. Shortly thereafter, Telee lost his—which might have made me feel a little better except that we *needed* his. In a trice the canoe swung right around, heading downstream toward a barracuda mouthful of rocks, but Charles was able to hold us long enough for Telee to retrieve his pole.

Progress became so arduous that Charles decided to risk using the engine. The propeller had barely got a grip on the water when it hit a rock and the shear pin broke. Poling our way to shore to put in a new one took thirty minutes and led to the unnerving discovery that we had only three spare pins.

It took hours of exhausting effort to work our way through Nilee-Deesee. By the time we escaped from the upper end of that torment, I had received my whitewater induction. None of the rapids we were to climb (or run) from here on would seem quite so fearsome.

It was almost dusk before we entered Itooee (Sandy) Lake. The low, boggy country through which we had been traveling was now giving way to parkland laced by a series of eskers. Itooee derived its name from one of these which ran like a massive railroad embankment along the southern shore.

Halfway across this lake we encountered a molting red-breasted merganser whose new flight feathers were not sufficiently developed to enable it to fly. It flopped noisily away with many a worried glance at us, but we were too hungry to be merciful. We pursued and killed it then went ashore and made camp below the esker.

Telee, who had been more than pulling his weight, now further distinguished himself by "ponassing" the duck. Having skinned and cleaned it, he spreadeagled it on a double cross made of willow branches, the lower ends of which he thrust into the sand so the cross leaned over a bed of coals. There the bird roasted slowly in its own juices, while strips of bannock Telee had wound around individual slanting sticks baked to a crusty golden brown.

Charles and I pitched our tent on a mossy carpet surrounded by scattered birches, while Telee made his bed beneath the canoe. As soon as we had eaten, we all sought the shelter of our mosquito nets. I lay awake for a while, listening to the baleful whine and speculating on what would happen to anyone trying to travel in this country without a mosquito bar.

A Canada jay—whisky-jack—woke us early by upsetting our tea billy. He was the first of his kind we had seen, and we welcomed him as a sign we were making progress south.

The day became very warm as we worked our way upstream from one rapid to the next. Warm or not, we wore our thickest sweaters. Better to sweat to death than be eaten alive. Tea breaks were appreciated even more than usual because the tea fire provided smoke, which gave some relief from our tormentors.

In the north almost anything serves as an excuse for a brew-up: a portage, a broken shear pin, an empty gas tank, emptying one's bladder, or just a whim. Somebody gets a fire started and slants a pole over it with a tea billy (in our case a bacon can) suspended from it. Apart from providing a temporary substitute for food, tea seems to be an excellent lubricant for storytelling, which is a quintessential aspect of life in the bush.

We crawled slowly up several rapids to the foot of Tebannay Chah, a half-mile torrent of whitewater which was too much for the likes of us. Getting around it necessitated a carry of 760 yards (I know the exact distance because I paced it) on Mud Portage, so-called because it consisted of a series of bottomless morasses separated by rock ridges.

The river now paralleled an enormous esker, a sandy embankment as much as ninety feet high which shut us off from the world to the north. Someone had taken advantage of the shelter offered by this bulwark to build a cabin at its foot. Only one wall still stood—the rest having fallen into rubble. Nearby was a mound surmounted by the debris of a rotted-out birchbark canoe. We were abreast of this mound when the Lockwood sputtered and for no discernible reason stopped.

"A grave there," Charles commented as we grabbed our paddles and headed to shore.

"Grandfather's," said Telee quietly.

The canoe grounded, whereupon Telee jumped out, walked over to the grave, laid a package of cigarette tobacco Charles had given him on top of it, and silently returned to climb into the canoe again.

Nobody said a word as Charles spun the flywheel. The motor started instantly. Whatever had needed to be done had been done.

The next ten miles consisted of little lakes separated by stretches of swift water. Because the river here was relatively narrow, the rapids were deep, so we were able to climb most of them under power, but they tried the kicker to its limit. While Telee and I bent over our paddles trying to provide a little extra bit of push, the canoe fishtailed frantically from side to side, gaining a few feet here, losing a few there. We worked our way up like a salmon, making good use of eddies and occasional pools of still water behind whirlpools and rocks.

Beyond Sucker Lake we were forced to make a one-mile portage which nearly broke both my back and my heart. The ancient trail, such as it was, had recently been swept by a forest fire and was now a hazardous shambles of fallen trees, as if giants had been playing pick-up sticks with the forest. Charles and Telee each made two carries. I made one and then collapsed. In self-abasement I built a fire, brewed up, then fried a pair of bannocks using the last of our butter as grease.

We were now down to a ration of two bannocks twice a day shared among the three of us. After I finished cooking these two, only enough flour remained for half a dozen more.

Soon we reached a place where a steep rapid breached the esker wall. Driving the canoe up and through the gap, we found ourselves in the labyrinthine approaches to Kasmere Lake, which, with its several extensive arms and inflowing streams, forms the main headwater of the river.

Going ashore to fill the gas tank, Charles and I came upon a low palisade of birch posts surrounding a dozen graves, each marked by a rectangle of logs and a pitiful little cross of branches tied together with rawhide. These graves were recent, but there were also many old interments from some of which fragments of bones, brightly burnished by wind-driven sand, spilled down the slope.

Telee would not go ashore here but sat mutely in the canoe. He did not need to tell us this was where some of the many victims of the spring epidemic lay.

Having refueled, we made the fifteen-mile traverse of Kasmere Lake. Entering it had been easy; departing was considerably more difficult, requiring a mile-and-a-half-long portage around the impassable Kasmere Gorge.

It was late in the day, we were half-starved, and the portage was bloody awful. Low and boggy, it had once been corduroyed with poplar and birch logs so dogs could haul canoes across it. Subsequent decay of the logs had made it into one continuous man trap ready to break the legs of anyone trying to pack a load over. My mind dwelt bleakly on the prospects for our return journey, when the canoe would be deep-laden with freight.

It was evening and growing dark before we completed the carry. The nights were drawing down as we got farther south. I was ready to collapse where I stood, which was near the ruins of a Revillon Frères' outpost called Red-head House, now reduced to a mere outline of rotted logs. But Telee hustled us into the canoe and soon we were well out into the inky waters of Thanout Lake (Fort Hall Lake of current maps). Here we encountered another southerner—a beaver. Curious about us, he swam alongside until Charles grabbed the rifle, whereupon Canada's national emblem very smartly submerged.

The fearlessness of the wildlife surprised me, especially considering that our old kicker had no muffler and sounded like a bad night on the Ortona Front. It was beginning to get a little grumpy, which made me hold my breath, for without it we would face a long, hard paddle, fueled by just two pounds of flour.

Halfway down this narrow-gutted lake we passed, but could not see, another abandoned trading post, this one grandiloquently christened Fort Hall, though usually called Eskimo Post because it had been built to trade with the handful of Ihalmiut bold enough to penetrate so deeply into Chipewyan country.

It was nearly midnight before we finally went ashore and Telee got a fire going and another fish duck ponassing. Not for the first (nor the last) time I wondered what we would have done without him. His abilities as a cook and his stamina as a packer seemed equaled only by his skill as a pilot. When the canoe was under power, he would sprawl amidships, apparently half asleep, until he gave a whistle and a wave of an arm, whereupon Charles would sheer off to right or left as indicated. Peering overboard from my seat in the bow I might glimpse the sinister shadow of a barely submerged rock sliding harmlessly past. It was as if Telee had built-in sonar with which he could scan the waters around us.

However, what really endeared him to me was the studious way he overlooked my inadequacies. Whatever I did wrong or failed to do right, he would give me a gentle smile and, usually, a helping hand.

He was a man one could easily learn to love.

CHAPTER ELEVEN

BROCHET

HUNGER ROUSTED US OUT AT DAWN, AND A twenty-mile-an-hour tailwind hustled us down the last few miles of Thanout Lake to the first of a series of eight portages over the height of land into the Cochrane River.

This was idyllic country consisting of open stands of birch, spruce, and Jack pine criss-crossed with eskers. A carpet of moss and lichens crackled underfoot. It was spangled with hundreds of little lakes surrounded by sandy shores. They looked beautiful, but I realized they would play the devil if one had to find one's way amongst them without a guide. Even as things were, Charles and Telequoisie had trouble enough locating the portages.

Most of the carries were good going, and I was happy to find I could now pack eighty or ninety pounds for as much as half a mile without a rest. The fact that Charles and Telee were packing half as much again did not lessen my satisfaction—after all, I was the new boy in the game.

While we were crossing a lakelet two-thirds of the way over the height of land, the kicker suddenly quit. We paddled ashore, and Charles set about disassembling the old machine, whose trouble proved to be a broken rotor. Since we carried no spare parts, I feared our motoring days were at an end.

Not so. While I worried about the future and Telee napped in the sun, Charles successfully created a new part out of bits and pieces of tin held together with solder melted from the seams of an empty condensed milk can. The kicker now ran like a charm, so we celebrated by brewing up our last dusty remnants of tea and eating our last bannock.

By 5:00 p.m. we had completed the final carry. We were tired, and God we were hungry! However, the Cochrane, our road to Brochet, now lay before us.

We had hardly begun the downstream voyage when we came to a set of rapids, wild and white. To my horror Charles headed straight into them with the kicker racing at full throttle.

This, my first-ever powered trip down rapids, was a terrifying yet perfectly reasonable procedure. The key to running any rapid lies in maintaining ample steerage way so the canoe can be made to change direction instantly. This the Lockwood enabled us to do.

"First time I seen it done with a kicker was with Dan Moberley," Charles remembered. "Was at Spruce Rapids. Instead of turning off his big Evinrude, he give her the gun, and we went down there like shit through a goose. Never touched nothing on the way. After that I used the kicker every rapid I run."

Swift water apart, the upper Cochrane was a big-hearted and lovely river running deep and sure between olive-green walls of spruce and tamarack bordered by an emerald-green fringe of reeds.

Before setting out on the trip to Brochet, I had wondered if I might not become bored penned up in a canoe for hours and days on end. In fact, as long as we were paddling my mind tended to remain in neutral, tranquilized by the rhythmic motion. Being under power was not dissimilar to being in a car on a long journey. I tended to become fidgety, but dealt with this by nature-watching and by working on a sketch map of the route. Not being the contemplative type, I failed to use this opportunity to explore the recesses of my soul.

Late one afternoon we emerged into a northern bay of Misty Lake and saw two dogs pacing back and forth on the tip of an island. Telee said they had been left there to guard a fish cache from foxes and wolverines. Such guard dogs might be left on their own for two or three months, scavenging a living and, if that failed them, dying of starvation. These two were emaciated. They howled beseechingly after us, but we had nothing we could give them.

As we entered the main body of the lake, the setting sun bloodied a group of tents pitched on the eastern shore of a well-wooded island. This proved to be the camp of fifteen families of Idthen Eldeli, most of what remained of the Misty Lake Band. As had been the case at Nileen, the people ranged themselves on the high ground and watched with the stolidity of a concrete wall as we beached our canoe. I knew the drill now, so out came my tobacco pouch, and the wall dissolved.

Telee introduced me to the nominal chief, Dettani (Big Bird), and to several other elders, including Tseekunee (Fish Guts), Lopeezin (Long Penis), and Deneyugun (Bent Man). A haze of tobacco smoke surrounded us as Telee did his best to explain who we were and what we were about. There was a ripple of quiet laughter when he rubbed his belly and sucked in his cheeks while describing how we had nearly starved him to death. The implication being that this kind of treatment was no more than was to be expected from white men.

Although the people were short of almost everything, they were generous with what they had, providing us with a ten-pound bag of flour (which we undertook to replace on our homeward journey), together with a large whitefish and a handful of tea. Dettani invited us to stay the night, but both Charles and Telee were so anxious to reach Brochet that they could not be persuaded. When we pushed off, Dettani gave us a small bag of dried, pounded caribou meat which, in those lean times, was no small gift. It looked like dirty sweepings from under a carpenter's bench, or perhaps from the floor of a stable, but was sweet to the taste and remarkably filling. We munched on it with satisfaction as Charles drove us at full speed down a wicked rapid separating Misty from Jackfish Lake, or Lac Brochet as it is sometimes called.

Our next camp was on a fly-free point where Telee cooked the succulent whitefish while Charles baked bannock strips peppered with dry meat. We ate to repletion for the first time in many days, and all was well with the world.

The back of the journey was broken now, and we had sufficient grub to get us to Brochet. Freed of immediate worries, Charles and I stayed awake until after midnight, smoking and talking. He wanted to hear more about the war, while I wanted to know more about him, his family, and the life he had led. Our friendship was maturing, and he was more forthcoming now, but some subjects were sacrosanct. One of these concerned his mother, Rose. Clearly he had worshipped her, yet he could hardly be persuaded to tell me anything about her life and absolutely refused, then or later, to discuss her death, the circumstances of which had evidently been traumatic for all concerned. His feelings toward his father and his relations with his brother Fred were also taboo topics. But he became almost loquacious on the subject of the barrenlands and his consuming desire to travel into their farther reaches.

We slept late and might have mooched around the camp all the next morning enjoying full bellies and balmy weather had Telee not been hot to hit the trail. Silently he loaded the canoe, gassed the kicker, then began pacing up and down the beach. It would have been cruel to have kept him waiting, so we departed.

Apparently I had served my apprenticeship satisfactorily, because when we embarked Charles settled himself amidships, lolling comfortably against our sleeping bags with my small-print copy of *The Travels of Marco Polo* in his hand. Telee took the bow, where he sat poised like an eager bird dog. The captain sat bolt upright in the stern, the Lockwood vibrating under his hand while her unmuffled voice rang out triumphantly across ten miles of open water.

I had never been more contented in all my life.

We ran on and on, stopping only briefly to boil the kettle and refuel. When we met more rapids, I expected Charles to take over, but he remained where he was. I took my cues from him. If he nodded, I would run the rapid. If not, we would go ashore and portage. By the time I had run three stretches of whitewater I had become an aficionado of shooting rapids under power, though the urge to empty my bladder when I looked down those foam-filled chutes remained almost irresistible.

We might have run on far into the night, which was moonlit, has not a sudden storm driven us ashore about fifty miles short of Brochet. We were away again at dawn, and shortly before noon an orange peel floating on the current warned us we were close to civilization. We came to a riverside cabin whose occupants waved us in, so we went ashore to be greeted by the Cooks, one of many Metis families of that name scattered across the north.

Sitting in the sunshine, smoking tailor-made cigarettes pressed upon us by Alphonse Cook, we exchanged gossip of the river. Ours was only the fourth canoe to come down the Cochrane that summer, so he told us. The several white men who had formerly trapped to the north and west had, with the exception of Ragnor Jonsson, abandoned the country, and the epidemic that spring had so decimated Crees and Chipewyans alike that a kind of paralysis seemed to have gripped the survivors.

"Nobody feel like travel now," Alphonse said sadly. "Too much afraid they get sick and die away from home."

Not far beyond the Cooks' cabin the Cochrane spewed us out into Idthentua, as the Chipewyans call Reindeer Lake. Clinging close to the northern shore, we soon raised a glittering, metal-sheathed steeple thrusting out of the black spruce pelt of this ancient land like the nose of an alien rocket. Brochet was in view.

Although *pedlars*—itinerant traders from Quebec—probably encountered the Chipewyans at Idthentua as early as the 1770s, the first European of record to reach it was David Thompson, a Hudson's Bay Company Scot searching for a more direct canoe route to Lake Athabasca and the far northwest. In 1796, with two Chipewyan guides, he ascended Reindeer River, traversed the 140-mile length of the island-filled lake of the same name, "discovered" the Cochrane, and paddled up it to eventually reach the eastern end of Lake Athabasca. Duty done, the three men then returned to Reindeer Lake and wintered on its western shore. Perhaps because he was feeling somewhat lost in time and space (he was more than a thousand miles by river from his base on Hudson Bay), Thompson gave his isolated refuge in the wilderness the comforting name of Bedford House.

By 1807, when the Company sent Peter Fidler to evaluate Thompson's route to the northwest (Fidler deemed the Cochrane too difficult for commercial transport), Bedford House, under the more appropriate name of Deer Lake Post, had become the principal contact point between Europeans and the Idthen Eldeli.

Fifty years later the Company built a second and larger post, Fort du Brochet, at the northern end of the lake. Brochet, as it soon came to be known, was a meat post whose primary role was to exploit caribou as a source of pemmican. Because caribou were nowhere more abundant than in the core wintering region around Reindeer Lake, Brochet became the principal abattoir of the new trade.

The lake in winter was ideal for caribou, providing innumerable openings between sheltering islands where the herds could rest and digest their food in relative safety from their only major enemies, wolves and men, who could neither surprise nor outrun them on the ice. Moreover, the myriad wooded islands were well endowed with mosses, lichens, and other edibles the deer could reach without having to wade through the deep, accumulated snowfall of the mainland forests.

Before white men and guns came on the scene, Idthentua and the surrounding country are thought to have harbored at least as many as a quarter of a million wintering caribou.

The new post at Brochet was soon exporting great quantities of pemmican, dried deer meat, deer tallow (fat), and smoked deer tongues. In some years a hundred bales of smoked tongues were shipped south by York boat and canoe, each bale containing up to two hundred tongues.

Even without producing much fur, Brochet was, from its early days, one of the more profitable of the Company's posts. Word of that affluence soon spread, and in 1860 the Roman Catholic order of Les Pères Oblats de Marie-Immaculée (the Oblate Fathers) founded the mission of St. Pierre du Lac Caribou a few hundred yards away from the Company compound, and Brochet became a full-fledged outpost of Commerce and Christianity, transient home to several thousand Cree and Chipewyans. On a summer day as many as twenty big York boats owned by the trading companies and a hundred or more canoes could be found hauled up on its sandy beach.

When Charles and I arrived there it was to find the beach deserted except for four canoes. The community itself had been reduced to about twenty mud-plastered log cabins haphazardly scattered over a few acres of dead grass and scrub between the gleaming waters of the lake and the encroaching darkness of the forest.

The Hudson's Bay compound stood primly at the eastern end of the straggle, its immaculate white-painted buildings with their bright red roofs dominating the scene, as they had done for almost a century. They completely overshadowed the scabrous cluster of shanties belonging to free-trader Israel Shieff.

Brochet's native residents, eighteen Cree and Metis families, were mostly absent at their summer fishing camps. None of the Idthen Eldeli lived permanently at the settlement, and only a few had as yet arrived to take part in the annual Treaty gathering, which was still two weeks away. Except for the traders, the mission, and a two-man army detachment running a weather and radio station, Brochet was an empty shell. When I remarked to

Charles that it looked like a ghost town, he replied grimly: "Plenty ghosts around since last winter. More ghosts than people...."

Rather to my surprise, he directed me to steer the canoe to the HBC's wharf. I had thought we would go to the free-trader since the Schweders were themselves free-traders.

"Nope," he replied with a scowl when I queried him. "We don't deal with that other fellow. There's stuff you hear about him. The Company sure don't like *me* but I'd rather deal there anyhow."

When I returned the following winter to spend some months at Brochet I, too, would hear disturbing stories about the free-trader. Nor will I forget a retarded Cree boy who one day showed me a bare arm covered with what I took to be tattoos, but which turned out to be scars from blows struck with a fur-marking hammer—a device having a number of needle points set in a lead base with which a trader stamped his logo into the pelts he purchased. The boy bore a dozen or more scars from such a marking hammer. He claimed he had been paid ten cents each time he allowed himself to be branded with the free-trader's mark.

Nobody was on the Company's rickety wharf to greet us, and when I walked up to the store followed (rather reluctantly perhaps) by Charles, there was nobody behind the counter either. We had to wait for some time before the manager emerged from his little office to casually inquire of me (he ignored Charles) what was wanted.

To my consternation I found that my relatively brief sojourn out of touch with teeming humanity had affected my vocal cords. I was experiencing something of the anxiety of a tribal man encountering strangers for the first time. Pulling myself together, I managed to explain who I was and why I was there.

The manager listened impassively. Charles then tried to describe his own situation, but could not do it. Abruptly he spun around and fled. Not until the next day was he able to make his wants known, and then it was to the Company's clerk, a Metis like himself.

The coolness of Charles's reception was due to his being that abomination of abominations in the Company's estimation: a free-trader. That I was associated with him made me suspect. It was not until I had established my credentials by producing an explorer's permit from the federal government and a letter of credit from a Winnipeg bank that the atmosphere thawed somewhat.

I bought a carton full of things that had been haunting my dreams for days: tinned fruit juices, apples (only moderately rotten), jam, honey, store bread (flown in once a month, and moldy), bologna sausage, canned milk, and an entire carton of candy bars; a new pair of pants to replace what remained of my old battledress trousers; and a garish plaid woolen shirt for Telequoisie as a token of my appreciation. After I had paid for everything, the manager somewhat grudgingly offered Charles and me the use of a bunkhouse kept for the use of his bush customers.

The place was a shambles, its floor covered with debris, including spilled flour, dirty burlap bags, and mouse shit. We took a look then went back down to the canoe and set up our own camp. Telee built a big fire, and we all three gorged ourselves. Then, after he had stuffed himself, Telee vanished. One minute he was there, the next he wasn't. Puzzled, I asked Charles where he had gone.

"Look for his girl. Stay away from us from now on, just in case we try to get him to go back on the trip home. Pretty hard for him to say no to a white man."

I never saw Telequoisie again, and for that I shall always be sorry. He was a truly admirable human being.

I spent the next day writing letters while Charles packaged our cargo for the return voyage and saw to it that all our running gear was in order. But he was thinking his own thoughts, as his diary tells:

I keep thinking of my trapline and if my camps are up or down, and if the water in the River of Graves is high or low, and how many portages there are on the way north to Dubawnt, and of a place near the east side of Dubawnt I tried to reach the last five years. What I want to see there I don't know. I don't think I will ever know but something seems to tell me to go there between Dubawnt and Thelon. I tried in the spring of 1946 but turned back because I had not enough grub. But there will come a day I hope when I get there. And a day will come perhaps when I will stop traveling but it may be a long time yet. Yet I might be lucky some day and then I can live quietly in a nice little home.

That evening I was frying a pan full of bologna when an old Fairchild float plane grumbled overhead. Grabbing my bundle of letters (including Harper's), I ran to meet it at the beach. The gum-chewing pilot reached out the window to take the mail, which he promised to post at The Pas before dark. In three hours he would cover a distance equal to that which Charles and I had taken two weeks to travel.

As I turned away, I almost collided with a human cyclone: a white-haired gnome of a man with the complexion of a mummy and the nose of a Viking who came running down the path in a billowing cassock that had once been black and was now rust-colored with age. "*Pardon, monsieur!*" he barked as he swept past me to thrust his own bundle of outgoing mail through the pilot's window.

Such was my first encounter with Father Egenolf, OMI, unofficial seigneur of a domain embracing forty or fifty thousand square miles with Brochet at its heart. Resented by most of the whites in the region (who called him Eggy, though *never* to his face) and feared by a good many of the natives whose spiritual servant he professed himself to be, he was a law unto himself. During his reign of forty-two years he had come as close as any man could to making himself the principal arbiter of human destiny in the vast realm of wilderness the Lord had entrusted to his care.

Joseph Egenolf was one of the last and one of the most remarkable of a breed of German and French priests who chose to dedicate their lives to the task of bringing native Canadians out of the "darkness" of paganism, *and* out from amongst the shadows of any non–Roman Catholic religious beliefs which might have infected them.

Through four decades, he had waged an often ruthless, always implacable war to reclaim the Cree, Chipewyan, and Metis from the Devil. In his earlier years he had shown no compunction about using force to save sinners. He had publicly punished backsliders with his long dog whip. Some, who were too stubborn to accept the light of the Lord, he had sent to Coventry to endure the truly dreadful ordeal of being cast out by their own communities. In times of severe adversity such as epidemic sickness or famine, the mission, which administered government assistance and relief, had been known to turn its back on those who rejected the true faith.

In his younger years (though no longer at the time I knew him) he had subscribed to the belief of the young priest who eventually replaced him, and who described the remnants of the Idthen Eldeli to me in these terms: "These poor people! They live like dogs. Perhaps it is better for them when they are dead and gone to heaven."

Father Egenolf also dealt in worldly things. The St. Pierre du Lac Caribou Mission held a trading license. Twice a year Father Egenolf visited every Idthen Eldeli camp by dog team, usually just before the people were due to come to the settlement to celebrate Christmas or Easter, and skimmed the cream of the fur crop, as it were. Not only did the mission trade for furs, it also took the Church's tithe, which amounted to at least ten per cent of the catch.

In effect, the mission financed itself from the avails of its parishioners. Very little support came from the outside world. Money actually went the other way, with the diocese benefiting from the father's acumen as a trader. On the other hand, the father held himself responsible for all the mission's requirements of food, fuel, and shelter. Insofar as it was possible, Oblates in the field always tried to be self-sufficient, which gave them a considerable edge over the Protestants, who never did succeed in establishing a foothold at Brochet.

During our stay the priest invited Charles and me to have supper in his spartan little house beside the squat frame church he had built forty years earlier, and which was now being replaced by a much more pretentious structure roofed with gleaming sheet metal.

The meal was cooked and served by a lay brother who seemed to have no name or, if he did, I never heard it. He was a fey-looking creature with a great bald head and a lopsided mouth. A hard-of-hearing and almost inarticulate orphan from Quebec, he had been sent to Brochet to serve his church thirty-three years earlier. There he had become an excellent gardener who somehow coaxed potatoes, carrots, and even beets from the cold mud and sand. He was also a chef of parts. He served us pemmican, boiled whitefish, smoked caribou tongues, potato salad, fried duck eggs (preserved in isinglass), homemade bread, doughnuts, and raisin pie. Washed down with generous pourings of the Father's berry wine, this feast almost made a convert out of me.

Joseph Egenolf had long been famous (notorious in some quarters) for his wine. In 1911 a young man named H.S. Kemp, who traveled to Brochet with the annual Treaty party, recorded that Father Egenolf gave the officials a bottle of his wine. Since they had been six dry weeks on the road, they finished it off in a hurry, and the question arose of how to get some more. Nobody cared to ask the priest directly, but Robert Hyslop, the then manager of the HBC post, knew the form. Acting on the visitors' behalf, he sent the bottle back to the mission accompanied by a note and a five-dollar bill.

Dear Father:

We realize more and more the need for the work of your Church in the north so please accept this money for furthering your work.

P.S. Perhaps you would be good enough to fill up the bottle?

Eggy's "bug juice," as it was affectionately known, became one of the region's most highly valued products, even upon occasion surpassing silver fox.

The pemmican and smoked tongue we ate were out of another time. Egenolf had prepared them himself and was happy to tell me how to do it.

You begin, he explained, by putting equal quantities of previously rendered caribou heart fat (which has a gluey consistency) and bone marrow (which produces an oil as light as olive oil) in an iron pot and gently bringing the mixture to a simmer. Then you add pulverized dried deer meat and small cubes of back fat and stir until the mixture becomes thick enough to hold together. At this juncture raisins or, better still, cranberries can be added. The result is then ladled into sacks made of scraped deerskin and allowed to solidify into something resembling slabs of brownish asphalt. He assured me that, properly made and stored in a cool place, it would keep for years. I sampled some that Egenolf had made several years earlier. Although rather hard on the teeth, it had as good a flavor as the best corned beef.

Smoked deer tongues were once the supreme culinary delicacy of the North. Egenolf made his by soaking fresh tongues for eight or nine days in strong brine; boiling them for an hour; then smoking them over a spruce and birch smudge for at least a week. Preparing them for the table required only that they be soaked in cold water overnight, after which they were boiled until the skin could easily be peeled off—somewhat as one might peel a banana. Indeed, smoked deer tongues were often referred to as Brochet bananas. The father told me that the mission still smoked two or three hundred tongues a year and that he ate one almost every morning for breakfast, along with a thick slice of pemmican.

The time I was able to spend with the priest on this first visit to Brochet was all too short. However, when in 1948 I lived in the settlement I saw a lot of him.

He seemed paradoxical to me. On the one hand he was clearly a man of stern and enduring faith; on the other he was a rationalist even to the point of thinking and acting in opposition to the beliefs and convictions of his church. He once frankly told me, "These people [the Idthen Eldeli] experience the world and the spirit differently from us. Perhaps they will never see things our way. Perhaps the good Lord understands that, and does not mind...."

He even speculated that the natives' pagan beliefs might have brought them nearer to God than did the garbled mumbo jumbo which constituted much of their understanding and practice of Christianity. Certainly, he himself was no longer straining every nerve to save their immortal souls. I had the feeling he continued in his vocation more from force of habit than from conviction. Perhaps there was simply nothing else he felt capable of doing after forty-three years of proselytizing.

Although he usually seemed full of vigor and vivacity, retaining a keen interest in everything around him, now and then it was as if the fatigue of a lifetime spent on what might after all have been a fruitless, even unnecessary crusade, shadowed his demeanor.

One winter evening in 1948, after he had mildly chastised a Cree man for getting a fourteen-year-old girl pregnant, Joseph Egenolf told me the story of a young priest with whom he had trained at an Oblate seminary in Belgium, and who had been posted to a mission on Great Slave Lake in 1905, the same year Egenolf had himself been sent to Brochet.

"You know the temptations of the flesh are not easy to resist? *Bien*. This young man, he was from Paris. He had a very nice native girl come to his mission, and he fought a long time with temptation, but one day it was too much for him.

"He sent a letter to his bishop renouncing his vows, then he went away into the bush with the girl and her family. That was in the fall of the year. He was a clever fellow, and soon he learned to hunt and trap like the rest of those people. It may be he was happy there, for by the spring the girl was carrying his child.

"So summer came and the girl's family went to trade their furs at the post. My friend would not go with them. He stayed in the bush and built a nice cabin, and the girl had her baby. When the others came back, they brought him goods bought with his furs, and I suppose everything looked peaceful enough.

"It was not so peaceful. The bishop could not do much in winter; he was too far away. However, that summer he sent two priests north to that place. They came in a canoe to my friend's cabin at the end of the summer and camped so they were right there whenever he stepped outside his cabin. They talked to him and prayed for him, and told him he could still be forgiven. They did everything they could to save him from eternal damnation.

"Well, you know, one day he broke down and cried like a baby. Then the two priests took him back to the Great Slave mission and told him what he must do to be restored into the Church again. He was to work as a lay brother at the mission and do all things required, but his special task was to go each summer in the canoe and collect dirt from the islands or wherever he could find it, and make a garden for the mission.

"As you know Great Slave is a long way north. There is very little dirt amongst all those rocks up there. My friend collected what he could find by the spoonful. On a good day he might get a pail full. It was years before there was enough soil at the mission to grow a few potatoes, if the frost did not kill them first.

"By that time there was a new bishop. He sent word to the mission to say my friend was now free of his sins. God had forgiven him. But perhaps my friend could not forgive himself, for soon after that he went out in his canoe and never came back. Nobody knows what happened to him. He just never came back.

"The old bishop had done what he could to save my friend's soul. But, you know, sometimes I still think about that because, you know, I have had thoughts myself... but it is not of him or myself that I am thinking now. I am wondering about that girl and her baby. Not so long ago I sent a message to that mission asking what had happened to the girl and the child. They did not know. It was so long ago, those two had been forgotten. Me, I would like to know what became of them...."

The last time I saw Joseph Egenolf was on a bitter January evening in 1949. I was to fly out of the country in the morning, and he had invited me to a final supper.

As I was pulling on my parka to go back to my own cabin, he came and stood in front of me for a moment, looking past, or maybe through me. And he said softly:

"I wonder, eh? Maybe it was better if I had never come to these people... better for them... I wonder..."

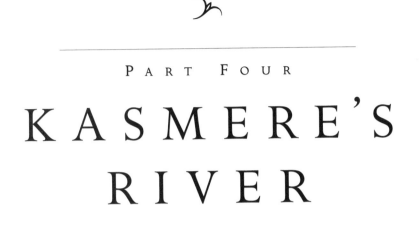

PART FOUR

KASMERE'S RIVER

CHAPTER TWELVE

CLIMBING THE COCHRANE

I T WAS NOW THE THIRD WEEK IN JULY, AND BAKER Lake lay nearly a thousand miles to the north by the route we planned to follow. Despite Brochet's attractions, we had to go. On the morning of our departure, I sought out Father Egenolf, who had promised to find a Chipewyan willing to help pack our freight over the portages as far as Fort Hall Lake, after which we would be traveling "downhill."

The Father was apologetic. He had been unable to persuade anyone to forgo the pleasures of Treaty time at Brochet. As a consolation he gave us a dozen smoked deer tongues and a slab of pemmican as emergency rations for our far-northern trip. He also gave me a note written in syllabic characters to Chief Dettani of the Misty Lake Band asking him to provide a couple of young fellows to help us over the portages at the height of land.

We loaded the canoe under the eyes of most of Brochet's residents. All too conscious of being closely observed, I struggled down the steep slope to the beach with enormous loads on my back. What the resident trippers could do, I *had* to do. Nobody offered to assist, nor would we have accepted aid. This was a personal affair.

I kept a tally of our load. Several of the most obnoxious items acquired their own personalities before the trip was over,

so I list them with the names we gave them. The weights are
approximations.

Big Coffin (a crate of tinned goods)	90 pounds
Candle Case	40 pounds
Ammo Case (.30-30 ammunition)	60 pounds
Charles's personal pack	25 pounds
my personal pack	35 pounds
The Body (a burlap sack stuffed with our sleeping robes)	25 pounds
Green Pack (miscellany)	40 pounds
sugar	100 pounds
flour	200 pounds
canned milk	60 pounds
gasoline (five 10-gallon drums, less a bit)	450 pounds
oil	40 pounds
tool box	30 pounds
grub box	35 pounds
junk bag	20 pounds
set of iron sled runners	60 pounds
a case of jam, honey, and bottled goods	15 pounds
tea chest	45 pounds
tarpaulins, spare paddles, axe, tent, rifle, etc.	30 pounds
	1,400 pounds

To this must be added the Lockwood (60 pounds); Charles
(160); me (130); and a dog called Bones (60). This brought our total
burden up to around 1,800 pounds, or as near as be damned to
three-quarters of a ton, which was almost as much as Johnny
Bourassa's twin-engined Anson had been able to carry in to
Windy Post. Fully laden, our canoe had a freeboard amidships of
just two and a half inches. A large fish flapping its tail alongside
might have swamped her.

To say that this weighed heavily on my mind would be an

understatement as well as a bad pun. I knew that between Brochet and Windy Post the canoe would have to climb twenty rapids and run down about forty more. We would have to carry everything over at least twenty portages. And there would be just the two of us to do it.

Father Egenolf arrived at a dead run, his rusty habit flapping around him. As he helped push us off the beach, he waved his cross above the bow and shouted a blessing which could barely be heard over the blatting of the kicker starting up. I'm not sure what he said, but it sounded like "*Au revoir, mes amis!* May we meet in heaven."

Shortly after entering the Cochrane, we paused to pick up one of Charles's dogs, which he had left with a Metis family after it had been injured in a fight during his sled journey south the previous winter. Bones was a big, hairy fellow who ought to have been cock-of-the-walk but was in fact a despairing pessimist. His drooping tail and head as he was hauled aboard suggested he believed himself doomed. Scrabbling nervously back and forth on top of the load, he added nothing to the precarious stability of our vessel.

Although the first rapid in the Cochrane was a minor one, the canoe at first refused to climb it. The Lockwood nattered furiously, shooting out clouds of blue smoke but getting us nowhere. The canoe fishtailed back and forth for what seemed like hours until, with both of us paddling full-out, we finally inched our way up. We went ashore then for a rest and a smoke, whereupon it began to rain as if God had opened a sluicegate in the sky.

Two miles farther on we were forced to make our first portage. Although a mere two-hundred-yard carry, it required seven trips apiece, each time packing roughly a hundred pounds, followed by an eighth trip carrying the canoe, which had become so waterlogged the two of us could hardly heft her.

Prospects for the journey did not look propitious. The flies made them seem worse. Most blood-sucking and flesh-eating flies hunt by smell, and the stench produced by men packing heavy loads in hot weather can attract them from miles around. After the portage Charles wiped the scum of sweat and flies from his face and grumbled, "If we was to go across one more time there'd be enough bugs under the canoe to carry it."

To add to our woes the Lockwood began to misbehave, forcing us to make camp early. While I cooked supper, Charles stripped the engine and removed a thick accumulation of carbon, which he said was caused by poor gasoline.

It had been a bad day, but the next one brought clear skies and a north wind that kept us cool and the flies at bay. The Lockwood was sweetness and light, and we climbed through all the whitewater below Mink Rapid, around which travelers usually portage; but we elected to track up the main rapid. This bravado involved us in an hour and a half spent wading waist-deep against a current so swift I could keep my feet only with great difficulty.

Tracking required us to attach a line to the center thwart (this being the strongest one), then run it under the forward thwart and over the bow on the shore side of the canoe. One of us would then take the free end over his shoulder and set off, wading and hauling, while the other, armed with a long pole, did his best to keep the canoe from running ashore.

This was a tricky business. If the bow swung too far out, there was a risk the current would seize the canoe and sweep it away downstream. Because of this danger, we tried to get Bones to go ashore and follow us on dry land, but he adamantly insisted on staying in the canoe, perhaps, as Charles suggested, because he was afraid we would jump back in and leave him behind. Ashore or afloat, he remained equally unhappy. As we sloshed up Mink Rapid, he ran back and forth on top of the load, howling so piteously he attracted an audience. First a bald eagle hovered ponderously overhead. He was joined by a bevy of ravens, then a family of crows, hooting hysterically. It was quite a show.

At sunset we camped near the mouth of La Pensie Lake in a little cove cradled between sandy, pine-grown points. This was perhaps the finest site we had yet encountered. Behind its saffron beach lay mile after mile of open parklands studded with big birches and poplars and carpeted with silvery reindeer moss.

Needing fish for Bones (who would not eat my bannock), we set one of the new nets we had bought in Brochet. All day long the surface of the river had been sliced by the fins of plump grayling harvesting gossamer-winged crane flies, so we expected a good catch, but when we hauled the net early next morning we found only one small lake trout and a northern sucker. This was just sufficient to make one meal for us and the dog. What few scraps remained were eaten by a family of whisky-jacks who were so delighted by our largesse that they followed us along the shore for an hour begging for more.

We stopped to boil the billy at a cabin where a free-trader named Louis La Pensie and his Indian wife and family had lived for thirty-odd years. The cabin was sheathed on all sides with flattened plug-tobacco cans colored yellow and red—a startling anomaly against the somber forest background. I noted that so thickly matted was the ground with three decades' accumulation of caribou hair and bones that nothing but mosses now grew in the vicinity of the cabin.

A massive cliff near the northwestern shore of La Pensie Lake seemed to promise a panoramic view of the countryside, so we headed for it. When, on entering a little cove below the stony wall, I killed the motor, the sound did not die away. What we at first took to be an echo turned out to be the putter of two other kickers, each propelling a big freighter towing several smaller canoes. Additional canoes were following along under sail and paddle power.

Through binoculars I could see that they constituted a sizeable fleet crammed full of people. Suddenly this land which had appeared devoid of human beings was swarming with them!

I experienced a moment of atavistic apprehension: "These are *Indians*... and one hell of a lot of them!" Then I was back in the present, knowing full well that the approaching armada was manned by Idthen Eldeli who, far from being on the warpath, were only bound for Brochet to celebrate Treaty.

Thirteen canoes filled mostly with men and older youths all clad in their best flannel shirts and flamboyant neckerchiefs pulled into our little cove. Only two or three women were amongst them, the rest having remained in the summer camps to tend nets and babies and look after the dogs.

Since 1907, when Treaty No. 10 between the King and the natives of northern Manitoba and Saskatchewan was concluded, Treaty day had been a banner one. Each summer saw the Idthen Eldeli gather at Brochet, where their adherence to the treaty that "extinguished their aboriginal rights" would be reconfirmed by their acceptance of an annuity and gifts from the Indian agent.

Essentially these consisted of five dollars in cash for every man, woman, and child, together with some ammunition, a fishing net, and a little tea, flour, and other comestibles for each family. The money and gifts were welcomed, but it was the coming together of the people that made Treaty a stellar occasion—a time and opportunity for visiting and for renewing friendships and relationships. Indeed, it was the highlight of the annual round.

If these Treaty-bound people looked forward to good times ahead, we did not. Their departure scotched any hope we had had of getting help in crossing the long portages that lay before us. We were a glum pair as we passed our tobacco pouches around.

The southbound travelers were soon on their way, cheerfully waving their paddles in farewell. Watching them go, I knew I was witnessing a moment out of another age—one which would soon exist only in memory.

After the departure of the flotilla, Charles drew my attention to a haystack-sized mass of branches and long-dead foliage clinging to the granite face of the cliff. This was a raven's nest and one which, judging by its enormous size, must have been in use for a long stretch of years.

"That's why the Chips stop here," Charles explained. "Would be bad business to just go on by."

He went on to explain that the raven was a being of deep significance in Idthen Eldeli culture. This particular nest was thought to be the home of raven "elders," and to have passed it by without some gesture of acknowledgement would have been to invite the ill will of its owners.

Soon we were back on the river again, working our way up toward Chipewyan Falls, where a wisp of smoke from a dying tea fire testified to the recent passage of the Idthen Eldeli. Here we were forced to make a long carry on the north side. My notebook described it as *a proper bastard. Two hours, and seven loads apiece. Hot as hell and I don't want to talk about the fucking bugs. Pushing ourselves to the limit. Mine is 100 pounds for the 600 yards carry, without a break. Charles is a goddamn bull. 150 pounds and he never even grunts.*

Some may wonder why we did not stop to rest. There were two good reasons: first, the flies; second, once you put down your load the odds were you would not be able to get it up again without help. It was simpler just to keep going.

We were now less than five miles from Sandy Rapids, a mile-long stretch of impassable whitewater and the last major obstacle separating us from Jackfish Lake. As we approached it, plumes of white smoke swirling ominously over the forest to the north gave us pause. Wildfire, perhaps born from the embers of an Idthen Eldeli travel camp, was threatening to deny us passage.

By the time we reached the portage, the acrid bite of woodsmoke was making me very nervous. Briefly we discussed whether to risk our gear (and ourselves) on the carry or to retreat downstream until the danger was over. The prospect of giving up so much as a yard of our hard-won upstream progress was simply not acceptable. Counting on the wind remaining easterly, we decided to risk the portage. Evidently Bones did not agree with this decision, for he resolutely refused to leave the canoe and had to be hauled out by the scruff of his neck.

The day was growing old as we packed our first load across the twelve-hundred-yard carry. I had the case of canned milk with a ten-gallon drum of gas balanced on top of it. This was the heaviest load I had yet attempted and, though the tumpline around my forehead took much of the strain, I was in constant danger of being driven to my knees.

Charles and I collapsed together at the northern end of the portage. The fire seemed no closer, though the smoke was thicker, so we decided to continue packing until fatigue forced us to quit. We each made two more trips before that moment came. By then it was past midnight, but we had been lighted on our way by the sullen red glow of fire reflected from a lowering mass of clouds that threatened, but gave no rain.

I spent the rest of that short night in a state of acute apprehension, and of acute discomfort from stiff limbs and sore muscles. It was well after dawn before I finally dozed off.

Charles kindly let me sleep until noon while he kept a wary eye on the progress of the fire. By the time he rousted me out it was less than a mile to the east of us, belching thick smoke and roaring like a pack of dragons.

"Better go now," he said, adding with masterful understatement, "or might be trouble."

By early afternoon we had managed to get everything over the portage except the canoe; then the wind veered and the fire began to bear directly down upon us. We brought Old Ironsides, as I had now named her, over at a blind run; or perhaps it was more of a stagger. Fortunately, the wind switched back into the west, leaving us to sprawl exhausted on the shore of a narrow bay, safe for the moment though almost too weary to care.

I was not, however, so weary as to be unaware of my filthy

state, so I peeled off and went for a swim in the icy water. Charles was amused by such idiocy, while Bones was filled with anxiety. Huskies do not swim if it can possibly be avoided, and he may have concluded I had been driven mad and was attempting suicide. Seizing a substantial stick from the edge of the beach, he rushed into the shallows and pushed it at me. I will never know if he hoped I would use it to float ashore or was trying to put me out of my misery.

Back in the canoe we soon met the fire, which had jumped a narrows separating the bay from open water. Trees were burning and exploding on both sides of us, and the smoke and heat were intense. However, with the Lockwood running at full throttle, we ran the gamut to reach safety on the wide waters of Jackfish Lake.

We decided to risk making a direct run down the middle but had gone only about ten miles and were in the widest part of the lake when the gas tank broke loose and would have gone overboard had not Charles grabbed it as it fell. He managed to reattach it and restart the motor, which now ran raggedly, coughing as if at death's door. Then a thunder squall smacked us with wind-driven rain. Bucking a swiftly rising sea, we scrambled for the shelter of the nearest island. Darkness had fallen before we got ashore there. Charles stripped the motor by the fitful light of our campfire and discovered the main seal was leaking oil, which had short-circuited the points.

"Can you fix it?" I asked anxiously.

Slowly getting to his feet, he shook himself. Then, with the trace of a grin, replied, "Don't think so. But she'll likely run if we keep her going slow. Don't you worry none. We'll make it, Farley…long as she don't quit cold on one of the rapids up ahead."

CHAPTER THIRTEEN

TWO TO REMEMBER

ON ENTERING JACKFISH LAKE, WE STEERED toward a densely wooded island upon which stood the abandoned winter house of Etzanni, once an elder of the Misty Lake Band but dead these past five years. According to Father Egenolf, Etzanni had been tall and rangy with an eagle's beak of a nose, brooding eyes, and the presence of an Old Testament prophet.

"He was a shaman, you understand, and sometimes I think he did the Devil's work. Many were afraid of him, even white men. The Indians listened carefully to what he said. He would tell them, 'Take what you need from the white man, but give him only what you must. Do not give him your heart.'

"Ah, he was an old-fashioned one, and strong for the old ways. The traders could not bend him. Nor yet the government. To tell the truth, I could not do so myself."

Rumor in Brochet had it that Etzanni's winter house and all that it contained still remained exactly as he had left it at his death. Curious to see if this was so, I had persuaded Charles to make a slight detour. He had not been enthusiastic, and when we beached our canoe at Etzanni's clearing he flatly refused to visit the house itself, claiming the Lockwood needed his urgent attention.

Leaving him hunched over the engine, I made my way to the large cabin, lifted the latch of the plank door, and cautiously entered. Small windows set high in the walls gave enough light for me to see that the single big room was, by northern standards, immaculate. Clean dishes were set out on the table as if in expectation of visitors. A large iron bed was piled with what the moths had left of many caribou-hide robes. The open door of a pot-bellied stove in the middle of the room revealed birchbark and kindling ready to be lighted.

The room was stuffed with an odd miscellany of things, including a keg of gunpowder; several guns (mostly of ancient vintage); rolls of tar paper; oil lamps; stacks of tin cans whose labels had mostly disintegrated; and a barrel of flour and one of sugar. There were countless other packages which I did not take time to investigate because of an uneasy feeling that the owner might appear at any moment and challenge me.

I now appreciated Charles's reluctance to intrude. Half a decade had passed since Etzanni's death, yet everything remained essentially as if he had just walked out the door. Nobody had helped themselves to what, in this remote corner of the world, was a treasure trove. Strangely, even squirrels and mice, usually quick to colonize abandoned cabins, seemed to have given this one a miss.

Carefully closing the door behind me, I went outside to look around. A hundred yards from the cabin stood the remains of another, much smaller log structure with its pole roof and one wall collapsed. A skewed and weathered cross of peeled spruce poles leaned in front of it. At the foot of the cross a big locomotive bell lay half sunken in the sand.

The ruin looked like the remains of some sort of chapel, but Father Egenolf had said nothing to me about a mission station here.

Charles was not so reticent. "Etzanni and the father was fighting a long time. One year the father sent a lay brother to build a mission right on Etzanni's island. Funny things happen then. That big bell was hanging up on three poles near the door, and one day it just fell down when the brother was walking under. Could have killed him easy. Some people say Jesus pulled him clear, but the brother went right back to Brochet and that was the end of it till after Etzanni died.

"Then the father sent a young priest to start up a mission for the Misty Lake Chips, to get them back to Church again. It never worked because the Chips wouldn't come near the island. Maybe scared of Etzanni's ghost. I don't know about that. I know everybody went away from here...and we should go too...not much daylight left."

Passing into Misty Lake, we found ourselves running between fires burning on two of the larger islands. These were spectacular blazes roaring through hundreds of acres of spruce and Jack pine, flinging flaming brands across a narrows that we shot through at the Lockwood's best speed, prepared to douse any brands that might fall aboard. None did, but some sparks settled in Bones's long fur and the smell of singed hair hung over us until we broke out onto open water.

Charles was phlegmatic about forest fires, while I, conditioned as most southerners are to the belief that they rob "us" of profitable timber, was irate about the wastefulness. Charles listened to my rant then shrugged. So far as he was concerned forest fires were part of the natural order of things. He pointed out that they mostly resulted from thunderstorms. Those caused by human beings were relatively few. And besides: "Big burns two or three years old is where the deer get most of their winter feed, from the new stuff growing up and the mosses that come after a burn. And wherever there's been a big burn is a good place for trapping a couple of years after. And there's lots of deadwood so you don't have no trouble finding firewood. Indians don't worry about fires 'cause they can just pack up, get out of the way, and go back when it's over. Trees grow up again. It's just whites, specially in the settlements; they're the ones really worry about fires."

The Idthen Eldeli camp we had visited on our journey south was now occupied solely by women and children. We stopped to replace the sack of flour we had borrowed earlier.

Charles thought that, in the absence of the men, the women might be shy of us, but the reverse proved to be the case. We had hardly beached the canoe before tea pails were boiling on half a dozen fires. Soon a crowd of women and children were clustered around us, laughing, talking, drinking our tea, and smoking our tobacco as if our supply of these luxuries (which they had been without for months) was inexhaustible.

I was truly sorry not to be able to speak their language. Judging from the bursts of mirth, a lot of funny stories were on the go, and I suspected Charles and I were the butt of some. Several not unattractive women made it clear we were welcome to stay the night, but Charles was having none of this and insisted we get on.

We were given three fat whitefish as parting presents. I reciprocated by giving the children some loose change I had acquired in Brochet, including a couple of mercury-plated U.S. pennies fabricated by American soldiers stationed at Duck Lake during the war and passed off to the Indians there as dimes. The natives had been aware of the swindle but valued the forgeries because some of them bore the profile of an Indian on the reverse side.

The passage into Misty Lake was a narrow, roaring gap in a rocky dyke. While tracking through it, I lost my footing and might have been swept away had not Charles dropped his pole, leapt out of the canoe, and anchored it long enough for me to seize a gunwale and save myself. He seemed to think nothing of this incident but it loomed large in my thoughts for a long time afterwards.

The Cochrane above Misty Lake boiled with whitewater, slowing our progress to a snail's pace. Cutbanks made tracking so difficult and dangerous that we elected to climb all but the worst rapids under power. Fishtailing madly back and forth, we broke many shear pins, but the toolbox was now well stocked with replacements in the form of pieces of four-inch nails bought at Brochet.

Dusk was falling before we came to the portage out of the Cochrane. The arduous passage to Fort Hall through the "little lakes" now lay before us, and Charles thought we should delay attempting it until the morrow, but I felt we ought to put the first portage behind us before we slept.

This was a short but brutal carry up the slope of a steep-sided esker and down an even steeper slope to the shore of the first pothole lake. By the time we had wrestled the canoe up to the crest, we were so tired we let her get away from us, and she bounded down the opposite slope like a hippopotamus seeking its native element. Charles was amused. I was not, for I had to swim out after her.

The previous night our net had yielded a whitefish, most of which we now had for supper, giving the offal to Bones. Dissatisfied with his portion, he set off hunting on his own. When he failed to return, I went looking for him and came upon what looked like the remains of a brush fence.

"That's a old-time Chip deer fence you found," Charles explained when I returned.

"You mean the Indians kept caribou penned up like cows?" I asked incredulously.

He grinned. "Nope. Built them things to point the deer to where they was waiting for them."

Five or six feet high, consisting of three or more rungs of saplings lashed or jammed between standing trees or posts, such fences channeled migrating deer to river crossings, into defiles, or into brush corrals where hunters waited in ambush. Charles knew of the remains of one such ancient fence near Kasmere Lake at least six miles long. Another, part of which I later saw near Nileen, was probably three miles in length, though so collapsed as to be barely recognizable. The labor expended making such structures must have been immense, but once completed they would have been relatively easy to maintain, and some may have served their builders for decades, if not generations.

Bones eventually rejoined us, and Charles nodded toward him, "Chips used dogs to hunt deer too. A man could have ten or twelve dogs. He'd keep six or seven to haul his toboggan and use the rest for hunting. The dogs knew to drive the deer to where the hunter was.

"Chips likely got as much meat in old times before guns come into the country as ever they do now. They could just about *think* like the deer and figure every move the deer was going to make. Used to wait for them at water crossings then paddle their little bark canoes—smaller than a kayak—right into the herd. Could spear a whole winter's meat in a couple of days that way. Would dry the meat and smoke it and fill big bark pails full of melted fat. If they happen to run short in winter or wanted fresh meat they dug pits in deep snow along deer trails, covered them with brush and snow, and got them that way. I don't believe they went hungry those times near as much as nowadays."

As we continued across the height of land, the flies became so bad that when we reached Wolf Island Lake we ran the canoe over the portage, launched her, and fled precipitously out onto the lake, leaving our freight to be picked up later.

We could see a high hill a short way down the shore and headed for it, hoping it might offer surcease from the flies. Climbing to its crest, we found ourselves in a grove of clean-limbed birches set in a lawn-like expanse of lichens swept by a fresh breeze. Here was a sanctuary fit for some northern naiad.

Gratefully, we pitched our tent, made a little fire, ate cold bannock, and went contentedly to bed. At least, Charles and I were content. Not so poor Bones. Because we had seen fresh bear dung on the portage into Wolf Island Lake, Charles had left the dog chained to a tree to guard our supplies. Perhaps concluding we meant to abandon him forever, Bones spent the night wailing to the world about what heartless bastards we were. When reprieved next morning, his relief was so extreme he knocked me down and sat on me.

The naiad of Wolf Island Lake not only blessed us with a fly-free night, next morning she sent some of her minions to extend her protection. As we picked up our first loads of the day, a squadron of giant dragonflies appeared and assailed our tormentors, especially the deer flies and even larger flies called bulldogs. The dragonflies, whose wingspreads were almost as broad as a human hand, flew with legs thrust forward, forming a basket into which they scooped large flies in full flight. Then they chewed the captives' heads off.

If the dragonfly clan is ever in need of a human champion, it can count on me.

In the middle of Long Carry Lake the old Lockwood blew her head gasket. Had this happened two weeks earlier I might have panicked. Now I nonchalantly picked up my paddle, and we headed for the nearest shore, where Charles performed another miracle. An hour later the Lockwood noisily returned to duty with a perfectly satisfactory head gasket made from a sheet of birchbark.

Crossing the height of land entailed ten portages, requiring us to walk in excess of thirty miles, half of that distance carrying loads of over a hundred pounds. The heat was intense and the blackflies and sandflies remorseless. As we reloaded the canoe after the last portage, Charles was moved to complain, "That's the worst I ever seen in this country! Nobody should travel through here in July, not without they had about a million of them dragonflies!"

It was a joy to launch on Thanout Lake's relatively broad expanse, knowing that from here onward we would be going downstream. After a leisurely four-mile run we reached a large esker that almost bisects the lake. A lob-stick—a partially limbed spruce tree retaining its bushy crown—stood atop this high ridge. I pointed questioningly at it, and Charles yelled over the blat of the kicker, "Old Kasmere's buried there. You want a look?"

Father Egenolf, who had known Kasmere through half a century, had described him to me as short but massively built; thick-necked as a bull caribou; broad of face with huge, square teeth.

"*Très formidable*, that man! But when he smile it was like the full moon. *Hélas!* He never have too many smiles for me!"

Kasmere was born around 1865, when the Idthen Eldeli were still living virtually as they had done since dim antiquity—their lives intimately intertwined with those of the caribou. Contact with Europeans or their institutions had still been so peripheral as to be almost irrelevant. There were no appointed or elected "chiefs" in those days. The most effective men supplied leadership as it was needed. Kasmere was one such. By the time he was twenty he was leading two hundred or so members of the Barrenland Band on their annual migration between Idthentua and Tobontua (Dubawnt Lake) far out on the tundra plains to the north.

By the turn of the twentieth century, Egenolf's predecessors had had some success with the Idthen Eldeli, but little with the Misty Lake or Barrenland Bands, a failure due largely to the resistance of Etzanni and Kasmere.

Kasmere was such an effective and powerful man that in 1907, when government came to the region to "make Treaty" with the natives, the officials selected him as Chief of the Idthen Eldeli.

The Indian agent duly presented him with the regalia of office: a medal on a ribbon to wear around his neck, a dark blue naval coat with lots of brass buttons, and a military cap sporting a gold tassel. Kasmere accepted these gauds with an indifference which might have warned the agent of trouble ahead.

Thierry Mallet, a trader for Revillon Frères who spent some time to the north of Reindeer Lake during the early and mid-1920s, wrote of Kasmere:

"A wonderful hunter and the shrewdest Indian I ever met.

Once a year the Government sends a Commissioner to Brochet to pay the Treaty to the whole tribe. For a small sum of money handed out to each head of the family, all the Indians accepted to recognize the Government and its laws.

"Kasmere was the chief by Government appointment. Each summer when the Commissioner arrived with his small fleet of canoes Kasmere was there.

"For some years he had fulfilled his task to the entire satisfaction of all concerned. He faithfully reported the deaths, births and the general state of health of his band.... Now and then he would have a brush with the local missionary, who also was a power in the land. Still he was a good chief and his wisdom in taking his tribe to the right place to hunt for food and fur each winter was greatly admired.

"Then came a year when Kasmere came to the conclusion that the Government owed him a brand new canoe. There was something about it in the Treaty, he said.

"For three years each summer he asked for his canoe but the Commissioner, who was on the point of retiring, told him to wait, that he would see what he could do about it.

"The fourth year a new Treaty Officer came who knew nothing about the whole affair. Kasmere made his request again. The white man curtly refused. Then the old Indian lost his temper completely. He beat his breast, quoted the Treaty, 'As long as the grass grows and the rivers flows, etc., etc., called the King a liar and gave an ultimatum. 'If he didn't get his chief's canoe he would refuse the yearly Treaty payment and so would every man, woman and child of his band!'

"The Treaty Commissioner was rather surprised but, wise to the ways of the north, he postponed his answer until the next day. Meanwhile his interpreter and the Missionary talked things over with each member of the tribe.

"The result was when the Government's Representative went to his tent under the big flag the next day and announced he was ready to pay Treaty, everyone of the band stepped up and got his money. Everyone except old Kasmere.

"The old chief had been so certain his authority was absolute that he hadn't even taken the pains to come over and see what was going to happen. He had remained quietly in his tent.

"An hour later a messenger came to him to tell him he had been deprived of his rank as chief and that he had to return immediately his blue coat with the brass buttons and his cap with the gold tassel.

"A few days later he left for the north surrounded by his entire family and close relatives. A little later the rest of the tribe followed. They had a new chief, but still they took no chances. Instinctively they trailed the old leader.

"Since that time Kasmere has remained far north on the edge of the Barren Lands. He absolutely refuses to go back to the settlement. He will not accept his Treaty money, neither does his wife, his children, his relatives, about forty heads in all. Meanwhile the money accumulates and the Treaty's bookkeeping is out of order.

"There is also another side to the situation. As Kasmere knows perfectly well, the new chief has no hold on the tribe. All the hunters still follow him and listen to his advice.

"How long will the situation last? Nobody knows. The Treaty Commissioner is displeased. The Missionary even more so. Half the tribe hasn't been to Mass for three years. Furthermore Kasmere has reverted to some of the old laws of the tribe. For instance, when two young people have started liking each other, the old man has promptly sent them to a teepee. 'Married.' Children have been born and Kasmere has put their names down in his books—that is in his memory. Meanwhile neither the Government census nor the priest has been advised.

"The more annoyed both are, the more resolved is Kasmere to remain north—serenely aloof—still 'the chief,' a peaceful but stubborn rebel—waiting!

"Waiting for what? Who knows. Justice? He doesn't believe in it! Arrest? Possibly! But he has so few years to live now, and his hunting grounds are so very, very far away...."[1]

Kasmere was more enduring than Mallet had thought. He continued to lead his band until the winter of 1939–40, when he was felled by a heart attack while driving his team across the ice of Kasmere Lake.

Before he died, he told his people, "Bury me standing on the high hill at the narrows on Thanout Lake. From there I shall watch you pass when you go north with your toboggans to hunt the deer, and when you return south in your canoes. I will watch for you as long as one of you is left."

[1] Captain Thierry Mallet, *Glimpses of the Barren Lands*, Revillon Frères, New York, 1930.

CHAPTER FOURTEEN

KASMERE'S GRAVE

FOR REASONS OF HIS OWN, CHARLES CHOSE TO remain with the canoe while I scaled the esker's steep slope to the narrow crest, which commanded a spectacular view of Thanout Lake. Not far from the lob-stick was an almost circular depression in the sand about three feet in diameter. It would have been a puzzler had I not known that a man was buried there—standing up. The concept was unsettling, and I could sympathize with Charles's unwillingness to visit the place.

Now he called from the beach below, "Storm comin'. We better get along."

"In a minute!" I replied.

I had caught sight of what appeared to be a collapsed log cabin to the south of the esker and wanted to investigate. When I slid down the reverse slope it was to find my "cabin" was a tangle of wind-felled Jack pines with a pair of fledgling merlins perched on a horizontal trunk. No adult falcons were in evidence. Instead of flying away as I approached, the pigeon-sized youngsters began jumping up and down, flapping their wings like hungry chickens. Amused, I went closer, whereupon they lurched into the air toward me, crash-landed on my shoulders, and began screeching in my ears.

Having played foster parent to many young animals, I knew what this was all about. Turned loose to fend for themselves by their parents, these youngsters were demanding food from the first comer. I was about to put them back on the windfall when I had a mental image of Charles's face if I descended from Kasmere's grave with a screaming hawk on each shoulder.

I acted on the impulse, and was sorry I did because Charles received us with a hard, unfriendly glare and demanded, "Where the hell you get them goddamn things?"

Taken aback, for Charles hardly ever swore, I apologetically offered to put the young birds back where I had found them. Surprisingly, Charles shook his head. "Maybe not...maybe we better keep them...maybe they supposed to go with us."

"Supposed" by whom? I did not think that adding two fledgling hawks to our passenger list was going to make life any easier, and I said as much. Whereupon Charles became insistent, so I acquiesced.

We had a couple of suckers in the canoe for Bones. Now we stripped some flesh off one and fed it to the young hawks, who ate voraciously. Then one of them responded to Charles's outstretched arm by scrambling up it to perch upon his shoulder, where it nibbled his earlobe.

Charles grinned with pleasure. "Likes me, I guess. We'll call this one Chief," he said.

Charles's discomfort at being so close to Kasmere's grave seemed to have dissipated. We made a fire on the beach, cooked and ate supper, then climbed the slope together. Charles sprinkled a packet of tea into the circular depression. Not to be outdone, I took out my tobacco pouch and contributed some of its contents. It seemed the right thing to do.

Dusk was falling by the time we got back to the beach. Bones was asleep beside the canoe, and the young merlins were perched on a gunwale, feathers fluffed and eyes closed. We took the hint, pitched camp, and spent the night under Kasmere's guardianship.

Although it was still July the weather looked and felt like October. Next morning a chill nor'easter bearing the sharp tang of woodsmoke was driving down the lake. The sun was bloodshot and obscure. When I went to the shore to fetch a can of water I came upon the fresh tracks of a lynx. Charles shook his head over that. "Lynx is pretty scarce. I only see their tracks couple times a year, just before freeze-up when they get restless and move around. Hope this don't mean we're looking for an early winter."

We had a wild, wet trip bucking wind and sea down the long gut of Thanout Lake. Perched on the baggage with wings spread as if about to take off, the young hawks seemed to enjoy it, though a minor contretemps developed when Chief tried to use Bones as a perch and was violently rejected. Chief thereupon retreated to the stern to seek Charles's protection. Presumably the second merlin was my protegé, but I did not name him (or her), concluding that within a week or so both would have flown away, out of our lives.

Hugging the north shore to avoid the heaviest waves, we came to some ruins that had caught my eye during our southern passage. There had been no time then to stop; but we made time now.

The ruins consisted of the standing walls of two small, conjoined log cabins whose roofs had long since been reduced to a skeletal filigree of rotted rafters. Charles told me the place had originally been home to one of Kasmere's uncles whose Dene name translated as Redhead. At the turn of the century Redhead's house had burned down with him in it. The site had remained unoccupied until 1908, when the HBC, wishing to lure the Kazan Eskimos south, sent a young employee named Herbert Hall to build a northern outpost. On Kasmere's advice Hall chose the place where Redhead's house had once stood. Kasmere's suggestion was undoubtedly self-serving, for his own winter house was not far distant and the presence of a Company store practically at his doorstep would have had obvious advantages.

Young, strong, and handsome, Herbert Hall had the appearance and aspirations of an empire builder. He renamed Thanout Lake, Hall Lake, and grandiloquently called the outpost he built there Fort Hall.

For a few years the place was visited by some of the more intrepid Ihalmiut, of whom the foremost was a man named Kakumee. A big fellow with a flashing grin, Kakumee had made a formidable reputation for himself amongst the Chipewyans in consequence of an incident near Fond du Lac on Lake Athabasca.

Despite the traditional enmity of the Dene people of that region, one winter Kakumee undertook to drive his big *komatik* to Fond du Lac to trade. He went alone because none of his own people would risk accompanying him.

On a bitter cold night en route Kakumee pitched camp close to Wholdaia Lake. He was a man who believed in looking after his dogs, so he cut spruce boughs for them to sleep on, then laid himself down and pulled his robes around him.

His fire continued to burn brightly for some time, and was seen by three Fond du Lac Chipewyans returning south after a fruitless deer hunt out on the barrens. They headed for the fire. According to his own account (and there was no other) Kakumee welcomed the strangers and hung a pot of soup to heat over the flames.

As Charles retold the story:

"Kakumee was pretty scared, but he never let on. At first the Chips was polite. Then when they seen there was only him and three of them they began to make jokes. Bad jokes about knocking him on the head. They never knew he could understand some Chip. They seen his dogs on the spruce boughs, so one of them unhitched his own dogs and kicked Kakumee's dogs off and put his own dogs on the boughs. Then the others did that too.

"Kakumee never said nothing. He just walked over to his sled and slid his .44.40 out of its deerskin case. The Chips went after their guns then but couldn't get them out fast enough, so in a minute they was all shot.

"Kakumee took off from there running with nothing but just his gun. Never took his dogs or his sled or his furs. He walked a hundred miles back to camp on the Kazan and never come south again for three years. Then he heard two of the Chips had died and the third had just made it home. The rest of the Chips were scared to death of him after that, so he started coming south again; and he kept on doing it until he died, an old, old man. It was mainly because of him this place, Fort Hall—Eskimo Post was what most people called it—got built. But once Kakumee was gone, no more Huskies come down this far, and that was the end of Eskimo Post."

When Charles and I stepped ashore we found a raven perched on the sagging ridgepole. He was a huge specimen sporting a cluster of white feathers around the base of his beak, an indication of great age. At our approach, he glided silently down and landed nearly at our feet. There he stood, almost within arm's reach, sagely watching every move we made.

This was too much for Bones, who jumped back into the canoe. I must admit I found the behavior of this big bird with his formidable, spear-shaped beak disconcerting.

Charles eyed the raven askance, then took a paddle out of the bow of the canoe and for a moment I thought he was going to use it as a lance. If so, he had second thoughts. "You can go on up there if you want," he said to me, nodding at the ruins. With which he too climbed back aboard.

As I walked up the slope, the raven kept pace, a yard to one side of me. I ignored his presence until, reaching a doorway in one standing wall, I turned to confront him. Looking almost as big as a turkey-cock, he put his head on one side and eyed me inscrutably before bending to pick up a stick with his fearsome mandibles and *tossing* it at my feet!

I usually feel comfortable in the presence of non-human animals, but the behavior of this bird unnerved me. I started back for the canoe. By the time I reached it, Charles was standing in the stern ready to start the kicker. I turned to see where the raven was. He had returned to the ridgepole and from there spoke for the first time: one clarion, bell-like cry that could have been either a benediction or a curse. Then the motor clattered into life and we were away.

The lake ended a few miles farther along, and we went ashore at the beginning of the long portage around the Kasmere Gorge. Near the landing place stood the crumbled ruin of yet another cabin; this one smaller and even more decrepit than those at Eskimo Post. Built about 1920 by Thierry Mallett of Revillon Frères, it had been intended to intercept the Eskimos before they reached Hall's post, but had been abandoned after only a year or two when no Eskimos showed up.

We were surprised, not to say startled, to find *another* raven on the decayed ridgepole of *this* structure. But *was* it another? Charles seemed to think it was the one we had already met. As we began unloading the canoe under its watchful eye, the bird tilted its head, gave the peculiar bell-like cry, and flew heavily off in the direction we were bound.

It was late in the day, and we had not eaten since breakfast, so we camped and cooked a meal—suckers for Bones and the hawks, bacon and bannock for Charles and me. Then we sat for a while, drinking black tea and pondering our immediate future.

Charles thought we might be able to run all but three of the many rapids which lay ahead. Vividly remembering their ferocity when we were ascending them, I did not share his confidence. In fact, I was severely frightened at the prospect of running them in our ponderous, overloaded canoe. Then I remembered the inscription carved into the transom of the old square-rigged ship in Joseph Conrad's novel *Youth*: Do or Die. In my mind's eye I saw the words emblazoned on the stern of our old canoe…and somehow felt a little easier.

A chill mist from the unseen falls overhung our camp when we awoke. We pushed off in a frigid drizzle. The hawks hated the wet and tried to shelter under Bones, who curled himself into a ball, refusing to even acknowledge he was in the world.

Soon we heard a guttural roar and went ashore—to behold a foaming torrent boiling through three consecutive chutes for a total fall of perhaps twenty feet.

As I stared, appalled, Charles gloomily remarked that the Chipewyans no longer ran this rapid, having lost two canoes and three men to it a few years earlier. My bladder constricted, and I felt a powerful urge to root myself to the riverbank forevermore. Charles, however, claimed he could see a channel and, after shaking himself like a dog about to take a plunge, headed back to the canoe, leaving me no choice but to stumble along behind.

A fierce current gripped us as we swung heavily into the slick water at the head of the first chute. Man-high waves backing up behind submerged boulders awaited us at its foot. The rock Charles had indicated as our leading mark flashed past, leaving us in a deep trough blocked by a great, curling wave. Charles whooped a warning, then we were heeling over between two granite obelisks surrounded by spouting water. I thrust my paddle between the nearest one and the canoe; pulled back for all I was worth; and I felt the paddle snap. The engine roared at full throttle and then, miraculously, the chute was behind us.

Moments later the second chute raced past, and then the third.

As the canoe steadied in the millrace below the rapids, Charles cut the engine and tossed me the spare paddle. The little hawks, both of whom had been soaked, burst into a chorus of outrage. Bones emerged from under my feet, gave me a hopeless look, then shoved his nose back under his tail. As for me, I was ecstatic—not because of any sense of triumph, but out of sheer relief.

Soon we were in the long eastern bay of Kasmere Lake and being buffeted by a strong southwesterly kicking up waves that threatened to swamp the Lockwood, whose sparkplug was unprotected by any sort of cowling. We crawled along under the lee of the high southern shore to land not far below Kasmere's empty house, which we had not had time to visit on our way south. Charles grabbed the bag containing our cooking utensils, I shouldered the grub box, and we climbed to the cabin up a steep path made slippery by the drizzle.

Everything about the house was unusual, including its location on the crest of a two-hundred-foot hill half a mile from the nearest water and exposed to every wind that blew. All the trees at the summit had been cleared away to provide an unobstructed view of almost the entire lake with its many deep bays and arms.

Kasmere Lake (originally Theitagatua) was the crossroads for several principal canoe and sled routes to and from the Barrenlands. It was not by chance that Kasmere's habitation commanded a view of all of them from its five large windows. Its single room, about twenty by twenty feet, had two entrances set side by side in the north wall facing the lake. One of these was for the use of Kasmere's own people; the other was for strangers. People who came through the right-hand door could make free of Kasmere's hospitality. Strangers coming through the left-hand door paid for the privilege.

The construction was also remarkable. Instead of being built in the usual "hog-pen" style with horizontally laid round logs, it was built of squared logs set vertically.

We entered (through the left-hand doorway) to find much of the roof collapsed and the hand-sawed floorboards reduced to streaks of rot. There was no furniture of any kind; but in one corner lay the body of a large dog, its muzzle distorted in the rictus of death. Untouched by scavengers, it appeared to have been mummified. Its presence bothered Charles, and only with difficulty could I persuade him to remain within the shelter of the cabin walls while I lit a fire on what had been the floor, made tea, and toasted some sodden pieces of bannock for our supper.

Charles, who had been fifteen when Kasmere died, had met the old man only three or four times, but he knew a good deal about him as, indeed, did every resident of the region.

"White trappers didn't like him. Traders didn't neither. They all had to pay for using his land. If they didn't—well, things happened.

"The smart ones, they'd stop when they came through Kasmere Lake and give him some flour, tea, sugar, ammunition, whatever he said he wanted. Then they'd go on about their business. He never kept all the stuff for himself. When things got tough for his people he'd hand it out to them.

"Once in a while a white trader or trapper might try to get by without stopping or leaving something. Next time that fellow come by he might get a .44.40 through his canoe. Or at night when he'd made his camp a bullet might come out of the woods and blow up his tea billy right in his face. Kasmere was a dead shot. Not too many tried to sneak past twice. Was smarter to stop and give him a present.

"Twenty or thirty years ago a few Eskimos still used to come down to trade at Eskimo Post. Kakumee was one. Another one was Kakut. Before Kakut died he told me when he used to drive his team across the lake he'd stop at Kasmere's house and give him a white fox skin. Once he even give him a muskox skin.

"He told me Kasmere's women would cook up a feed, then the men would settle down and play udzi—that's the Chip gambling game. Mostly Kakut would lose, but sometimes Kasmere would let him win a little so's he wouldn't be too mad about it. If you had a specially good dog, watch out 'cause Kasmere loved good dogs.

"He was the last Big Man among the Chips. So long as he was alive, all the country between the Crees on Reindeer Lake and the Eskimos out on the Barrens belonged to the Chips, no matter what white men might think about it.

"One winter when my father was working for the Company as

a camp trader, he tried to sneak around Kasmere Lake. He went south of it but got lost in the sandhills and muskeg country and ran out of dog feed and was pretty near starved when he broke out on the ice of Kasmere's River near Sucker Lake. He no sooner got a fire going than along comes another team with old Kasmere driving it.

"He pulled up at the fire, looked around and seen the dogs was about done and Father pretty near as bad, then he dug into his toboggan, hauled out a quarter of deer meat and slung it alongside Father and says, in Cree: 'Hard trip, eh? You should go the short way, past my house. Wife would have cooked you a good meal. Now you pretty near lost your dogs. But I will help you. I take two of your dogs home with me and feed them. There's enough on that quarter to feed the rest so you can go on.'

"There wasn't nothing Father could do about it. Kasmere went off with Father's two best dogs, and Father never saw them again until a year later Kasmere drove up to the Company post at Windy Lake and one of them dogs was his lead dog. When Kasmere saw Father looking at the dog he said, 'That's a good dog. I might sell him if the price was good enough.'

"My father hated Kasmere's guts, but the old fellow never done me no harm."

Father Egenolf had mixed feelings about Kasmere. When I asked him if the old Chief was a Christian, he took a long time answering.

"He was as good a Christian with his own people as you or me. What he had was theirs. He looked out for them. While he was alive, the Idthen Eldeli were strong for each other and the old ways. They did not often visit the settlements, and when they came they did not stay long. Kasmere and Etzanni and some others, they did not want their people to take up the white man's ways. Even today there is not one of these people really speaking English.

"He was not so good a friend of the Church as he should have been, and we did not agree about many things. But this I did agree with: the way Kasmere tried to keep the Idthen truly a people of the deer, and not let them turn into tramps hanging about some settlement looking for handouts from the white men."

CHAPTER FIFTEEN

KASMERE'S BIRDS

W E HAD THOUGHT TO CAMP ON A BUG-FREE islet a few miles east of Kasmere's house, but big waves breaking on its shore made landing our heavily laden craft too hazardous, so we continued on to Grave Rapid, which spans the narrows at the end of the lake and marks the rebirth of Kasmere's River.

Though rain, mist, and the onset of darkness had reduced visibility to a few hundred feet, Charles ran us through Grave Rapid like a man inspired. Emerging abeam of the extensive cemetery we had visited on our way south, we went ashore, got the tent up in jig time, and crawled inside.

Next morning we hung around the breakfast fire, swilling black tea, heaping green spruce boughs on the coals to produce a smudge, and talking very little. Charles seemed reluctant to make a start; then he did a peculiar thing. Catching up one of the little hawks, he held it at arm's length in front of him. "I dream about this bird last night. Show us the way down the rapids. So I guess we go now."

A short run of fast water brought us to a mile of chutes around which most travelers bound either up or down made a thousand-yard portage. We had done so ourselves on the journey south and would have done the same now if the prospect of spending the rest of the day in a swelter of sweat and flies while humping our enormous lading through windfalls and across muskeg had not been so appalling. Anything seemed preferable to that. *And* Kasmere's birds were riding with us....

Bones was not. When we pulled in to shore for a long look at what lay ahead, he jumped ship. Tail tucked between his legs, ears back, and with nary a glance in our direction, he fled into the woods. No amount of yelling could persuade him to return.

"He'll follow along," said Charles phlegmatically.

The first part of Charles Rapid, as I named it on my sketch map, was a straightforward chute through which the water raced so swiftly we were into it and out of it in seconds. But it turned out to be merely the bait in what threatened to become a lethal trap. The next section included three small falls throwing up backwash waves four to five feet high. The riverbed above and between them was strewn with frost-shattered rocks between which we could see no channels wide enough nor deep enough for our canoe.

We had no sooner entered this killing ground than the bow crunched against stone and the canoe instantly began swinging broadside. There was only one thing to be done. Both of us leapt overboard, scrabbling for footholds while struggling to keep the canoe from being swept sideways onto the *chevaux de frise* below. Somehow we managed to get her straightened out and off the underwater rock. We leapt back aboard like men mounting a running horse and an instant later shot over the first ledge, where a standing wave swept over the bow and carried my little hawk into the stern to join his saturated sibling under Charles's feet.

We grounded the canoe in a backwater to bail her out and to see what damage she had sustained. Her oaken bow timber was splintered, and another rib had cracked, but she was still seaworthy. Looking upstream, I beheld a basalt stairway built by titans, down which foamed a raving torrent.

The remaining section was so fearsome that we elected to line down it. Acting as brakeman, I waded along the shore gripping the end of a fifty-foot line tied to the canoe's stern, while Charles splashed along abreast using a long pole to keep her from being smashed into the shore rocks.

It was touch and go. We had to wade knee- to thigh-deep, slipping and sliding as we struggled to keep our footing, being pulled off balance and forced to sit down while the current poured over us. Then we came to a jutting point of boulders around which the canoe simply could not be maneuvered. In desperation we brought her close to shore, where I held her while Charles removed seven or eight hundred pounds of freight which he somehow managed to pack across the point without breaking a leg.

We then combined our strengths to shove the canoe far out into the stream, leaving the line slack. Free to go her own way, she behaved like a lady, and we hauled her safely back to the bank below the point. By this time I had fallen so many times I was reduced to flopping along like a seal.

While tracking around that last bend, I was startled to catch a glimpse of a red plane flying northward high above us. Nothing could be heard above the roar of the rapids, and by the time I was able to draw Charles's attention to it the plane was gone.

We went ashore to replace our load and to consider what the plane's appearance might portend.

"Hope it don't mean no trouble," Charles mused. "Maybe just a bunch of prospectors."

Bones rejoined us here, and his joy at doing so was unconstrained. Huskies are supposed to be undemonstrative animals, but Bones gave this canard the lie by jumping on Charles and sending him sprawling. When Charles threw him off, he came for me, and when I put the fire between us, he tried to lick one of the little hawks.

We slipped on downstream until we came to the head of Sucker Rapid. I had expected to walk around this one, but Charles elected to run it. First, though, we carried some six hundred pounds across the portage, not just to lighten the canoe but to ensure that if there was an accident we would not lose everything.

The river here became a maelstrom funneled through two successive chutes. Entering the upper one at full gallop with the Lockwood blaring, we shot out of the lower one in something less than a minute. Reloading our freight, we then puttered out onto the calm, sunlit waters of Sucker Lake, where we came upon an islet harboring a colony of about a hundred arctic terns. Fate had not been kind to them. Although there were a good many live fledglings, there were even more dead ones wedged in rock crevices or drowned in pools. Rotting eggs in what passed for nests littered the foreshore. Since we could see no indications that the rookery had been attacked by predators, we concluded the terns were the victims of their own fecklessness.

The first of August dawned gray and chill after a night of wind and pelting rain. That day's run began with a mile-long stretch of whitewater, then the river surged deep and swift under the high shoulder of a great esker to Spruce Falls, whose six-foot drop gave us no option but to portage.

Tebanaycha—Mud Rapid—was next. We paused here to brew up and eat cold bannock while our hawks dined on the corpse of a dead tern we had brought along for them from the charnel islet in Sucker Lake.

Having run Mud Rapid, we slalomed through a boulder field awash in raging water, zigzagging from side to side like a frenzied rabbit. At one point we unexpectedly reversed direction so that Charles perforce became bowman and I steerman. This was the last straw for Bones, who threw back his head, closed his eyes, and gave his rendition of the Huskies' Last Lament.

A flightless merganser surfaced so close beside us in the pool below that I was able to belt it with a paddle. As we entered the quiet waters of Sandy Lake, Charles plucked the duck, leaving a trail of feathers floating in our wake.

We went ashore at the foot of a high, mustard-colored esker

snaking sinuously along the shore and soon were eating ponassed duck, crisply charred and oozing oil. Although it was only mid-afternoon, neither of us felt like resuming the duel with Kasmere's River, so we elected to stay put for the night.

The wind dropped at dusk, and mosquitoes emerged en masse. Their appearance triggered a kind of dementia in me, and I built up a big bonfire and began leaping through it, hoping to effect a mosquito holocaust. However, I made one leap too many and landed on a stone. My right foot snapped sideways and I collapsed in agony.

Pain kept me awake most of the night. In the morning Charles insisted we stay put, so I spent much of that day in the tent fretting about the mess we would be in if my ankle proved to be broken. Strong and energetic as Charles might be, I did not see how, single-handed, he could move our enormous load over all the many portages which still separated us from Windy Post.

I was brooding over that bleak prospect when we heard the grinding roar of an aircraft engine and the red plane flew over again, this time heading south. Charles recognized it as a Lamb Airways Norseman and concluded it must have been to Windy Post. He wrote in his journal:

I am getting worried if they keep flying up and down from Nueltin like that. We are both wondering what is going on at home. Well, if they don't do one thing I wouldn't worry at all, but I guess I can't help it. I hope to God the plane can stay away from home and the Kazan River.... I am thinking of a nice little dream that someday her and I will be on our own. I am going to build a nice home somewhere soon. I have three nice places picked out. One near Big Point [Hidden Valley], one close to Kazan and one [near Dubawnt Lake].

Although Charles did not identify the object of his concern by name, there can be no doubt but that it was Rita.

A sense of impending catastrophe descended upon us, and neither of us could sleep that night. I found a codeine pill in my kit and with its help was able to catnap, but I dreamed dark dreams in which I was being attacked by a red fighter plane spitting incendiary bullets.

The next two days were uneventful; however, on the third the Norseman reappeared, this time flying at an altitude of only a few hundred feet. The pilot spotted us, banked steeply, and landed on an expansion a mile downstream. We motored toward the plane filled with a disturbing mixture of excitement and apprehension.

As we came alongside, Tom Lamb, the pilot-owner, thrust his beefy face out a window and greeted Charles in friendly fashion. "Climb into the cabin, son. We've just come from Windy. Dr. Yule wants a chat with you."

Wordlessly, Charles did as he was bid. The door closed behind him, and Lamb turned his attention to me.

"I guess you're Mowat. You had enough of roughing it in the bush yet? How'd you like a free flight back to The Pas?"

Completely taken aback, I stammered something to the effect that I had no wish to go to The Pas and in any case could not leave Charles here on his own.

"Not to worry about him," Lamb responded heartily. "I'll be back up here again in a couple days. Pick him up and his stuff and fly him to Windy. I could bring your gear out on the same trip. Dr. Harper's got it all ready to go."

"Why would he do that?" I asked, nonplussed.

Lamb's smile vanished and his expression hardened. "When we was at Windy, Dr. Harper says he fired you. With good reason. He don't want you back there, so you might as well get your ass into my plane right now and I'll take you out of the country. It's the best chance you're going to get."

Although I had no way of knowing it, I was about to make one of the most important decisions of my life. If I had accepted Lamb's offer, I might not have gone north again in the succeeding years and, even had I done so, would probably not have had the experiences which led me to write *People of the Deer, The Desperate*

People, and *Never Cry Wolf,* three books which became foundation
stones of my writing career.

Sitting in that old canoe, with Tom Lamb in his miracle of
technology looming over me, I was becoming angry. "Thank you,
Mr. Lamb, but no thanks. I don't know what you've been told, and
I don't give a damn. I'm not pulling out! It's a free country and I've
just spent four bloody years fighting to keep it that way. I'll leave
when and *if* I please!"

Now Lamb was angry, his red face becoming redder still.
Glancing disdainfully at the army cap I retained as a kind of tal-
isman, he had the last word. "Suit yourself. But you ex-service
guys don't cut any ice up here. War's over, you know. Maybe
Charley'll make you see sense." With which he slid his window
shut, perhaps to keep out the mosquitoes.

Half an hour passed before Charles climbed down from the
cabin. A rather cadaverous-looking middle-aged man, presumably Dr. Yule, appeared behind him in the open door.

"Here!" he said, tossing a burlap bag into the canoe.
"Government fish nets for the Indians at Putahow. Didn't have
time to stop. Drop them off on your way past."

If this man *was* a doctor, he was what I needed.

"Don't want to hold you up, but I've got a wonky ankle. Mind
taking a look at it?"

He glanced at Lamb in the pilot's seat. Lamb shook his head.
The doctor looked down at me, smiling apologetically. "We're in
a great hurry. Bad weather's on its way. Besides, I've no equipment
for a proper examination.... Tell you what. Climb aboard and fly
with us to The Pas and I'll fix your foot up there."

I turned to Charles.

Crouched over the Lockwood, he would not meet my gaze,
but in a voice so low I could hardly hear him, he muttered, "You
want to go in the plane with them, you go. I'll make out."

"Screw that!" I said and pushed the canoe away from the
pontoon. Charles started the motor and headed downstream.

Soon the roar of a Wasp engine drowned out all other sounds. The Norseman thundered past and took to the air. We were alone again on Kasmere's River.

We went ashore on an island in Long Lake to brew up and to calm ourselves. There Charles told me what had transpired in the Norseman's cabin, but several months would elapse before I was able to reconstruct, and understand, all that had taken place.

On March 13, 1947, Dr. Robert Yule, the federal Department of Indian Affairs official responsible for the health and well-being of natives in the region, chartered a Lamb Airways Norseman at The Pas to fly him and a load of relief supplies to the Eskimo band on the Kazan River. Charles had reported that they were in dire need.

For reasons never given, that flight went only as far as the mouth of the Putahow River on south Nueltin, where the relief supplies were unloaded and abandoned on the beach. The plane went south to Brochet to spend the night but the following day flew direct to Windy Post, where it paused just long enough for Dr. Yule to tell Charles he would return in a few days with the relief supplies and, using Charles as a guide, fly on to the Kazan. The Norseman and the doctor then returned to The Pas.

That was on March 14. Dr. Yule and the plane did not come back *until four and a half months later*, when, on July 31, I saw them passing overhead. They were then en route to Windy, where the good doctor and his wife intended to enjoy a barrenlands holiday.

They had chosen the right time for one. The flies were thinning out; the weather was at its most clement; wildlife was abundant; and the relatively virgin waters of Windy Bay offered sport fishing as good as was to be found anywhere. The Yules doubtless expected to have a splendid time.

And so they did.

Delighted by the unexpected arrival of a congenial white couple, Harper turned over the Schweders' cabin to them and volunteered the services of Fred, Mike, Anoteelik, and Rita. The visitors reciprocated by listening sympathetically, and indignantly, to the catalogue of difficulties my actions or lack of action had inflicted upon this eminent American scientist.

Harper explained that he had been forced to sever my connection with the Keewatin Zoological Expedition, whereupon I had "seduced" Charles into making a canoe trip to Brochet, and intended to follow it with an even longer trip north on some foolhardy adventure which would deprive Harper of Charles's services for the balance of the summer season.

As a Canadian government official, Dr. Yule was anxious to make amends for my behavior to the American. He decided that the best way to do this was to get me out of the country. Which is how it came to pass that when the Norseman headed south from Windy Post, its pilot and passengers were intent on finding us.

Charles also told me Lamb and Yule had insisted that for his own present and future good he must sever all connections with me. They impressed upon him that any attempt to travel with me to Baker Lake would see both of us leaving our bones on the barrenlands. And if by some miracle we should survive to reach Churchill, we would be too late for Charles to be able to return to Windy on the expedition's plane.

Why so?

Because, so the doctor claimed, he was carrying a telegram from Harper instructing Johnny Bourassa to fetch the expedition from Windy on September 10, rather than October 20 as had originally been arranged.

Whatever else this change might have been designed to accomplish, it would effectively scuttle our travel plans. What Charles and I did *not* know (although presumably Yule and Lamb did) was that Harper had no intention of leaving Windy until he had filmed the mass southern migration of the caribou, an event not to be expected before mid-October.

Something else had occurred during the session in the Norseman's cabin which caused Charles acute distress. Lamb announced that he was considering taking Rita ("cute little kid," he called her) out to The Pas to live with him.

"Dr. Yule said he could fix it for Mister Lamb to do it. He said Rita was an orphan, so the government could decide what to do with her, and Mr. Lamb would give her a good home and see she got a education.... Seems like they might do it if I don't do what they say."

Charles and I crouched beside our tea fire in a state of deepening depression. I found the prospect of spending the next several weeks having to share the poisonous atmosphere of Windy Post with Harper intolerable. And there was also the distinct possibility of my becoming estranged from Charles. Although he seemed to want to keep our comradeship alive, he was now under great pressure to do otherwise—pressure which I knew would increase when we reached Windy. The possibility of losing Rita constituted a threat I doubted he would be able to withstand.

We might have remained immobilized beside the dying fire indefinitely had not the glare of distant lightning given warning of a storm. Since the island offered no place to camp, we reluctantly got back into the canoe and set off down the penultimate stretch of river.

Soon we were at the head of Nilee-Deesee—the four-mile rapids. Such was our state of mind we did not give a thought to portaging. We did not even go ashore for a reconnaissance. Charles hardly slowed the Lockwood. We ran as recklessly into the whitewater as if we bore charmed lives—and perhaps we did. There followed another confusion of standing waves, falling water, roaring torrents, and glimpses of rocky teeth set in a primordial jaw. Then we were through and in the clear.

But not unscathed.

Unnoticed by either Charles or me, the little hawk named

Chief had been swept overboard. Although we searched for him in the slower water, we found not a feather.

We carried on across Nahali to land at the upper end of the portage around Nileen Falls. By then the storm was almost upon us, so we pitched our tent on a broad strip of beach where, through the millennia, countless others had camped before us.

Kasmere had been kind, and his river was now safely behind us. But before us lay a prospect as ominous as the black clouds rolling overhead.

CHAPTER SIXTEEN

PUTAHOW

T HAT NIGHT AT NILEEN WAS SINGULARLY TRYING. An almost palpable shadow had come between Charles and me. We no longer felt at ease in each other's presence. I lay awake for hours, listening to the rain beat against the tent, growing more and more morose as I contemplated the way my post-war search for solace and purpose seemed to be degenerating into a welter of acrimony and frustration.

I was in no hurry to face the new day, which broke chill and bleak. Charles, who was usually up at the crack of dawn, lay inert in his sleeping bag. Only the pressure of a full bladder kept me from doing likewise—that and the piteous hungry shrilling of our surviving hawk.

I lit the fire, fed the bird scraps of raw bacon, and had the billy boiling before Charles emerged from the tent—and turned the day around. He was smiling broadly, something I seldom saw him do. He walked briskly over to the fire and poured a cup of tea.

"Tell you what," he said, "if we got no time to go to Dubawnt or Baker, we could go another way to Churchill."

So he had not—as I had supposed and feared—been thinking about ways and means of disassociating himself from me. To the contrary, he had been mulling over ways to keep us together. My spirits soared as he continued: "A big river runs out of Seal Hole Lake at the north end of Nueltin. The Chips call it Thlewiaza—

means big fish, 'cause white whales supposed to live in its mouth; but we just call it Big River. Runs right down to Hudson Bay. I never met nobody traveled down it, but Joe Highway been to Seal Hole and seen Big River. Says it's bigger than the Cochrane. Says a long time ago, before there was even a post at Brochet, the Chips used to go that way to trade at Churchill. Would take them about a month."

He paused to refill his cup. "If you and me went down Big River, we ought to make Churchill easy by September 10…."

"Well, Jesus Christ, yes!" I cried. "I bet we could!"

We spent most of the morning talking it over. Though not as grand as our original plan, it had its inducements. It would take us through virtually unknown territory, much of which was, or had been, Inuit country. It would be a continuous water route, so we would be able to go all the way by canoe and not have to undertake cross-country travel with pack dogs.

There were some drawbacks. For one thing we had no map of the greater portion of the country we would be passing through. In fact, no accurate map of it then existed. Canada's National Topographic Survey maps showed the course of the upper Thlewiaza River only in dotted lines. We did not have even this approximation of its middle and lower reaches, so could only guess at where it debouched into Hudson Bay, or how far we might have to travel along an exposed sea coast to reach Churchill. And we knew nothing about the nature and character of the river itself except for the little Charles had been told.

Nevertheless, the more we talked, the more enthusiastic we became. Before we knew it we had reached an agreement to tackle the Thlewiaza. But first we had to complete the journey to Windy Post, and the immediate task in hand was to move our freight around Nileen.

Though my ankle was somewhat better, I could only carry light loads, so Charles had to do most of the portaging. It was dusk before we had everything across and could set off down the entry bay leading into south Nueltin. The Idthen Eldeli were no longer at the camp we had visited on the way south—Charles said they had probably gone to Putahow River, where the fishing was better—so we did not pause until we reached the mouth of the bay, where we took aboard a crate of hardware Charles had left there the previous winter. The additional weight brought the already heavily laden canoe's freeboard down to about two inches—precious little with which to face the open waters of Nueltin. Before dealing with that problem, we had first to deliver new nets to the Indians at Putahow, then, if we could find it, collect Fred's elusive cache.

Summer was now well advanced and the night sky considerably darker than it had been on our way south. Even the glaucous glare of a rising moon could no longer dim the profusion of stars. A cat's paw of wind riffled the surface of the runs between the islands, setting the shadows all aquiver. It was a magnificent night to travel, so we kept going until 2:00 a.m., by which time we were approaching what we hoped was the lagoon at the mouth of Putahow River. The moon had set and the darkness had become nearly absolute when we glimpsed what might have been a couple of fireflies—except there are no fireflies in the north. Charles headed for these pinpricks of light, which turned out to be the flare of matches being struck by someone on an unseen shore.

Just sufficient light remained to dimly silhouette three tents pitched on the crest of a long embankment crossing the estuary of the Putahow River: part of a great esker we had encountered several times before, and which, according to Charles, could be traced all the way from Windy Bay to Brochet. This camp was occupied by three men, four women, eight children, and a dozen or more dogs, all of whom we had met before.

The distant throb of the Lockwood had brought Madees down to the shore to beacon us in. Meanwhile Angela, his wife, had built up a fire in front of their tent and started ponassing a trout with which to regale the visitors, whoever they might be.

This time we experienced none of the diffidence that had attended our first meeting. We were greeted with friendly smiles and laughter. A young man secured the canoe as we were escorted to Madees's fire, where the aroma of trout fat vaporizing on glowing coals started my stomach rumbling.

There was no tea in camp, nor any flour or lard, but we remedied that, and in no time kettles were boiling and bannocks frying. Soon everybody, ranging from a child too young to walk to an elderly woman too old to do so, was sitting about eating and drinking.

And talking.

Angela, I now discovered, had been educated for a season at a mission school and spoke some English, in an appealing if fragmented manner. She had not revealed this ability during our previous meeting, presumably because my alien presence had inhibited her. But now that I had been accorded a measure of acceptance she became so busy interpreting what was being said that she allowed the trout to burst into flames, an offence for which she was reprimanded by the old woman.

The mood about the fire was cheerful, though what the people had to be cheerful about was difficult to discern. They had been out of flour or any other kind of store food for weeks, and their supplies of dried meat had long since been exhausted. Subsistence fishing, upon which the Idthen Eldeli normally relied in the summertime, had become very difficult because new nets (part of the Treaty obligations of the government) had not been forthcoming.

Shortly after our earlier visit to the camp at Nileen, the situation had become so critical that most of the people had fled to Duck Lake hoping to obtain relief from the trader there. All the band would have gone except that there were too few canoes to carry everybody and everything, and they would have had to abandon much of their gear and many of their dogs. In the end

Madees, together with two of his adult nephews and their families, volunteered to camp at Putahow, where they hoped to be able to catch enough fish with their torn and rotten old nets to feed themselves and all the dogs.

They had also counted on word of their plight reaching the Indian agent via the trader at Duck Lake and a few days before our arrival had thought help was at hand when a red float plane flew over their camp.

"Plane come real low," Madees told me through Angela. "Wag wings, don't stop. See us for sure but don't stop. Maybe come again?"

"Maybe," I said cravenly. "We met it at Itooee [Sandy Lake] and they gave us some nets to give you. The doctor said to tell you to send him lots of moccasins."

Behind my back I heard Charles mutter: "Them nets was likely bought with the Chips' own Family Allowance money. Shouldn't have to give him nothing."

The people at Putahow were getting by on two or three whitefish or lake trout a day. The dogs were starving. Several had already died, and unless the fishery could be dramatically improved, the rest would probably die too. Madees had found himself in a terrible dilemma. He could not crowd all his people into the one remaining canoe in an attempt to reach Duck Lake; nor could he have sent his nephews in the canoe to seek help, for then there would have been no way for those who remained to work the nets.

Despite the shortage of fish, Charles and I were served embarrassingly large portions of trout. We ate what we were given because this was expected of us, but quietly we made plans between ourselves. There was supposed to be plenty of flour in Fred's cache, so we decided to give these people fifty pounds of the flour we were carrying, together with the requisite amount of baking powder. If and when we found Fred's cache all would be well. If not—there might be a shortage of flour at Windy Post next winter.

We told Madees what we were going to do, and he informed the others. Nobody said much, but everyone, including the children, found an opportunity to mutter or whisper the word *mairtzee* to Charles or me. Whether the resemblance to *merci* was accidental or due to borrowing from the French, its meaning was unmistakably heartfelt.

The mood around the fire now became positively gay. Nobody, not even the youngest children, showed the least desire to go to bed. We laughed, talked, and sang together. The men told us about the appearance of a mysterious entity who supposedly haunted south Nueltin. According to Madees, man-like tracks had appeared on the crest of the esker less than a mile from camp, a discovery which had frightened the women and children and made the men uneasy. Madees would show us the tracks when daylight came.

Who did he think had made them? I asked.

He shrugged and lit his pipe (stuffed with my tobacco) before replying. It might be a spirit, though he himself did not believe in such things anymore. (I suspect this was said in deference to white attitudes and was not strictly true.) Most likely it was some man who had done wrong in the south and did not want to be found by anyone . . . but . . . what a *clever* man he must be to avoid being seen by the Idthen Eldeli. Ah well, whoever or whatever he was, he seemed to mean no harm, and as long as things stayed that way there would be no trouble.

The people were apparently content to adopt a live-and-let-live policy toward the mystery being, but such a *laissez-faire* attitude did not apply to sea monsters.

Every large lake in the north is reputed to have its resident monster. If they are difficult to find in the flesh, stories about them are not. In keeping with the mood of the moment, we were discussing the legendary monsters of Nueltin when a boy galloped up to the fire yelling his head off. Everyone sprang to his or her feet. Women and younger children fled into the tents. The men scattered to get their rifles. As Madees emerged with his .30-30 in hand, Charles demanded to know what was happening. For answer Madees pointed his rifle toward the lagoon.

A pre-dawn glow silvering the surface of the water revealed what looked uncommonly like the looped humps of a traditional sea serpent moving slowly across the lagoon. Then Charles too was running for his rifle. Before he could get it, a fusillade broke out from the crest of the esker, and within seconds the monster had vanished. It did not dive or sink. It *flew* away. Seven Canada geese—probably an entire family swimming in line—flapped frantically off into the opalescent sky, filling the departing night with cries of outrage.

Indians are popularly believed to be an unemotional people, but that night at Putahow I watched grown men and women actually rolling on the ground while some of them literally laughed themselves sick. The Night the Monster Came to Putahow will be long remembered.

This incident seemed to bond us with our hosts. Barriers dissolved—on both sides. Having observed how I favored my bad ankle, Angela prepared a compress for it compounded of used tea leaves, unidentified herbs, and a pinch of salt and baking powder. Applied steaming hot, this remedy was so efficacious that I was able to hobble around without pain.

I did not, however, feel ready for promenades and so did not join Charles when he was taken to view the tracks of the mysterious stranger. On his return he reported seeing the moccasin footprints of an exceptionally big man, almost certainly a European since the toes pointed outward, whereas the toes of most natives tend to point inward. The stranger had apparently observed the camp for a time then turned about and gone off to the west.

"Glad he did," said Charles, with no pretence of courage. "I sure be scared to meet that guy."

When the new nets were hauled next day, they yielded more

than a dozen fat whitefish and lake trout, and there was jubilation in the camp. The emaciated dogs got an adequate meal and their howls of hunger ceased. We humans feasted too.

Charles and I were reluctant to leave this place and these people. We felt we had fallen amongst friends, which was a wonderful relief after having so recently felt we had been amongst enemies. It is one of my enduring regrets that this interlude at Putahow was the closest I would ever come to the Idthen Eldeli, who, for a brief time, almost made me feel like one of them.

As we were preparing to depart, Angela shyly gave each of us a pair of superbly made and beautifully bead-and-quill-decorated moosehide moccasins.

"Make for Madees," she told us, smiling, "for wear next Christmas at Brochet. He say give to you boys. Me too. Give to you."

I hesitated to accept, but Charles urged me to do so.

"Take them," he said *sotto voce*. "If you don't they will be sad."

On the morning of our departure the sky was ominously hazed by smoke from far-distant fires. We motored off to Jonsson's Island to replace the supplies borrowed from Ragnor's cabin on our trip south. A wolverine had been there in the interim and had eaten the rawhide lashings off Ragnor's two sleds, reducing them to piles of lumber. The mosquitoes seemed as bad as ever, so we did our duty then quickly fled. I complained in my journal, *Damn Ragnor. Why doesn't he feed his pets!*

We spent most of the rest of the morning and a couple of precious gallons of gasoline searching for Fred's cache. Although we checked a score of islands, we never found it. Charles charitably concluded his brother must have placed it on shore-ice, which had gone out with the thaw. I had my own opinion, but kept it to myself.

We were now very much on edge, if for different reasons. Charles was increasingly anxious about Rita, and I was dreading the prospect of having to deal with Harper. Tension mounted, but we kept our tempers. We had now been on the trail together for a month without unpleasantness between us, a fact I found worthy of note:

We seldom disagree. My propensity for getting on people's nerves notwithstanding, I don't seem to get on his. Nor he on mine. If I bother him, he has never showed it by word or deed. My old man would have called him a "stout fella."

Abandoning the search for the cache, we headed north. The water was glassy and the calm uncanny. Although the sun was obscured, the heat grew hellish. Mirages rose and fell in shimmering curtains over the surface of the lake, blurring images and outlines. Bones became so restless I had to sit on him, and the little hawk flapped his way anxiously back and forth from one end of the canoe to the other.

When we paused in the middle of the Big Opening to refuel the Lockwood, the silence was hugely oppressive. We seemed to have become part of a fantastic dream. The rows of naked islands with their boulder-strewn crests and wide bands of ice-scoured rock around their shorelines appeared to float between wind and water. I thought they looked like the barnacled carapaces of antediluvian monsters trapped in a sea of amber, a sea across which we crawled with such infinite slowness we seemed mired in it.

As we came close to an island at the mouth of the Narrows, our little hawk suddenly abandoned us and flew to shore, there to perch on a rock and shriek what sounded like maledictions. He had by this time lost his juvenile down, but not his singularly penetrating juvenile voice, in consequence of which I had begun calling him Windy, a name which would become permanently his as time went on.

We landed and took him back on board, but did not linger even long enough to boil the kettle. Inner turmoil combined with a sense of looming disaster drove us on until dusk, by which time we had reached the cache at the north end of the Narrows.

Here we loaded several additional bundles and boxes whose weight reduced our freeboard even more.

Ahead of us now lay twenty-five miles of open water. Considering the ominous weather, I was about to suggest making camp where we were when Charles clambered into the stern of the canoe and started the motor. Nothing was said, but he was clearly determined to reach home that day.

The old canoe was a mile offshore, laboring along like a semi-submersible, when a puff of wind struck us from astern. In minutes it was blowing hard. There was no going back, for we would have been unable to face into it. We could only carry on, angling to the west in a bid to gain the shelter of the coast under the lee of Big Point.

Although we were soon taking a lot of water over the stern, with both of us bailing we managed to keep abreast of the inflow. I could not see Charles because of the mountain of gear between us, but after a while I heard him shout, felt the canoe lurch, and turned my head in time to catch a glimpse of an almost submerged barrel floating away astern. To lighten the load he had jettisoned a ten-gallon drum of precious gas.

The spirits of Nueltin may have taken this as an acceptable offering. In any event the wind fell off a little, and we were able to waddle into the lee of Big Point. Despite Charles's impatience, there could be no question of proceeding any farther until the wind dropped out, so we rounded into the little bay behind the point, went ashore, and made camp for what remained of the night.

I was more than ready to crawl into my sleeping bag, but Charles said he could not sleep so I kept him company by the little fire.

Restlessness of spirit seemed to be eating him up. That, or something else. He was unusually talkative, but I found it hard to follow what he was trying to say. He was vague about details, maybe on purpose. I gather he's adopted the Eskimo custom of early betrothal and had intended to marry some Eskimo kid called Pama when she was old enough. I guess he would have brought her to Windy Post and treated her as his daughter until she was old enough to be his wife.

Well, Pama died last year. He didn't say how or where. I gather her death was a hell of a blow and he can't get over it. Maybe he's trying to replace her with little Rita, hoping she'll become another Pama....

PART FIVE

ARCTIC PRAIRIE

CHAPTER SEVENTEEN

HOMECOMING

FRED AND ANOTEELIK HEARD THE VOICE OF THE Lockwood from several miles away and came out in the little canoe to escort us to the beach where Mike and Rita waited.

It was a subdued homecoming. The tethered dogs contributed a hungry chorus, but Mike, Anoteelik, and especially Fred seemed oddly restrained. Only Rita showed uninhibited delight at being reunited with Charles.

I turned reluctantly toward the cabin. Steeling myself, I walked up the slope, actually *knocked* on the door, and went in. Harper was skinning a mouse. He did not look up when I entered. When I said, "We're back," he only pursed his lips.

"Brought some fresh stuff from Brochet," I ventured. "Oranges and apples."

There was no acknowledgement, so I retreated to the shore. There the six of us unloaded the freight and stowed it away, after which we retired to Ano and Rita's shack, where we sat waiting for Harper to go to bed.

The environs were a shambles. Working gear, including several torn and twisted fishing nets, littered the yard area, along with empty cans, household garbage, and fish and caribou bones. The dogs, still chained in the same places where we had left them a month earlier, were mired in their own feces and skeletal with hunger.

Mike was a distressing spectacle, wraith-like, his eyes so deep-set as to be almost invisible in a shrunken face resembling that of a half-starved monkey. He had been existing largely on bannock and tea, although several cases of dehydrated vegetables and fruit juices remained untouched amongst the Keewatin Zoological Expedition's supplies.

Fred seemed hardly healthier. Hollow-cheeked and lean as a whippet, he was dressed in disintegrating rags whose rents and tears had not even been roughly repaired. It was apparent he had been making little attempt to care for himself, Mike, or the dogs. He seemed sullen and withdrawn.

Only the two young Eskimos appeared to be in good shape. They had largely fended for themselves, and for each other, by catching their own fish, killing birds and small mammals, and gathering early berries. Harper had had little to do with them. As he would later note in an academic journal: "Since they ate their fish raw and their meat half-raw, segregation was understandable."

When Harper eventually withdrew to the privacy of his tent, we six trooped up to the cabin. It had begun to rain, and our mood was hardly effervescent. Charles and I each had a splash of alcohol in our tea, after which I wrote in my journal:

I think I can stand the atmosphere here just about long enough for us to get things running before we push off for the trip to Churchill. Fred will hardly talk at all, but makes it clear he doesn't want to stay on here with Harper. There's no choice. Somebody has to stay. The dogs have to be looked after and Ano and Rita can't just be abandoned. We could perhaps take them and Mike with us, but Charles is afraid to do that because of the risks of running an unknown river. In any case Charles should be back by plane in a month or less with a full load of supplies and, if needs be, Mike can then go out to Churchill with the plane. Meantime it's going to be tough to avoid open warfare between Harper and me.

Fred had taken over Charles's tent during his absence so, since Charles and I did not expect to remain for long at Windy Post, we spread our sleeping bags in the cabin.

By the time I woke next morning, Charles was already up and gone and Harper was at the table skinning another mouse, or perhaps it was a bird. The tension in the air was almost tangible. In what I hoped might be taken as a gesture of goodwill, I offered to fire up the big iron stove and make a batch of bread. When the offer was met with stony silence, I abandoned the cabin and went to join Charles in the Eskimos' shack.

Tried to discuss the Big River trip with Charles but he is so upset about something he can't concentrate. Says he will only be free again when we start traveling. I know just how he feels.

Although it was still raining, Charles, Ano, and I ignored the downpour and rigged a new net at the mouth of the river. When we hauled it only a few hours later it yielded enough fish to feed the dogs and ourselves to repletion. Any shortage of fish at Windy Post had not been due to a shortage of them in nearby waters.

That afternoon I tried a new tack with Harper. I wrote him a humble-pie letter acknowledging that I was a poor specimen of a scientist and accepting responsibility for most of the things he felt had gone wrong; however, although generally adhering to the *mea culpa* tone, I intimated that if he persisted in acting like God with a grudge I would be unable to help him get specimens of the freshwater seals which were reputed to inhabit the north end of Nueltin Lake. I knew that Harper very much hoped these seals would prove to be an unknown subspecies of which he could become the official discoverer. My reference to them may have done the trick. He read my letter, took an hour to cogitate, then spoke to me at last. In truth, he preached a sermon about my manifold faults of omission and commission, concluding with: "All my life I have tried to do only what was right. I could wish that others were like me."

Communication (of a kind) having been restored, I invited him to share the homecoming dinner I was about to cook, but he was not yet prepared to accept such overt peace-making. He prepared his own meal from his private cache of supplies and ate it in silent dignity, after which he retired to his tent.

We six stuffed ourselves on roast bacon, fried trout, and potatoes and carrots which had been more or less fresh when I bought them in Brochet. The meal was good, but not sufficiently so to dispel the gloomy atmosphere. It was only when Charles remarked that the deer ought soon to be returning from the north that animation returned.

The deer! Fresh meat and fat! Even the prospect of such things seemed to act as a powerful stimulant. Before going to sleep that night I noted: *Truly, caribou are the blood, the flesh, and the essence of human life in this country.*

Next day brought more rain, inducing a fit of depression from which I was rescued by a dilapidated book found amongst the debris at the back of the cabin. *Old Junk* by H.M. Tomlinson was an extraordinary thing to come across here. I immersed myself in this English author's memories of his years as a journalist in the First World War and aboard the great clipper ships sailing to China and beyond. For a few hours I was free of the miasma that pervaded Windy Post.

Late one afternoon Charles stuck his head through the doorway of the Eskimo shack, where I was reading, and, giving me one of his rare smiles, asked what I would *really* like for dinner.

"Steak and mushrooms," I replied grumpily.

His smile widened. "Come see what Fred's got."

Early that morning Fred had intercepted the advance guard of southbound caribou and had brought home a hind quarter and a sirloin strip. He was greeted with jubilation. Even Harper agreed to join us for dinner. That evening we demolished an inordinate amount of meat garnished with dubious-looking mushrooms gathered by the Eskimo kids as their contribution to the feast.

Rita and Ano were bright sparks at the table that evening. Ano entertained by drawing remarkably apt and expressive caricatures of each of us, drawings which provoked Rita to such peals of mirth as to almost drown out the yammering of the dogs, who, having smelled the meat, were hysterically demanding a share.

I am falling for Rita. She is a miracle of vivacity and charm, imbued with a scintillating sense of humor. Although only six, she has the aplomb and self-confidence of a woman of the world, and the panache of a lady of society. I can understand if Charles is in love with her....

Excitement ignited by the return of the deer kept us awake until dawn, drinking tea, snacking on underdone meat, making Inuit string figures under Rita's bubbling direction, chatting, and sometimes breaking into song.

At dawn all hands except Harper and me went hunting. I stayed behind to pack my surplus belongings so they would be ready for shipment out when and if an opportunity arose. Harper and I worked warily around one another, observing what I referred to in my journal as "the truce of the caribou."

Fred, Ano, and Mike came back at noon, having shot two deer. Ano cut some meat into small pieces to feed Windy the hawk, whom he and Rita had adopted and were spoiling rotten. Unfortunately, they clipped one of his wings, which meant he was effectively grounded and would have to remain as a dependant until the feathers grew out and he could fly again.

Rita returned alone to the cabin at suppertime. She was so unusually subdued I feared something might have happened to Charles. When I asked about him, she pointed to Soapstone Point, a hook of granite with an embedded vein of steatite (soapstone), thrusting out into the bay a quarter mile from camp.

I found Charles there, sitting on his bedroll, staring morosely into a small fire. He acknowledged my arrival with a grimace but did not look at me. Clearly he was in no amiable mood. Thinking to cheer him up I went back to the cabin and fetched a can of bug juice. He took it from me, drained it, and flung the empty can amongst the beach stones, all the while preserving a chilling silence. I had no idea what was in his mind but recognized the behavior of someone dangerously near the breaking point.

Suddenly he kicked at the fire, sending sparks streaming in all directions, while muttering fiercely: "Could get hisself killed!"

I assumed he was referring to Harper. Had I been able then to read Charles's journal for the day I would have been disabused, but that opportunity did not occur until several months later. His own words express the essence of the agony he was enduring that August evening at Soapstone Point:

Fred has taken my tent up the hill for himself and Rita. Oh what a place is home now! I just can't stand it no more. And I might not come back here. I might come back but only for one day because I am afraid of something that might happen. I feel tonight to be a lot better away from home. Nice night tonight and it makes me feel [like the] night when I traveled fast to Kazan River. The night which makes all this trouble today.... What Rita said to me when she saw where I was sleeping [alone by the shore] was enough to make me feel awful again. But am going to say nothing to Fred who has no feeling for anybody but himself. He did more to me now than of all the bad things that happen in my life.

Although I did not realize it at the time, of all the Schweder brothers Fred was the one with the most reason to be resentful of Francis Harper. In the absence of Charles and myself, Harper had treated Fred as he might have done a servant on a southern plantation, telling him he would "get a dollar a day" for keeping the big stove fueled; providing fish and meat; doing the other onerous camp chores and acting as guide and bearer whenever Harper went "out into the field."

Fred had reacted by keeping out of Harper's sight as much as possible, sometimes vanishing for several days on end. Initially he had taken Mike with him but later had begun taking Rita, leaving Mike and Ano to care for the dogs and to deal with Harper as best they might. Fred also instituted other changes. To Mike's great distress he was sent to sleep with Ano in the tiny shack Charles had set aside for the two Eskimos...and Rita was moved in to share Fred's tent. And bed.

Although he could hardly have failed to be aware of what was happening, Harper did nothing to interfere. Perhaps he felt this was the way natives could be expected to behave.

All hands had been greatly excited when Lamb's plane arrived, bringing the Yules to Windy Bay for a barrenlands holiday. Fred was instructed to serve as their fishing guide and warned he might be wanted to guide the plane to Eskimo camps when it came back to collect the Yules. Fred did not want to fly, so when the plane did return he was relieved to hear that the long-delayed visit to the Ihalmiut had been postponed yet again. Before departing, Dr. Yule told him to remain close to camp and assist Dr. Harper in his investigations, and cautioned him to have nothing further to do with me for I was a mischief-maker whom the police were going to send out of the country.

After rebuilding the fire at Soapstone Point, I put the tea billy on to boil and waited for Charles to calm down. This took a while, but eventually he began talking, mostly generalities at first, then zeroing in on the poisonous attitude suffusing Windy Post. He longed to be free of it, an emotion I felt just as strongly. When he proposed that we make a quick overland trip to the Little Lakes country so he could put his dogs in the custody of the Ihalmiut during his absence on our trip to Churchill, I was delighted. My foot had almost healed, and I dearly wanted to see the Ihalmiut on their home ground.

We decided to head north next morning, expecting to be back at Windy in a week. We also decided that when we set out for Churchill we would take Harper and Fred with us in the big canoe as far as Seal Hole Lake, towing the small canoe behind. Once at Seal Hole, Charles and I would shift ourselves and our gear into the smaller craft and head off down the Thlewiaza, leaving Fred and Harper with the big freighter and the Lockwood to hunt for seals and, in due course, return to Windy Post.

In a much better mood, we set out another three hundred feet of new nets. While we were about it, we recovered those Fred and Harper had been relying upon to feed the camp. These were reduced to slimy twine, waterlogged floats, and broken anchors, their catch consisting of one solitary sucker which, as Charles remarked, must have worked hard to get itself entangled.

Soon after dawn we hauled the new nets and took out nearly two hundred pounds of whitefish and lake trout. For the first time in weeks the dogs were able to gorge.

With the addition of Bones, Charles's team now consisted of six dogs. Since one man can comfortably control only two pack dogs at a time, Charles enlisted Ano to accompany us on the trek north.

The term "pack dogs" is misleading. Instead of toting a load on its back, each of our dogs pulled a "summer sled," a miniature version of the horse-drawn travois used by the Plains Indians for transport in the days before wheels. These dog travois, copied from the Ihalmiut, consisted of pairs of flexible, eight-foot spruce saplings whose front ends were attached to chest-and-neck harnesses, leaving the rear ends to drag upon the ground. A foot-square platform fixed between the two poles at a safe distance behind the dog's tail could carry a load of up to thirty pounds.

As we were about to start, Charles noticed that Windy the hawk was not with us. I had purposely left him behind with Rita, but Charles insisted he must travel with us, "for luck," so I went back and got him, and he settled contentedly upon my shoulder.

A week of rain had turned the low land into a super-saturated sponge, and the going was very tough, especially for the dogs, who, with the exception of Bones, were still in poor shape. Scamp soon played out completely, and Charles had to shoulder her load on top of his own pack.

Ten or fifteen miles north of Windy Post we paused on a high ridge crowned by an inuksuak stone marker. From here we watched apprehensively as a procession of black clouds resembling warships steaming into battle came sailing up from the south. We sought shelter in the lee of a house-sized glacial boulder. And none too soon. Within minutes a wind of hurricane force was unleashing torrents of pelting rain upon us. The dogs curled head to tail to avoid its lash while we three humans clung to each other behind our boulder.

This miniature typhoon lashed us briefly, then wind and rain ceased and the sky blew clear. But it was in a chastened mood that we continued on into what explorer Vilhjalmur Stefansson was fond of calling the arctic prairie.

Although the cross-country travel was demanding, it had its compensations. I almost stumbled into a white fox's den, sending an adult in its dun-colored summer coat streaking away from between my feet. The little beast did not go far before sitting down facing us, ears cocked forward, black eyes gleaming, to challenge our presence with a yodel-like cry. As we passed the den, three half-grown pups cautiously emerged to watch us go.

We made an early camp. Charles and I strung my little travel tent between two summer sleds planted upright in the muskeg. Ano constructed his own shelter from a ragged piece of canvas to which he had stitched an old mosquito net. We tethered the dogs and fed them the small quantity of meat we had been able to carry with us. From now on they would eat only when and if we were able to make a kill. Although we had seen a few distant caribou, we had been too concerned with putting distance between ourselves and Windy Post to hunt them.

Next day we came to a hill sporting a cluster of inuksuak. We climbed to the crest, where we found a small cache containing a three-pronged fish spear made of caribou antler; a pair of intricately carved wooden snow goggles; a homemade fire drill; and, inside a piece of caribou hide, a packet of Philip Morris cigarettes in an unbroken cellophane wrapper. This last find might well have mystified an archaeologist, but Charles had the explanation. Several winters earlier he and the Ihalmiut shaman Pommela had visited a detachment of American soldiers stationed at Duck Lake. The cigarettes were souvenirs of that visit.

"Pommela owe me lots of tobacco," Charles said apologetically as he opened the pack, helped himself, and passed it to Anoteelik and me. "Anyway, I leave a box of .30-30 he can get if he ever comes back here."

We were now crossing a seemingly endless plain dotted with low hills that seemed to swell beneath the tundra like waves beneath the surface of the sea. The intervening hollows were morasses of muskeg dotted with occasional shallow ponds and crevassed by streamlets.

The going was so bad that by noon we were carrying most of the dogs' loads on top of our own. In my mind's eye I saw us as little blobs of animate matter about to be absorbed into a semi-aquatic void.

Next day we encountered two deer but, since there was no cover for miles in any direction, could not get close enough for a shot. However, one of the pair decided to follow us, presumably curious to see what manner of creatures we were. This was too much for Ano. Handing his dog leads to me, he hid in a willow swale while we continued on.

The sound of a shot was our signal to stop and pitch camp. Ano soon rejoined us, grinning from ear to ear and laden with meat. Since there was almost nothing with which to fuel a fire, we ate our supper virtually raw. The entrées consisted of slightly singed slices of liver, dripping red steaks, and jelly-like marrow from the deer's leg bones.

We led the dogs back to the kill, where they ate whatever they fancied, which was just about everything. I was astonished at how much they could cram into their bellies. Each must have filled him- or herself to the brim at least twice over before we were ready to depart next morning, and very little of the inquisitive buck remained to be scavenged by foxes, gulls, and ravens.

Charles and I were entertained that evening by Ano creating a number of little animals out of scraps of vegetation, which he then made to jump, dance, and sing. After this exhibition of puppetry he became an acrobat, executing cartwheels, handstands, and somersaults around our tiny fire under the light of a pallid moon. Then he transformed himself into a clown, executing such riotous (and ribald) imitations of Harper, Charles, myself, and some of his own people, that Charles laughed out loud, one of the few occasions I ever knew him to do so.

Anoteelik's one-ring circus staged in the midst of the barrengrounds had been a memorable success.

CHAPTER EIGHTEEN

LAND OF LITTLE STICKS

T IS A PLACE WHERE CURLEWS CIRCLE IN THE WHITE SKY above icily transparent lakes. It is a place where gaudy ground squirrels whistle from the sandy casts of vanished glacial rivers; where the dun-colored summer foxes den and lemmings dawdle fatly in thin sedges by the bogs. It is a place where minute flowers blaze in microcosmic revelry and where the thrumming of insect wings assails even the greater beasts and sends them fleeing to the bald hills seeking the long wind to drive the unseen pursuers away. It is a place where the black muskox stands four square to the cautious feints of the white wolves; and where the shambling giant of the land, the massive Barrens grizzly, slouches solitary and untouchable. And it is the place where the caribou in uncountable hordes once inundated the world in a river of life that rose below one far horizon and flowed, unbroken, to the opposing one.

So, in later years, would I write about the arctic prairies. In early August of 1947 I was still a newcomer to them, but I already realized that they were the kind of reality I was seeking—a multifaceted world where ancient and immutable laws still governed; a world where every living entity was part of one intimate and sustaining relationship. In short, a pre-eminently viable world relatively undefiled by modern man.

Then one afternoon as we descended a long tundra slope toward some nameless lake upon whose surface hundreds of geese had gathered, the peace that had begun to solace my soul was shattered by a hateful sound. I stopped so suddenly that Bones ran the pole of a summer sled into my leg. The sound was the voice of the Machine. As it swelled viciously out of the south, instinct urged me to take cover as I would have done from a Messerschmitt with Nazi crosses on its wings. But when I recognized the rapidly approaching plane as the same red devil that had assailed us on Kasmere's River I was tempted to lever a shell into the chamber of my rifle.

It roared low over our heads, imperiously waggling its wings as a summons before descending onto the small lake a mile distant.

"The hell with those bastards!" I exploded furiously. "They can go fuck themselves!"

Charles was irresolute. "Dunno...better see what they want. They get mad at me...could lose my license...could lose..." he stopped, and I knew we would have to face the music.

Unwilling puppets dragged by invisible strings, we made our way to the lake, where the Norseman lay with its tail to the shore. We were met by Tom Lamb, all bluff geniality, and by a silent Fred, both standing on the floats.

Lamb issued orders like a general. "You, Freddie, get ashore! Charley! You climb aboard."

Meekly the Schweders did as they were told, then Lamb turned to me. "I'm flying Dr. Yule to the Eskimo camps. Charley's going to guide us. No room to take you along. Full up. We'll drop Charley off here tomorrow sometime and pick up Fred." Then, as if an afterthought, "You could fly south with us. Offer's still open."

"I'm not going south. I'm going north. And if the doctor's on board, I'd still like him to look at my foot."

Lamb grinned cheerily. "The doc's in a hurry to check out the Huskies." With which he swung himself into the pilot's seat. The engine belched, the prop spun, and as the plane slowly drew away from shore, I could see the doctor's long face at one of the windows. He seemed to be taking my picture.

Now what was I to do? At first Fred was so sullen and taciturn I could get nothing out of him except that he intended walking back to Windy Post immediately. He wanted to take Ano's .22 rifle with him. I had given Ano that rifle, the first he had ever owned, and the prospect of having to part with it was now enough to send him off on his own heading north. Running after him, I assured him the rifle would stay in his hands. Reluctantly he returned to the lake shore to help me set up camp. Fred observed us with a furious disregard, making no move to assist. I had the feeling he was about to explode and I shouldn't turn my back on him.

The situation was resolved, and perhaps saved, by the deer. Bones whined and we looked up to see a small herd of bucks passing to the west of the lake. Instantly my two human companions became partners ready for a hunt. Answering the question in Fred's eyes, I handed him my gun, and he and Ano slipped away into the rolling tundra, leaving me to quiet the dogs and to wonder what malign consequences Lamb's visit would have this time.

An hour later Fred and Ano were back, toting most of the meat from a prime buck. Now our little camp became the happy, cheerful center of the world. Fred gave up his intention of walking home alone and, wonder of wonders, began to talk. At first he spoke mainly in monosyllables but, as the night advanced, pent-up emotions burst their bonds and he became almost loquacious, though sometimes incoherent.

I was astonished and alarmed by the nature and intensity of his feelings for his elder brother. It appeared that Fred had been Charles's loyal acolyte until first Pama, then Rita, had appeared upon the scene. Thereafter, he had felt himself displaced in Charles's affection and regard. What seemed to have made this all the more infuriating for him was that he shared his father's contempt for Eskimos, whom he considered of little more consequence than any other local fauna—to be made use of as circumstances required, but certainly not to be included in one's clan.

His resentment of Charles and his jealousy of Rita seemed to come together in one brooding remark I chose not to pursue: "Thinks she belongs to him...maybe they find out different!"

There were sundry other disjointed and enigmatic references to Charles and Rita, which gave rise to some disquieting speculation about the relationships between *both* brothers and the girl, but this was not something I was anxious to explore.

These uncomfortable thoughts were temporarily banished when Fred turned his attention to Harper...and to me. His animosity toward Harper was evidently due to the servile role Harper expected him to play. As for me, he resented my developing friendship with his brother. His feelings about both of us outlanders were perhaps summed up in one muttered remark which he delivered with an unconvincing smile: "Since you fellows come there been lots of trouble. We got along good before you fellows come."

On that unsettling note he drifted off into the night.

The three of us were eating a silent breakfast next morning when the plane returned. I made myself scarce. The Norseman lingered only long enough to put Charles ashore before picking up Fred and roaring off to the south.

The story Charles had to tell me was deeply disturbing. "They say I could have a government job looking out for the Eskimos. Tom Lamb would fly in the stuff they need, and I would hand it out. Doctor Yule says I got to have a better storehouse though. He and Tom Lamb say I should go up to Simmons Lake and take down Simmons's old house. Float the logs to Windy Post and put up a new storehouse."

With a hollow feeling in the pit of my stomach, I asked when this work would need to be done.

"Start now, should finish before freeze-up."

"What about us going out to Churchill? The Big River trip?"

"They don't want for me to make that trip."

I sat in desolate silence for a time before suggesting we at least go on to the Eskimo camps before returning to Windy Post.

Charles shook his head. He was obviously determined to go home as fast as possible.

Although bitterly disappointed at not being able to visit the Ihalmiut, at this time I had no alternative but to acquiesce with what good grace I could muster. Charles thereupon decided Ano should go direct to Simmons Lake while Charles and I returned to the Post, collected Fred, loaded a canoe with the requisite gear, then traveled up Windy River to begin dismantling Simmons's house. He intimated that once this work was well in hand he might be able to leave Fred in charge while we two set off for Big River and Churchill. This sounded like a long shot to me but one I chose to believe in because I so much wanted it to happen.

The account of the Norseman's visit Charles wrote in his journal was laconic:

They just would not take Farley along. Tom Lamb said that he was too heavy loaded but he did not have much in the plane that I could see. After we got up he said he felt sorry for the little captain whatever he meant by that.

Charles had much more to tell as we sat around the fire that night.

Although all five of the Ihalmiut camps lay within ten minutes' flying distance of each other, the inspection party visited only one: that of the shaman, Pommela. Dr. Yule looked at people's teeth and peered down their throats before pronouncing them all to be in good health. This constituted the full extent of the medical examination of the Kazan Eskimos, as Yule called the Ihalmiut in his report.

Thereafter the visitors went sightseeing. They were much interested in the grave of Kakut, the "big man" of the Ihalmiut during the previous decade. When Kakut died in 1943, many of his possessions were placed on top of the stone cairn containing his body. Now, while Charles watched, Lamb, Yule, and the mechanic picked through the grave goods, removing a kayak paddle, a number of soapstone implements, a ladle made of muskox horn, and some other things. Perhaps aware that Charles might not approve of what was being done, Dr. Yule claimed that he and Lamb were collecting artifacts for a museum.

Additional souvenirs were obtained at Pommela's camp, where, according to Charles, Lamb spent the night with Pommela's younger wife (the shaman had two wives) while Dr. Yule slept chastely in the cabin of the Norseman.

Yule and Lamb questioned Charles closely about our plans, then did their best to scuttle them. They warned him that any attempt to descend Big River in a sixteen-foot canoe would be suicidal. Lamb claimed to have seen part of the river from the air and described it as having "the worst rapids in the North!"

Charles was also given to understand that if he continued in my company not only would he be likely to spoil his chances of getting a job as agent to the Ihalmiut, but he might also find himself in difficulties when it came to renewing his trading and trapping licenses.

"They say best thing I can do after I make a new storehouse is help Dr. Harper with his work. They say he's a important man down in the States, so the government won't forget the help I give him."

I listened to all this with sinking spirits and a growing conviction that our journey to Hudson Bay would not take place. But I was misjudging Charles. Far from intimidating him, these heavy-handed attempts to bring him to heel had determined him to remain his own man, as he made clear next evening.

"Don't you worry, Farley. We'll make our trip. Only we'll have to take the big canoe and the Lockwood so we can travel faster 'cause we won't have much time. Dr. Harper can have the small canoe, and Fred can paddle him around where he wants to go. They got more time than us."

"What about the job of agent for the Ihalmiut?"

"I can do without it. Anyway, not sure I'm going to stay at Windy. Maybe I'll build a new house at Hidden Valley, or a long way north at a place I know about where nobody would bother me, not even if they got a plane."

"How about your licenses?"

"They take them away, not much I can do about that. But I guess I know a few things happened up around here would be better kept quiet...."

This was a Charles I did not know.

"What about Rita? What'll happen to her if we leave her at Windy and go down Big River?"

He smiled somewhat wolfishly. "If Tom Lamb comes near Windy Post, I tell Ano to take Rita off into the Stony Hills. There's an old cabin in there they can hide in till the plane goes."

Things looked much brighter now, though there were still clouds on the horizon. How would Fred react to these new plans? Well, that was something Charles would have to deal with, and I was prepared to believe he could handle any problems that might arise. I went to sleep that night in an optimistic frame of mind.

As I perhaps ought to have realized, there never was any real intention of appointing Charles to be an "agent" for the Ihalmiut; in fact, no such job description existed.

After Dr. Yule returned to The Pas from his visit to Pommela's camp, he submitted a report to the federal authorities strongly recommending that the surviving Ihalmiut be moved 150 miles northeast to Padlei, an HBC outpost of Eskimo Point, and placed under the de facto control of the post manager there. Yule further recommended that in the meantime they be given only minimum assistance so as not to make them "dependent."[1]

---

[1] This deportation was eventually carried out, with disastrous results. See Farley Mowat, *The Desperate People*, McClelland & Stewart, Toronto, 1959, and *Walking on the Land*, Key Porter Books, Toronto, 2000.

Next morning we continued retracing our steps. Late in the day we saw something moving toward us from the south. We took it for a deer until it resolved itself into the figure of a man. It was Pommela, who had been given a flight to Windy Post in the Norseman, perhaps as a gesture of reciprocity for favors received. Now he was walking home.

He was a squat, powerful fellow with a tuft of black whiskers on his jutting chin and a wispy, snot-soaked mustache. He was in an ebullient mood, having just had his first flight in *tingmeaktuk,* the big goose. He admitted to Charles that he had been a little frightened, but only a little because, as a shaman, he had often made spirit flights on his own.

We visited together for a while, drinking tea and cracking the marrow out of the leg bones of a caribou Pommela had shot. Pommela told Charles that while at Windy Post he had seen the white men load several cases into the plane, cases which, from his description, I thought I recognized as mine. Apparently I was being moved out whether I wished to go or not. In answer to an anxious question from Charles, he reported that the plane had taken off for the south without Rita.

Pommela departed. That night we made our supper fire on an ancient battleground—not one where men had fought but where trees and tundra had struggled to prevail against each other. Several hundred years earlier, when the climate had been warmer, outriders of the forest had advanced this far into the arctic prairie. Their failure to endure was attested to by a boneyard of wind-scoured, frost-whitened stumps.

These old wooden bones burned with astonishing heat. We built an extravagant fire upon which we boiled a deer tongue Pommela had given us. Afterwards we contentedly smoked our pipes as the late summer sun went down in a lurid burst of flame. Although we were then within a few hours' walk of the cabin, we did not wish to complete the journey until we were reasonably sure Harper had gone off to his tent. We arrived back at Windy

Post after midnight, lighted on our way by a gibbous moon.

Next morning's meeting with Harper was notably unpleasant. He called me a fool for not accepting Lamb's second offer to fly me out of the country, and I was equally offensive in insisting that he had robbed me of some essential equipment by shipping all my gear out on Lamb's plane. By the time I stormed out of the cabin, we were both inarticulate with fury.

Harper then called Charles inside to assure him that attempting the Big River trip in a sixteen-foot canoe would be the death of us. He was hoist with his own petard when Charles deferentially agreed that Big River might prove too much for the small canoe.

"So we have to take the big canoe and the Lockwood. I guess you and Fred can get around all right in the little one. It sure is easy to paddle!"

Harper's response was a theatrical "You'll regret this!"

By noon the atmosphere at Windy Post had become unendurable. Fred and Charles were like two hostile dogs, barely acknowledging each other's presence. When Charles suggested we all go to Simmons Lake to rendezvous with Ano, Fred chose to set off on some mysterious journey of his own.

Mike and Rita joined us in the big canoe. Our departure for Simmons Lake was ignominious. During our absence someone had poured water into the Lockwood's fuel tank. In consequence the motor stalled halfway up the first rapid. Despite some frantic work with paddles, we were washed down it again—backwards. I could imagine Harper stealthily watching this debacle from a cabin window, and I cursed him loud and long.

We started the Lockwood again and made our way slowly upriver with so many stops and starts it was dark before Ano's signal fire on the shore of Simmons Lake guided us to a landing. We had a mug-up and I crawled under my mosquito net, but Charles slipped away by himself. When I asked Mike where his brother had gone, the boy shrugged and muttered one word: "Mama."

Later I learned Charles had spent the remainder of the night across the lake beside his mother's grave. By the time I woke in the morning, he had returned and was busy cooking breakfast bannocks. As we sipped our tea, he told me he was not going to tear down Simmons's house after all; that he had never had any real intention of doing so; and that he had really come to Simmons Lake because this was where he had spent the happiest years of his life and he wanted to remember them again as an antidote to the bad times he had experienced during the past several months.

"Mother made me feel this was my place...where I belonged. She knew I was happy here. Never had much to be happy about herself, though. Good times for me was bad ones for her, but she never kicked...bad times now make me think about her...."

I broke the long silence that followed by asking why he had agreed to move Simmons House.

He chuckled. "Mr. Tom Lamb and Dr. Yule and them tell stories sometimes. Guess it don't hurt to tell them some."

The day was so superb—clear, warm, and bright—that we made it a holiday. Charles and I loafed by the fire while the three youngsters played a wild and noisy game with a ball made of scraps of deerskin stuffed into a sack; went berry picking; and fished for arctic char, squatting like little bears on slippery stones in the adjacent rapids to grab at jumping fish and sometimes to catch one.

Charles talked about the "old days" when his father had run the HBC outpost, first at Windy Lake then at Simmons Lake. He reminisced about free-trader Del Simmons, who had built the post here in a determined effort to challenge the Company at a time when a good white fox pelt was worth fifty dollars and a silver perhaps two hundred.

"Del and the Company bid each other up 'til they was both losing money. The Company could afford to lose more than Del, so that was the end of him. Then the price of fur fell and the

Company pulled out. That was when we come to live at Simmons Lake. Nobody here now, nor ever will be no more, I guess. It sure is nice and peaceful now."

Something—perhaps the quality of the day, perhaps the sense of being relieved, if only temporarily, from our trials and tribulations—set us to pondering the nature and purpose of our personal hopes and aspirations. Just for the hell of it, we each decided to draw up an assessment of who we thought we were, and where we might be going. Withdrawing to opposite ends of the clearing, we worked at our notebooks for the next few hours. I don't know what Charles wrote, because after scanning the pages he tore them up and burned them. My notes amounted to a confession that I didn't know who I was or where I was bound, but was certain I wasn't going to be trapped in some conformist cul-de-sac. Categorically rejecting my old ambition to become a biologist, I concluded it would be infinitely preferable to be a dedicated drifter and that *bullshitters and money men run the world, but they bloody well won't run me! I'll outrun the buggers!*

As the lazy afternoon waned, Ano inveigled us into accompanying him to a stand of stunted little spruce trees, where he had found a peculiar mound of mossy stones. We poked about for a while but could not decide what it was. Mike offered the most intriguing explanation. He thought it might be the grave of a grizzly bear, and not just any old grizzly, but the *king* of the grizzlies. I had not suspected him of possessing such a vivid imagination, and I wondered what else might be going on behind his inscrutable countenance.

After an enormous meal of fried char garnished with slices of puffballs the youngsters had found, Charles and I agreed that if I could raise the money and find a willing photographer, we would combine our talents and make a film about the Ihalmiut, the Idthen Eldeli, and the caribou. It was a day to dream.

Soon after leaving Simmons Lake next morning, we encountered a mighty bull caribou whose velvet-covered antlers spread above him like a living tree. He was swimming in the river and, when we appeared, came directly for us. We stopped paddling and watched as he approached to within fifteen or twenty yards. Then, a little worried that a collision might ensue, Charles started the kicker and we headed downstream at a good clip. Effortlessly he accompanied us, his powerful legs swirling the water into circular eddies behind him.

We were so impressed by this performance that not a hand was raised against him. Even Windy, the chatterbox, seemed awed into silence. The bull kept us company for a quarter of a mile before sheering away to the far shore, where he climbed the bank and made off over the tundra without a backward glance. I wondered if his interest had been in the nature of an invitation to stick around. Or a warning to go away.

It was time now for Charles and me to start for Big River. Harper and I engaged in a final round of mutual recriminations that accomplished nothing. The rift between us was final and unbridgeable. With disdain he refused Charles's offer of a tow as far as Seal Hole Lake, perhaps because he may have overheard Fred tell Charles, "I'm not going on Nueltin with that man. Could drown us both."

It was as much as Charles could do to persuade Fred even to remain at Windy Post. Although he did finally agree to do so, and to look after the youngsters and the dogs, he had the final word as we departed, shouting so loudly the whole camp could hear: "You don't come back and everybody going to starve! Don't forget that!"

It was hardly a farewell benediction.

CHAPTER NINETEEN

THE DEER'S WAY

ON AUGUST 14 I FINISHED A LAST LETTER TO MY parents in Ontario—"last" not in the sense that I did not expect to live to write another, but because I expected soon to see them in person.

What do we know about the Thlewiaza, or Big River as they call it here? Not much. A trapper named Joe Highway, who's been to north Nueltin in mid-winter, says he found seal breathing holes in the ice there. He and the Catholic missionary in Brochet say Chipewyans used to travel down Big River a hundred years ago. It has the reputation of being a bad canoe river, but that may be no more than rumor. My map only shows the headwater region, on a scale of 8 miles to the inch and in broken lines because it's never been surveyed. We don't even know where it runs into Hudson Bay. Charles thinks somewhere near a trading post called Tavanni, 250 miles north of Churchill. Harper has a small-scale map of the eastern arctic that probably shows the outlet but claims he's lost it.

Well, not to worry. We'll just travel east until the water gets salty then turn south till we hear a train whistle. Piece of cake!

One good thing, we won't be burdened like pack mules this time. Our out-fit looks about like what a couple of boy scouts might take on a weekend hike. A bedroll each. My two-man pup tent. Enough spare clothes to allow for a change of underwear. Add my army compass and binoculars, Charles's .30-30, and some fish line. The grub box is so light I can hoist it with one hand: some flour, baking powder, sugar, can of jam, couple of pounds of

lard, chunk of caribou, lots of tea. The idea is to leave as much food as pos-
sible here for Fred, Mike, Anoteelik, and Rita. But not to worry, there'll be
plenty of fish, caribou, ducks, and other stuff to fill our bellies.

We're going in Charles's old freighter canoe pushed by an outboard
engine about as old as Charles. It won't be much use though because we've
only got a few gallons of gas. Mostly we'll paddle like old style voyageurs.

Windy, the young pigeon hawk, is coming with us because Charles thinks
the scruffy little character (he's now almost blind in one eye from an infected
mosquito bite) is our good luck.

We got away at 9:00 a.m. after tearful farewells from Rita, Mike,
and even Anoteelik. Fred unbent enough to wave us off, though
with neither tears nor smiles. Of Francis Harper there was no sign.

Charles ran the Lockwood full bore until we were out of sight
of camp then slowed to a crawl in order to conserve fuel.

We headed down Windy Bay in a dead calm under a surly-
looking sky. The feeling that I had escaped from a pressure
cooker was so overwhelming that I burst into a raucous army
song.

Fuck 'em all! Fuck 'em all! The long and the short and the tall! There'll
be no promotion this side of the ocean, so goodbye my boys, fuck 'em all!
The sound of feet banging on the canoe's thin wooden slats made
me turn, and there was Charles, beaming like a happy drunk,
waving his free arm over his head while joining in the chorus.

Even Windy seemed to share our feelings. Perched at the
extremity of the bow like a one-eyed avian figurehead, he spread
his poor, truncated wings and shrieked almost in harmony. For a
moment I wondered if he thought he was returning to Kasmere's
River, then I remembered that the river we were heading for was
the extension of the Kasmere, carrying its waters on down to the
salt sea.

As we rounded the northeasterly headland of Windy Bay and
opened the full hundred-mile sweep of Nueltin, my spirits continued to soar. The dismal miasma of Windy Post was well astern.

Ahead lay a world which would deal with us according to how well we dealt with it. A world over which mankind had no claim to dominion. Remembering the battlefields of Europe, I was thankful that this was so.

Oddly luminous clouds towered in the northern skies, releasing streamers which descended to form a kind of wavering curtain, veiling the windless surface of the lake and the vast spaces into which we were venturing.

When hunger made itself felt, we beached the canoe on a strip of sand on Nueltin's western side and fried up a pan of tenderloin. This lunch stop provided us with a benediction, or so I interpreted it. We were shoving off when a white wolf stalked down to our smoldering fire and sniffed at it casually before raising his shaggy great head to stare at us drifting in the canoe a few yards from him. We were so close I could look into his amber eyes. They were not inimical. To the contrary, they seemed to reflect a kind of camaraderie. Charles must have felt it too. Instead of reaching for his rifle, he grinned at the wolf in friendly fashion before pulling the Lockwood's starting cord. Later he would tell me: "That was his place we was into. But he never minded 'cause we was just passing through."

The lake remained oily calm as we puttered along its western coast past mounded, boulder-strewn hills and yellow eskers with tundra valleys splayed between them. The innumerable islands seemed afloat upon a mirror. The lake slowly narrowed, and some twenty miles after leaving Windy Bay, we passed through a strait which, according to the map, should have led us over a long rapid into Seal Hole Lake. It was a bewilderment to find ourselves faced with another great opening seemingly as vast as that we had just traversed, an opening also rimmed with islands but which, instead of being oriented north and south, stretched away to the northeast.

Unable to correlate these features with the map, I set it aside for the moment. I would have been wiser had I tossed it overboard, for in the days ahead it was to prove itself a delusion and a snare. However, such was the power of my conditioned belief in human wizardry that I could no more bring myself to discard it than a Jehovah's Witness could have been persuaded to discard the Holy Bible.

When I complained to Charles that the map and the reality were hopelessly at odds, he only shrugged. At some point along the hundred or so miles of shoreline facing us, Nueltin would transform itself into Big River. One had only to "read the water" to find the way.

This Charles proceeded to do, though just *how* he did it I still cannot say. When I pressed for an explanation, he seemed no more capable of providing one than a fox can explain how it follows the old and invisible trail of a rabbit. I suspect that in both cases the brain routinely synthesized evidence collected by all the senses then cued the conscious mind to the right conclusion. Reason and logic were not even involved.

Whatever. With Charles piloting from the bow and the motor stilled, we paddled through a labyrinth of islands and channels, following a current that was imperceptible to me. So we backed and filled amongst the faceless islands until Charles suddenly held up his hand. I stopped paddling and listened. Far to the eastward I could hear the rumble of falling water. Windy heard it too and began chittering a whitewater warning.

A visible current was now drifting us toward the unseen exit from Nueltin and the beginning of Big River. But the day was old, and we were in no hurry to seize the moment. In truth we were somewhat apprehensive of what might lie ahead, so we made camp.

That night we all three dined on steaks done very rare, not from choice but because we were now beyond the Land of Little Sticks and the only available fuel consisted of moss and the twigs and roots of dwarf birch and willow shrubs. We made gluttons of ourselves, perhaps stimulated by the instinct that impels soldiers to eat, drink, and make merry to excess the night before going into battle.

It is poor policy to camp within earshot of any rapid you have reason to feel apprehensive about. Certainly the muted but insistent vibrato of the one lying in wait somewhere to the east of us impinged heavily on my consciousness this night. Primordial phantoms kept insisting I empty my bowels, presumably so I would be in better condition to outrun the saber-toothed tiger that had selected me as his next meal.

Things looked better in the morning. The day dawned warm and clear. When we launched the canoe into the unknown, the current quickened under us and the rumble of the rapids soon mounted to a roar.

A mile along what had now definitely become a river we came to an island splitting the flow into twin cataracts. These were flinging foam and spray high into the air with a thunder that obliterated Windy's screams of alarm. Landing some distance short of this maelstrom, we climbed a hill for a reconnaissance. The eastern channel seemed one mass of foam dropping at least fifty feet in the first hundred yards. The western cataract descended in a series of frothing chutes to terminate in a five-foot fall. Having learned that too long a time spent weighing the odds can induce paralysis, we made our decision quickly. The west channel it would be.

Wordlessly, Charles got into the stern and started the Lockwood. When he gestured that he was ready, I shoved off. Such a volume of whitewater was storming through the chutes that we were swept clear of all waiting rocks. Seconds later, with the Lockwood blatting maniacally and Windy wailing like an air-raid siren, we came to rest in a back eddy at the lip of the falls. A short carry around these and we were clear—though not yet free to enter Seal Hole Lake.

Three or four miles of fast water brought us to a serpentine rapid whose lower reaches were concealed in a steep-walled canyon. I would have preferred to run this one under paddles alone, but Charles insisted on using the motor. Rightly so, as it turned out. Halfway down, the river abruptly veered toward a wall of rock against which we would certainly have been flung had not the Lockwood's thrust carried us clear.

When the canoe spun into a pool of relatively quiet water, we seized the chance to get ashore. I climbed a nearby hill, and there before me lay Seal Hole Lake: a shimmering expanse of turquoise. A light breeze off the water brought a faint scent of fish. I searched for a seal but could see no living creature except one distant gull.

Windy, too, had gone wandering. Charles found the little bird perched on one of a pair of silvery-gray sticks protruding from a pile of lichen-covered rocks. The sticks proved to be ancient Chipewyan paddles—long, slender, and knife-bladed, designed to serve both as paddles and as poles. Although of obvious antiquity, they were still strong and supple.

Supposing the mound to be a grave, Charles was for leaving these relics where they were—but I suggested that their discovery was almost too providential to be accidental.

"We've only got two paddles. Bum ones at that. And we're not likely to lay hands on any more. And don't forget—it was Windy found them."

Charles mused over this, then nodded. "Maybe somebody's *supposed* to take them, eh? Sure must have been waiting a long time.... We could leave some tea."

We took them, and they served us well until the end of our journey, long after our factory-made paddles had been splintered to almost useless stubs.

As we entered Seal Hole Lake, a long gravel reef caught my eye. It looked to be an ideal sort of place for seals to sun themselves so we searched it, but found only hordes of little flies of some species unknown to both of us. Then we paddled eastward across the lake in the direction in which we supposed the exit lay.

Landing upon a curving sand spit on the far shore, we climbed the bank and were surprised to find ourselves on a mile-wide isthmus separating Seal Hole from an even larger lake to the eastward.

Beyond this new lake (whose existence was not even indicated on our map) the horizon erupted into something resembling a tabular iceberg. Flat-topped and vertically walled, it appeared to be a plateau hundreds of feet high and five or six miles long composed of a substance so white and glittering the light reflected from it almost made me squint. The resemblance to a giant iceberg was so compelling I could almost have believed I was looking at a last remnant of the titanic glacier which had overlain this land ten thousand years earlier.

Charles was as dumbfounded as I by this colossus about whose existence he had never heard so much as a rumor. We concluded it must be a mountain of quartz. I admit that visions of a motherlode of gold flickered in my head. We might have succumbed to temptation and rushed off to prospect this potential Eldorado had not time been more valuable just then than gold. In less than twenty days we *had* to be in Churchill.

First we had to find our way out of Seal Hole Lake. We could see no indication of an exit, but three prominent hills at the northern end of the isthmus promised a wide view of the countryside, so off we went to climb them.

We found ourselves on a veritable highway churned into muskeg muck by countless caribou hooves. Although not a single animal was then to be seen, it was clear that multitudes must recently have passed this way, heading north in the peculiar reverse migration that sometimes occurs in late summertime.

We slogged along in their wake, ankle-deep in muck. The distant hills seemed to become higher while remaining just as distant, but we pressed on, certain the view from the summit would reveal the channel we were seeking.

It was not to be. Well before we could reach the crest, the pale, piercing tundra light began to fade and somber dusk drew down. Although it was not yet mid-afternoon, a stygian darkness descended. Bewildered and somewhat fearful, we turned and hurried back down the long slope toward the illusory security of our canoe. Stumbling through bogs, we sometimes lost sight of one another and had to shout to keep in touch. The shouting was almost the worst of it, for a terrible silence had come over the land and our voices seemed to reverberate like explosions in an empty building.

It was as if the walls of the world had collapsed letting in the darkness and silence of outer space. I don't know what caused the effect. I do know I don't ever want to experience anything like it again.

Reaching the sand spit, we hurriedly pitched the little tent, crawled inside, and waited tensely...and nothing happened. Eventually we emerged and, somewhat ashamed of ourselves, cooked supper, by which time the unnatural darkness had been replaced by normal night. We went to bed no wiser as to the location of the exit from Seal Hole Lake and slept uneasily.

The next day broke calm, hot, and hazy. I was up at dawn and sleepily climbed the bank between our campsite and the spine of the causeway. A moment later I was wide awake. Caribou were flooding southward over the three hills, inundating the slopes and pouring onto the causeway. They came in herds of hundreds, wavering skeins of living beings that wove and interwove a tapestry of life as far as the eye could see.

This was la Foule! And now the causeway between the two lakes truly became the Deer's Way.

Charles joined me, and together we almost timidly approached the verges of this river of life. The air was warm with the throng's warmth, heavy with its smell, and loud with breathy grunting. The castanet-like clicking of ankle joints was an insistent pulse felt rather than heard, as was the semi-comic rumbling of guts filled with fermenting lichens. The overall effect was so hypnotic we were not even aware that the little rise upon which we stood had become an island until we found ourselves surrounded by a flow of heavily antlered bucks.

The antlers seemed like a moving forest. I would have made a break for the shore if Charles had not gripped my arm.

"Don't you move now. They won't hurt us unless we get them scared and get in their way."

He was right. Although the bucks were certainly aware of our presence, they ignored us, some passing so close I could almost have touched them as they glanced at me out of the corners of huge, moist eyes.

We were not the only watchers. A flight of ravens floated like kites above the causeway, keeping pace with the herds as if attached to them by invisible wires. Then a family of wolves appeared on a knoll on the far side of the Deer's Way: four gray ghosts emerging out of nowhere to sit in a row like attentive patrons of a theatrical show. Although they too must have been fully aware of us, the wolves hardly glanced in our direction, their attention concentrated on the passing parade.

The deer paid no heed to them or us. Neither the presence of wolves nor of men could distract la Foule. When one wolf made a brief sally toward a group of does accompanied by their fawns, the deer bunched briefly, broke into a trot for perhaps a hundred yards, then slowed, stopped, and stared disdainfully back at the wolf before resuming their trek. The wolf nonchalantly rejoined its fellows.

"Testing them deer," Charles explained, "to see if one was sick or hurt or old so it would make an easy meal. Them other wolfs is likely young ones learning the way to get along."

Leaving the pack to its lessons—if that *was* what they were about—Charles and I cautiously made our way to a small pond that diverted the flow of deer and sat down in its lee where there was less likelihood of being trampled. Probably we were never in any danger, but the magnitude of the passing hordes intimidated me and I was relieved to be out of harm's way.

Although most of the animals were moving at a steady walk, occasionally some broke into a slack-legged, awkward-looking gallop. Then they moved at speed: I guessed as much as thirty miles an hour. At one point a herd of galloping bucks spilled over the crest of the distant hills, swept down upon and past us, never slowing so long as they were in sight. Yet none of the other deer on the isthmus paid any attention to their swift passage, which may have been no more than a display of male braggadocio.

Charles and I spent all that morning watching the herds go by. By noon the flow was still unabated. A barnyard stench hung heavy in the air. The center of the Deer's Way had become a quagmire into which hooves rose and fell with a luscious, squelching sound. It was hypnotic. My senses were sated by too much life impinging too heavily upon me. Charles roused me from a near trance.

"Better get going. Got to find Big River yet. Sure nice to see this big bunch of deer, though."

"Nice" hardly seemed the appropriate word, but I let it go.

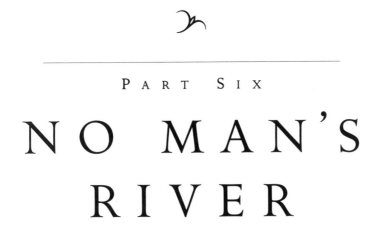

PART SIX

NO MAN'S
RIVER

CHAPTER TWENTY

BIG RIVER

BECAUSE THE DEER'S WAY BARRED OUR PASSAGE east and there appeared to be no channel through it to the north, we had no choice but to go south. The country in that direction looked very formidable. Naked granite ridges seemingly devoid even of moss and lichens quartered a wasteland of splintered rock. How the deer managed to make their way through such a desolation posed a mystery. How Big River did so, *if* it did, was another. We were uneasy as we pushed off from the sand spit and paddled south into what appeared to be a deep bay of Seal Hole Lake.

There being no river within his hearing, Windy snoozed in the bows, his one good eye closed. The afternoon was well advanced before he crouched down and turned on his warning siren. Although we strained to hear whatever had alerted him, a considerable time passed before we detected a low-pitched and menacing vibration, as of a swarm of giant bees.

We went ashore, climbed a hill, and there was Big River—a mighty cataract spewing over a shattered landscape with the kind of chaotic violence that might follow the collapse of a major power dam.

I found it an appalling spectacle.

"My God!" I thought. "If it starts like this, what in hell's name will it be like farther on?" In the initial grip of panic, I was not at all soothed by Charles's reaction.

"Sure don't like going down there," he said, and I could hardly hear him over the massive tumult. "Tom Lamb said Big River was a killer...might be right.... One sure thing, we start down, there won't be no turning back."

Instinct shrieked at me to reject Big River, even if that meant having to return to Windy Post. I was about to say so when my army training came to the rescue: when faced with an impossible choice, leave the decision to someone else.

"You're the boss," I mumbled. "What you say goes."

Charles slowly nodded his head, and I knew we were committed.

By the time we got back to the canoe, the Worm of Fear was writhing in my guts. I did what I had learned to do before going into action: I poured each of us a drink. And when one had burned its way down, I poured another.

Having seen to it that everything was properly stowed, and having tied Windy to a thwart to prevent him from being washed overboard, we pushed off.

The sensible thing would have been to portage around this first set of rapids or, at least, to have tried lining the canoe down. Instead, Charles started the Lockwood and we flung ourselves into Big River's maw.

The initial challenge consisted of five chutes separated by three ledges, each of which spilled into a boiling vortex that flung the canoe about like a lotto ball. Charles's skilled piloting and the trusty Lockwood carried us safely through, and almost before we knew it the canoe bobbed out from below the final ledge. Although we never ceased to treat Big River with all the respect it so obviously deserved, henceforth our fear of it was manageable.

Once clear of the first set of rapids, we rode a millrace through shallow, diverging channels between islets that had been swept as bare as a baby's buttocks by ice floes pouring out of Seal Hole Lake during the spring melt. The current seldom flowed less than eight miles an hour, to which our paddling (we were conserving our small supply of fuel) added another couple.

Neither of us had ever before experienced a river like this one. It was a primordial force unleashed. The Cochrane and the Kasmere had been tricky, but Big River did not stoop to trickery, relying instead on brute power. Feeling as if we were being whipped down an aquatic ski run laid out by a fiendish slalom master, I began to experience an irrational exhilaration that almost overmastered terror.

Map-making—even sketch mapping—was out of the question here, even supposing I could have kept my sketch pad dry. Nor was sightseeing an option. Many deer idled along the low shores, but we had no time to spare for them. The foaming waters were so full of obstacles that all our senses had to be concentrated on avoidance. When we clawed our way ashore to catch our breath and brew up, Charles ruefully suggested that perhaps we should slow down before we were flung halfway across Hudson Bay. I was not so concerned about our speed as I was about the direction in which we were being taken. Big River appeared determined to carry us southward instead of eastward.

"Way we're heading, if we *get* to Hudson Bay at all we'll be lucky," I replied.

Almost as soon as we pushed off again, the river changed its shape. Instead of spilling all over the landscape, it now squeezed itself into a single channel no more than two hundred yards wide. Such was the volume and velocity of the constrained flow that the surface erupted into boiling waves of almost oceanic magnitude. The increased depth made for a safer passage but the headlong rush brought my heart into my mouth. It seemed downright *unnatural* for a canoe to go so fast.

An hour before sunset we came upon a herd of several hundred bucks massed on the riverbank at a place where the channel widened and the current eased somewhat, giving us an opportunity to rubberneck. They were so densely crowded that their tall antlers, silhouetted against the fading sky, resembled rifles being shouldered by a massed infantry regiment.

They were preparing to cross the river, and some had already been pushed into the shallows by the press behind. Although we swept past only a few yards away, they paid us not the slightest heed. They had more vital matters to consider. I could understand their preoccupation. It did not seem possible for any creature to enter that millrace on foot and survive.

A shriek from Windy claimed our attention and soon the river's heavy voice again swelled to a thundering obligato. We went ashore for a chilling look at a rapids with two ledges and a total drop of perhaps forty feet. Having agreed upon a plan of how it might be run, we hurried back to the canoe before our nerve deserted us.

The current proved so powerful that even at full throttle the Lockwood could not provide steerage way. Unable to avoid the lip of the first fall, we momentarily became airborne before the canoe plunged into the backwash, burying herself for half her length. I was still frantically bailing when we shot over the second one, from whose eddy we emerged like a piece of water-logged flotsam.

Big River allowed us no respite. The next eight or ten miles were virtually one continuous rapid down which we skittered like a dog chased by hornets. We were still in this roaring run when our nerves gave out. Charles ran the canoe into a backwater and we scrambled ashore to stand, shaken and shivering, determined to venture no farther that day. Windy, who had been saturated time and time again and now looked more like a drowned rat than a bird, voted in favor of taking a break by scuttling under a rock and adamantly refusing to come out.

Since our departure from Windy Bay, we had been traveling through totally treeless country but had now made so much southing we were again close to the treeline and able to camp alongside a clump of dwarf spruce, which provided the fuel for a fire.

That fire almost made an end to Windy. While trying to scrounge a piece of meat from the frying pan, he slipped into the flames. I grabbed him before he could be fatally scorched, but he emerged looking scruffier than ever. Most of his feathers were already frayed and frazzled; now the fire had wrecked his tail as well. Yet despite his many disfigurements, he remained indomitable—and companionable. Although he had always had the freedom to come and go as he chose, he seldom strayed far from the side, or the shoulder, of one or other of us. Afloat he stubbornly insisted on riding right up on the bow, where he could best herald the approach of each new rapid, even though his warnings were sometimes cut short by a wave washing him back into the canoe. As a pilot he was without peer. Whenever Kasmere's bird ruffled his mangy plumage and crouched down, shrieking, we knew trouble was coming and were on guard.

Next morning brought an easterly gale laden with frigid rain. Conditions were so unpleasant we decided to lie up for the day, but we were made to pay for this dereliction of duty. Although the tent floor was waterproof, rain dripped freely through the roof. The water, unable to escape, formed puddles under our sleeping robes, puddles which could be drained only by stabbing holes through the fabric floor.

Fortunately, there was some distraction from the consequent misery. I had brought along India-paper and small-print books: an omnibus volume called *The Forsyte Saga* for me and *The Travels of Marco Polo* for Charles. This was his first venture into such an exotic literary world and it engrossed him, while visiting Victorian London gave me a respite from the problems of the moment.

Although the weather did not noticeably improve next day, we decided to travel anyway. Another stretch of "quick water," as Charles nonchalantly called it, brought us into a small lake boasting a grove of spruce trees, some of which were ten feet tall. This was a welcome find, and we took full advantage of it, loading up with dead spruce boughs before we went hunting the exit from the lake.

After three hours of fruitless searching, we found it at the bottom of a *northwestern* bay—in the opposite direction to the way we wished to go.

As soon as we re-entered the river, the sonorous thunder of rapids threw Windy into hysterics, and at the same moment the heavens opened and drenched us with sleet. Although Charles pulled furiously at the starter cord, the waterlogged kicker refused to start, so we were swept into the vortex at the head of the rapids with only paddles to help us deal with what lay ahead.

The sleet almost blinded me, which may have been just as well. Charles would later claim we passed between the bodies of two drowned bucks stranded amongst the rocks, through a gap that was barely the width of the canoe.

"Horns was right up against us," Charles commented. "Good thing they was in velvet or we'd-a been tore in half." Whereupon he gave me a slow wink, in case I missed the joke.

While crossing the next lake, we encountered a yearling buck with a broken back stranded on a gravel bar—doubtless a casualty of Big River's violence. Charles shot him and we hauled the carcass to the nearest shore. The sun broke through while we were butchering him, so we seized the opportunity to build a fire, dry ourselves, and cook a feast. The *pièce de résistance* was blood pancakes, which Charles made from fresh blood drained from the yearling's body cavity mixed with flour, baking powder, and a handful of cranberries. The resultant flapjacks were as leathery as old boot soles and nearly as enduring. One survived at the bottom of the grub box until the end of our journey.

While we were eating, Charles remarked on the fact that we had seen no trace of human beings since leaving Nueltin: no tree-fellings, campsites, graves, not even any of the ubiquitous little stone pillars that sprout like mushrooms wherever Eskimos live and travel.

This dearth of human detritus seemed ominous. Even in the most remote parts of the north, travelers expect to occasionally find indications that others have passed the same way. We wondered if we had entered some kind of no man's land between the ancestral territory of the Idthen Eldeli and the inland Eskimos— a region avoided by both.

Dry and well-fed, we continued on our way until an armada of roseate storm clouds sailing in from the west warned us it was time to camp. Before turning in, I tried to determine where we were. According to the elapsed time and distance traveled, it appeared we ought to be halfway to Hudson Bay, though far to the south of the route we had expected to follow. But if we *were* halfway we should already have reached an unmistakable large lake known variously as Edehon or Edehontua Lake. According to Father Egenolf, it had once been a kind of Indian Shangri-La located at the base of a salient of spruce copses that thrust almost a hundred miles beyond it into the barrenlands.

"Lots of trees there," Father Egenolf had said. "And very big caribou herds. Many, many years ago the Idthen Eldeli used to walk up there cross-country in summertime to meet la Foule. They carried little canoes made of birchbark with them on their backs to cross the rivers. At Edehontua they would spear many, many deer and smoke their tongues and make much dry meat.

"When autumn came they would make new and bigger canoes covered with deerskins, then travel downstream to salt water and go south to the Great Stone House—that was what they called Fort Prince of Wales at Churchill. There they would trade pelts and dry meat and tongues for powder, shot, tea, and tobacco. When the snows came, they would *walk* all the way back to their own country.

"They would walk anywhere, those people. Walking from Reindeer Lake to Edehontua was just a holiday for them."

Concerned about Edehontua's non-appearance, I began to wonder if we were even on the right river. Perhaps Thlewiaza and

Big River were in fact different entities? Well, there was no point in worrying about it. All water eventually finds its way to the sea—and so in due course would we.

Whatever its identity, the aquatic monster we were riding continued to hurl us southeastward. The roar of the rapids and Windy's warning screeches punctuated the daylight hours and reverberated through my dreams. We saw very little of the land we were passing through. Our senses were so concentrated on the river that we were only peripherally aware of anything else.

The sound and fury of the river exerted a hypnotic effect, which may have been why Windy failed to sound his alarm as we rounded a hairpin bend to find ourselves facing a stretch of whitewater worse than anything Charles or I had ever imagined.

The river plunged into a mile-long gorge, splitting into twin cataracts around a whale's-back island of ice-and-water-polished rock. The western cataract was so clogged with boulders an eel would have had difficulty slipping through. The other was a flume built by colossi down which the bulk of the river thundered over a series of ledges with such cacophony we could hardly make ourselves heard.

Such was the effect of this spectacle that Charles, a whitewater man for most of his life, did something he almost never did. He swore, loudly and with passion. "God-damn son-of-a-bitch!" he cried, and frantically headed the canoe for shore....

Too late. We were caught in midstream, and the vortex sucked us in. Seconds later it spat us out onto the sloping nose of the stone whale. Slipping and sliding on the wet rock, we somehow managed to drag the canoe to temporary safety on a narrow ledge.

Now we were marooned in mid-river with a chilling choice. We could either attempt to run the eastern cataract, or we could try to portage the whole length of the whale's back across a web of crevasses filled with lesser torrents that were nevertheless capable of sweeping us away like errant leaves.

Having assured himself that the canoe had not been seriously damaged, Charles braced himself with one of the old Idthen Eldeli paddles and looked around.

"Maybe could pack our outfit to the lower end of the island then run the canoe down light," he shouted. "We smash her up, we still got our gear. We try to run her down full, could lose everything...."

It seemed like Hobson's choice to me, but I nodded in fatalistic acquiescence.

We spent the next couple of hours on the whale's back, slithering, slipping, falling, sometimes crawling as we portaged everything except the engine and two paddles. Then it was time to run the gauntlet.

Launching was tricky. We managed by throwing the canoe into the torrent and leaping aboard as one might mount a running horse. The canoe *acted* like a runaway horse, but she struck only once, ripping a foot-long strip of canvas from her flank and cracking a rib. Then we were out of the dragon's mouth.

Drunk with relief and now as cocky as if we had just won Olympic gold, we went ashore below the last overfall to reload our gear. And to suffer a severe deflation of our egos.

As we watched incredulously, a lone doe stepped delicately into the torrent we had just come through and waded slowly across the rapids. At times surging back waves obscured her from view, and we were sure she must have been swept off her braced and quivering legs. Yet somehow she kept her footing and struggled on. Making it to the whale's-back island, she shook the water from her coat, glanced nonchalantly about, and, evidently concluding this was not where she wished to be, *swam and waded back to the mainland shore from which she had come.*

To complete our ignominy, as we ran the next set of rapids we shot into the midst of a herd of about a hundred does and fawns crossing to the south. Multiple collisions threatened. There was much yelling from us, snorting from the deer, brandishing of paddles, and flinging about of antlered heads, but no damage resulted. A backward look revealed the herd scrambling ashore to stand looking disdainfully after us.

On and on we ran and still there was no sign of Edehontua. We had almost concluded we were indeed on the wrong river when the canoe shot round a bend to come upon a vista of open water stretching to the far southeastern horizon.

Edehontua? Our hopes seemed confirmed by the presence of extensive stands of good-sized spruce trees. We went ashore to examine one of these and, when a stiff southeast breeze sprang up, decided to camp there for the night.

I began unloading the gear while Charles went off to gather firewood. Soon I heard him calling. I found him examining some brittle, ash-gray sticks which he identified as teepee poles. Nearby were many firepits filled with a rich growth of lichens. All around were the seemingly petrified stumps of felled trees.

"Big old Chip camp," Charles said, casting about like a hound looking for a scent. "Lots of people must have stayed here a long time ago. See the axe cuts? They wasn't made with steel or iron axes. Them trees was likely beavered off with stone axes like the old people used."

He shook his head in wonder. "Stumps must have been here before any whites come to this country." He paused. "I found one of them old axes once. Tied it onto a hardwood haft with deer thongs and tried it out. It cut pretty good, though I never did figure how to sharpen it."

He paused again, this time to stare out over the broad expanse of the lake. "Got to be Edehon. Looks like pretty good country around here too. Lots of wood. Lots of deer. Likely lots of fur. Good place to build a cabin. Sure wouldn't be too crowded."

That night, sitting beside a fire on the shore of Edehon Lake, I was in a mood to celebrate. Not so Charles. Something, perhaps a joking remark of mine to the effect that I wished Rita had come along to do the cooking, made him retreat to an inner fastness where I could not reach him.

On several previous occasions I had encouraged him to talk about his troubles, but he had often ignored such opportunities. He did so now. He had nothing to say except that he was glad that it was I, rather than Fred, who was with him on this trip. Then he betook himself to his journal.

There has been trouble between Fred and I since I left Putahow River with the last load of freight last spring. What is the matter with me? I can't write decent today making lots of mistakes. Well I guess because my mind is on something else and I know what it is too but I am afraid to say.

Fell asleep at last after thinking of home and what Fred said to me before I left. Wonder what he is doing now and if he done what he should do. And will he keep his promise that he said he would keep, and will it be all right I hope.

CHAPTER TWENTY-ONE

RIVER DOGS

EDEHONTUA WAS CERTAINLY A LIVELY LAKE. THE skies cleared during the night, but at dawn the wind switched right around to blow half a gale out of the northwest. This made for a gorgeous day, if a challenging one. Waves soon built to form a sea difficult or impossible to handle under paddle power alone. Although the Lockwood could perhaps have enabled us to deal with it, we were now down to our last gallon of gas and wished to preserve that for running rapids.

Perhaps we could sail.

This was my department, so for a change Charles ran about doing my bidding while I cobbled together a more efficient version of the lateen rig we had used on south Nueltin. A stouter mast and a longer boom and gaff transformed the tent into a much more effective pulling machine. I also contrived a leeboard out of a paddle and showed Charles how to use it to give the canoe (which had no keel to speak of) a better hold on the water. We solved the steering problem by removing the propeller from the Lockwood, allowing the shaft to remain in the water so the tail fin could be used as a rudder.

Having securely stowed our gear, we climbed aboard and set sail. Running "full and by," the old canoe went charging down the lake at six or seven knots, almost planing off the crests of the following seas. Charles was astonished if somewhat intimidated by this performance. Windy was ecstatic. Perhaps he felt that this was flying.

We cavorted before that spanking breeze for three hours while the seas got higher and the canoe became ever more difficult to handle, sheering wildly from side to side. It was time to seek shelter, but I dared not alter course because that would have put us into a beam sea with the very real risk of capsizing. So we continued to scoot before the wind, hoping a safe haven would present itself before we ran out of lake.

The shores, which had been as much as five miles apart, drew together until at last we found ourselves in a deep terminal bay at whose foot the breakers were piling up on a rocky coast. Somehow we got the sail down without going broadside, then managed to slew the canoe into the lee of a little point and beach her on a providential strip of sand.

Edehontua had been lenient with us, but she had not dealt in kindly fashion with ten or twelve caribou fawns whose swollen corpses littered the beach. We could only suppose they had been overwhelmed while trying to swim across the open lake with their mothers and that their bodies had been driven, as we had been, into this cul-de-sac.

And a cul-de-sac it truly was. Though we walked the shore for a couple of miles in either direction and climbed several hills, we could find nothing suggesting a river exit. I went back to the beach to cook a meal while Charles ranged cross-country. He returned to report another big bay five or six miles farther east, but still no sign of an outlet.

We would have to make a search by water, though not yet. Until the wind died down we were trapped, able to do little more than stuff our bellies, dry our gear, and possess our souls in patience. Not to worry. We had made an extraordinarily swift passage through Edehontua. That night I dreamt I was sailing around Cape Horn in a canoe, and woke up in a cold sweat.

The wind fell light next morning as we set off to search for the outlet. By now we were resigned to the fact that exits from all Big River's lakes were never where they ought to be. Edehon was no exception. We eventually found its outlet in a north-western bay into which we were directed by Windy sounding his whitewater alarm.

We entered the river under power, prepared to run a rapid, and found ourselves bearing down upon a mixed group of bucks, does, and fawns crossing diagonally in front of us. Since I was at the tiller, I seized the opportunity to fool around a bit by sliding the bow up on the back of a big buck. He retaliated by trying to sideswipe us with his arching antlers. Fortunately he had no solid footing. Hurriedly sheering off, I ran alongside a fawn. Charles grabbed it by its skinny neck and hauled it aboard, where it protested in such a gruff voice that we burst out laughing. As Charles said, it sounded like a fat man with a bellyache. "OW-OH! OW-OH! OW-OH!" it cried hoarsely. Its mother, who was not amused, came for us, flailing long forelegs which looked quite capable of slicing the canoe open. Charles hastily dumped the fawn overboard.

A preliminary rapid was followed by a long cascade. We went ashore for a reconnaissance of it and ended spending an hour watching a steady flow of deer crossing through a relatively quiet stretch between two rapids. Charles drew my attention to a long row of stone pillars on the far bank that seemed to be directing the animals toward the crossing.

"Spear place, down there. Chips or maybe Eskimos came here one time with their canoes or kayaks. Hid in them willows. When a bunch of deer was in the river, they paddle right into the herd. Just like we done. Their spears was about as long as a paddle, with a wide head. What they did was stab the deer in the back to let the air out of its lungs so it couldn't breathe and it would drown. A good hunter could kill a big bunch of them that way."

Caribou seem almost semi-aquatic, nearly as agile in the water as out of it. Their hollow hair gives them great buoyancy; their powerful legs driving big, splay feet can move them through the water at considerable speed. They have been known to make forty-mile open-water crossings and emerge with strength enough remaining to gallop away.

Although they are not aggressive, their flailing legs and many-pronged antlers posed serious risks to spearmen in fragile canoes and kayaks. Deer were not the only creatures whose corpses were sometimes swept downstream. Even in modern times it was a rare Ihalmiut family that had not lost a man at the spearing places.

Swollen by many new tributaries, Big River was becoming ever bigger while at the same time losing some of its hard-muscled character. It no longer appeared to be committed to one continuous rampage, or perhaps we were simply growing used to it.

We relaxed. The sky was clear, the sun hot, the flies negligible; even caribou along the low and stony riverbanks seemed somnolent. Charles slouched at the tiller while in the bow I actually dozed off....

...To be brutally awakened by the roar of a .30-30 a few feet from my ear. Dazed, I heard Charles yelling: "*A seal! A seal!*" I glanced astern to glimpse a pair of big black eyes staring from a sleek, dog-like face.

The vision vanished in a flurry of foam. The canoe lurched over a rock, and I had to grab both gunwales to steady myself. In that instant the seal reappeared and Charles fired again. The explosion was deafening. The bullet probably came closer to me than to the seal, which promptly dived but popped up a hundred feet away in time to watch Charles struggling to get the motor going before we crashed into a line of boulders.

There followed an insane game of hide-and-seek during which seal and canoe were swept down the next set of rapids. Charles snapped off half a dozen shots, but the seal remained unscathed.

Charles was devastated. This was his first encounter with a seal, and his desire to kill something so unusual was reinforced by the knowledge that, according to Dr. Harper, science valued a specimen of the legendary freshwater seal as a rarity almost beyond price.

We went ashore to bail out the canoe.

"Don't know what's wrong," said my companion disconsolately. "Never shoot so bad in my whole life."

"Not to worry, chum. Where there's one river dog—that's what Egenolf says the Chipewyans called them—there's likely more. That fellow sure *did* look like a dog!"

An hour later we encountered a second seal, asleep on a reef below a rapid. Charles fired a shot at it and missed again. Grayling were jumping in the pool below this rapid so, concluding that the seal might stick around, we went ashore in hopes of surprising it later that evening. By now I was almost as anxious as Charles to see what a river dog in the hand was like.

It had been a busy day. In addition to discovering that freshwater seals really did exist—something I had had my doubts about—we had seen several thousand deer crossing or preparing to cross the river in herds numbering as many as two hundred individuals, mainly does and fawns but including small parties of yearling bucks.

"Big bucks don't hang around much with the does except at breeding time," Charles explained. "Old does that lead the herds won't put up with it. That's the only thing a big buck is scared of—an old doe."

Charles was not really interested in deer that evening. River dogs engrossed him. He sat with one eye cocked on the nearby reef, oiling and cleaning his rifle but, as it turned out, failing to examine it as carefully as he might have done.

We were up at dawn next day and when no seal had appeared by the time breakfast was over decided to push on. Charles took the bow seat with the rifle across his knees. I was happy to be in the stern, out of the line of fire.

The previous evening I had scouted the next stretch of river and glimpsed what appeared to be a large lake a few miles farther on. A brisk westerly breeze was blowing that morning so I hoisted the sail in expectation that open water lay close ahead. The river began to widen as it usually did before entering a lake, and even Windy was taken by surprise when, on blithely rounding a bend, we found ourselves looking down a mile-long cataract.

Since we were already in the slick water at the head of the chute, there was no time to get the sail down. We had no choice but to go down that rapid under full sail.

I managed to steer clear of some of the worst obstacles, and Charles clawed us clear of others...until we were pitched over a ledge with a jolt that unstepped the mast and smothered both of us in the tent's flapping folds.

By the time we got ourselves untangled, the canoe was drifting toward a gravel reef in the pool below the rapids—a reef from which we were being observed by two surprised seals.

Seen out of the water and near at hand, they appeared enormous. Five or six feet long, they vaguely resembled a couple of bloated beach bums. Heavily whiskered beach bums with large and lustrous eyes.

We crashed into the reef (it was the only way we could stop in a hurry) and the startled seals plunged into the river with a resounding splash as Charles fired...and missed again!

This so infuriated him he refused to pause long enough to install the propeller so we could use the motor in pursuit.

"Get going!" he bawled. "Got to kill one of them things!"

Re-stepping the mast took only a minute or two. The sail billowed. We swept downstream and soon caught up with the two seals, who were making no great effort to outrun us. Charles blazed away at their bobbing heads, but with no effect except to make them decamp, this time for good.

Windy was warning of whitewater ahead. I suggested we cease

pushing our luck and get the Lockwood back into service. Charles would have none of it, so we sailed on into a lake-like expansion of the river. It was either devoid of seals or they were learning to keep their heads down. We did, however, spot five Canada geese feeding in a grassy swale. Hungrily I shifted course toward them, and we were almost within range when a wolf reared up from a patch of willow scrub to stare balefully at us. Presumably he had been stalking the geese. Now, seeing we were about to spoil his chances, he spoiled ours by making a dash, which sent the big birds splashing heavily into the air as Charles belatedly fired at them. And missed again.

By this time he was so mad he would not even respond to my meek suggestion that we go ashore. So on we sailed over another and quite severe rapid into another lake, then to the bottom of yet another dead end, where we were forced to spend the next several hours climbing hills searching the landscape for the outlet. Meanwhile, sable clouds rolled up, warning of a storm in the offing.

The country hereabouts was aquiver with blackflies of a new and virulent breed, and ominously devoid of deer, which was a matter of real concern, for we were out of meat. Well, not *quite* out. We still had a piece of brisket, but blowflies had colonized it, and their innumerable eggs were hatching into voracious little maggots. Besides which, Windy had pre-empted it. Crouched over it with wings extended, he warned us off with a possessive display that would have done credit to the imperial American eagle.

That evening, as we were eating a soggy meal of rain-soaked bannocks, a seal surfaced right in front of camp and swam over for a closer look. I would have left him in peace, but the sight was more than Charles could bear. Up came the rifle. A shot roared out. And the seal swam saucily away.

When Charles flung down the rifle in disgust and stormed off into the hills, I picked the weapon up and casually glanced down its barrel. Something about the foresight seemed odd.

Closer inspection revealed that the front sight was twisted out of line. The mystery of Charles's execrable marksmanship was no longer a mystery.

Through the years following my first meeting with river dogs, I inquired about them throughout Canada's eastern arctic. Chipewyans told me freshwater seals once inhabited most of the major rivers draining into Hudson Bay from the west, especially the Thlewiaza, Th'anne, and the appropriately named Seal River. When I asked if the Dene people had ever hunted them, my informants shook their heads. Why not? Because, they said, river dogs shared common ancestors with their own dogs, and who but a fool would risk offending the dog spirit?

When I inquired of the coastal Inuit what they knew about the matter I was told that freshwater seals also lived in several river systems running into eastern Hudson Bay and Foxe Basin, including the Kogaluk and Povungnituk rivers of northern Ungava. They were said to be especially numerous in Baffin Island's Koudjuak River and in the two very large lakes, Amadjuak and Nettsilling, associated with it. Nettsilling is, in fact, an Inuktitut word for seal. However, the coastal Inuit seldom if ever hunted the freshwater kind, considering it inferior in flavor and blubber content to saltwater seals.

"Besides," one of them explained, "they can duck bullets. Very hard to shoot."

Charles Schweder would have appreciated that comment.

The inland-dwelling Ihalmiut, who knew almost nothing about saltwater seals or the sealing culture that sustained their coastal relatives, were knowledgeable about the freshwater kind.

"Seal people" (they did not call them river dogs) once lived in all of the barrenlands' big rivers and lakes, an Ihalmiut elder told me.

"They were in Tulemaliguak, Hicoliguak, Angikuni, even when those lakes were covered with five or six feet of ice. They kept holes open with their claws so they could breathe. They had their young in an iglu under the snow on top of the ice. If the ice got too thick, or they were lazy, they swam to a rapid or a falls where there was open water or thin ice all winter. There they lived like otters, catching plenty of fish.

"A long time ago when there were lots of our people and lots of seal people, some Ihalmiut were living beside Hicoliguak [Ice-shores Lake]. One autumn they missed the deer, so the families were hungry. They had nothing to feed their dogs, but they noticed the dogs did not get thin. A man wondered about that, so he watched the dogs and saw they went a long way out on the lake ice, and when they came back they smelled of fish.

"The dogs were going to a hole in the ice and the seal people were bringing fish to those dogs. The man asked the dogs if the seal people would bring fish to the Ihalmiut too. And that is what they did.

"After that the Ihalmiut never hunted the seal people. I have never hunted them myself, nor has anyone I know. Yet, though nobody was killing them, they still got scarce. Maybe the sicknesses that killed so many of us killed them too?"

CHAPTER TWENTY-TWO

ESKIMO CHARLIE

BIG RIVER NOW RAN RESOLUTELY SOUTHEAST-ward, hemming us in between high gravel banks so that we felt as if we were being flushed down a gigantic sluice. The high banks shut us in so completely we could see no deer, which distressed us, for we were hungry.

Charles finally spotted the antlers of a solitary bull cresting the bank. The moment the bow touched shore he was overboard, rifle in hand. He reached the top of the bank in time to watch the buck gallop out of range. Then, "Come on up!" he called. "Something here you oughta see."

Set into the side of a hill littered with granite slabs was a semi-subterranean vault about nine feet square and four high. Its domed roof had been crudely shingled with flat stones supported by the twisted trunks of dwarf spruce trees. Walls and roof may originally have been chinked with moss and lichens; if so, the caulking had mostly vanished, leaving a multitude of holes for the wind to whistle through. The whole structure had a singularly desolate feel about it.

"Think it's a grave?" I asked.

"Maybe. Sure don't look like what a Chip or a Eskimo would make though. More like a white." Then, with a sly look at me, "He could still be in there."

Taking this as a challenge I got down on hands and knees and peered through a low doorway gaping darkly like the mouth of a badger's burrow. There was a fetid, vaguely skunk-like odor. I lit a match, but its brief flare revealed nothing recognizably human: no bunk, table, stove. The floor seemed to be covered with hair—and with bones.

Backing out somewhat hurriedly, I described what I had seen. Charles appeared relieved. Gathering a handful of moss he rolled it into a makeshift torch, lit it, and thrust it into the cavern.

"Wolverine been living here, but he hasn't been around for a while. Good thing. Sure don't want to tangle with no wolverine in his den. They're mean enough and tough enough to take on a wolf. Even a bear."

Since he still seemed reluctant to enter, I offered to explore. Inside the dark interior I found two brass .44-40 cartridge cases, the broken spring of a fox trap, and a small glass bottle tightly stoppered and sealed. I assumed this must be some kind of medicine but Charles identified it as a vial of holy water.

"People out here like to carry some holy water 'cause you never know when someone's going to die. No priest anywheres around, so you got to do whatever you do yourself."

Charles concluded that the cabin, as he generously styled this sorry hovel, had been built by one of the shadowy fugitives from civilization who are an integral part of the mythology of the Canadian arctic.

"Maybe a fellow come up here to get away from some war, figuring to hide out 'til it was over. Quite a few did that.

"Loners, the most of them. Some got along with the Eskimos. Some never did, and never come back out. Not hard to figure why. Didn't know the country. Didn't know how to make out. Turned the natives against themselves the way they acted... not much chance they'd ever come back out.

"Could be what happened to the fellow made this cabin. Some of the bones in there could be his.... Sure reminds me of Eskimo Charlie. You know about him?"

I didn't then, but after hearing what my companion had to tell me my curiosity grew until in years to come I made it my business to find out more about Eskimo Charlie.

Janez Planisek was born around 1890 on a hardscrabble little farm in Slovakia. While still in his teens, he set off to make his fortune in the New World. He worked his way across America to San Francisco, then went hunting for gold in Alaska and Yukon. Failing to find a fortune there (and having been accused of being an accessory in a murder), he drifted to Herschel Island, near the mouth of the Mackenzie River, where he signed on an arctic whaler. The vessel sailed east a thousand miles, to be wrecked close to the mouth of Back River. The crew managed to return to Herschel in their whale boats. All except Janez Planisek, or Charlie as he now called himself.

A slightly built man with a narrow face, black eyes, and what were described as "ape-like arms," Planisek had trouble making friends with his own kind. His way of dealing with natives was to try to outwit or intimidate them.

He spent the next year or two with the Utkuhilingmiut, the Soapstone People, an isolated group of Inuit living near the mouth of Back River. When his welcome began to wear perilously thin, he commandeered a dog team and sled from his hosts and fled southward into the territory of the Thelon River Inuit.

Here Charlie struck gold: not yellow metal, but white gold in the form of arctic fox, whose pelts were then becoming wildly fashionable in Europe and the United States.

Charlie went after the foxes, but became so unpopular with the Thelon people while doing so that he found it expedient to move even farther south, into Ihalmiut country between south Nueltin, Kasba, and Ennadai Lakes. Here, about 1914, he built a cabin on the shore of what is still called Charlie Lake.

Charlie inveigled the Ihalmiut into trapping for him in

exchange for tea, tobacco, a little ammunition, and trinkets he obtained from a trading post at Fond du Lac on Lake Athabasca. He himself did not set many traps. They were expensive, heavy to transport, and a nuisance to maintain. Poison, on the other hand, though illegal, was cheap, light, and fatally effective. Strychnine was Charlie's choice.

Caribou carcasses baited with "fox sugar," strychnine's *nom de plume*, would kill anything that ate the meat, firsthand or second-hand, including ravens, eagles, jays, wolves, foxes, weasels, dogs, and sometimes hungry human beings. If, due to its popularity with white trappers, strychnine was sometimes hard to come by, Charlie made do with ground glass, which he manufactured by pounding broken bottles into a lethal powder.

Poison did have one disadvantage. Before the victims succumbed, they were often able to drag themselves so far from the bait that the "trapper" never found them. However, foxes were then so abundant that such losses hardly mattered.

Charlie did very well until the First World War turned white gold into dross. In 1916, with fox pelts almost valueless, Eskimo Charlie, as he now proudly called himself, traveled still farther south to enjoy a long holiday in the forested country south of Reindeer Lake. Here he got himself a young Cree woman, and here also he encountered Fred Schweder senior. The two men established a wary friendship.

When fox prices began rising after the war, Charlie took himself and his woman back north and began "trapping" again. But there was easier money to be made as an illegal trader to the Ihalmiut, so this is what he mostly did until the mid-1920s, when licensed traders began establishing outposts close to his baili-wick and cut him out of the business.

By that time Charlie had seriously alienated the Ihalmiut. Pretending to be a shaman possessing powerful magic, he had exploited them at every opportunity. One of his gambits had been to take furs on consignment to trade at a legitimate post then fail to bring back the goods, claiming he had been robbed en route by the Itkilik—the forest Indians.

He took advantage of the Ihalmiut in other ways as well. Eventually, a man whose wife and daughter Charlie had sexually abused took a shot at him. The bullet missed, but the message went home. Soon thereafter, Charlie pulled up stakes and retreated to the country south of Reindeer, where he remained for the next several years, scratching a living as a sometime trapper, trader, and even subsistence farmer.

In the spring of 1929 he embarked on a bizarre enterprise which he called the Planisek-O'Grady Expedition from Arctic to Tropic. Accompanied by two of his younger children, four dogs, and a recent Irish immigrant named O'Grady, Eskimo Charlie undertook to make a journey by dog sled and canoe from Chesterfield Inlet on Hudson Bay to the Gulf of Mexico.

He hoped to make a fortune by giving lectures and exhibitions along the way. Clad in caribou skin clothing, he would be joined on stage by the dogs hauling a sled upon which rode his dark-skinned, black-eyed children wearing beaded buckskin jackets and feathered headdresses. Charlie would introduce himself as the chosen leader of forty thousand Eskimos who called him the Master of the Barrengrounds. Then he would tell tall tales of his experiences in the wild and woolly arctic.

The "expedition" continued for three years, during which Eskimo Charlie entertained in schools, prisons, convalescent homes, legion halls, churches, or anywhere else an audience could be gathered. His travels took him through Winnipeg, down the Mississippi valley to New Orleans, briefly to the Bahamas, then north again to Canada via Florida and the eastern United States.

What happened to his earnings is a murky question. At some point O'Grady and the dogs fell by the wayside. Charlie and his two children showed up in Montreal in July of 1932, broke and sick. He was hospitalized and the children were placed in a foster home. They never saw their father again.

Released from hospital in the spring of 1933, the Master of the Barrengrounds made his way back to Reindeer Lake, but found no welcome there. His woman had died during his absence and his three other children had been consigned to a church-run orphanage...where Charlie let them remain while he returned to the long-derelict cabin at Charlie Lake.

There he became a virtual hermit. The Cree had rejected him. The Ihalmiut wanted no part of him. The Chipewyans feared him. Most of the few white men in the country gave him a wide berth. His only human contact was with the Schweder family at Windy Post, and eventually even this tenuous link disintegrated.

Charlie concluded that the natives, and especially the "huskies," were out to kill him. To protect himself from them he raided native graves, collecting Inuit and Chipewyan skulls, which he placed on long poles surrounding his cabin. Convinced that he was under deadly siege, he kept his dogs barricaded in the cabin with him to prevent *their* being poisoned!

In later years he never went outside without a cocked rifle in the crook of his arm. So did the Master of the Barrengrounds live out his time.

In 1941 Fred Schweder brought word to Brochet that Eskimo Charlie had not been seen for a year or two. This news reached the RCMP, and in the winter of 1942–43 a patrol was sent to investigate. When the policeman and his Indian guide reached Charlie's cabin they found the door barred from within. They burst it open to be met by a nauseating stench and an appalling spectacle.

According to Charles Schweder, "Looked like he died in there along of his dogs. There was nobody to feed them then so I guess they ate him. Hope he was dead when they done it. The Eskimos don't think so. They think the dogs killed him because of the way he was."

This was wishful thinking. When the policeman searched the charnel hovel he found this note:

April—I guess it is the 12th.

For four days I am feeling rotten. I can neither eat nor sleep. I have pains in my chest. For four days I haven't been able to pass water, or bowel. I have no laxative. I had some Epsom salt but I cannot find it. Last night I passed out for some time. I guess this is the end. So long everybody.

P.S. I have the following fur. 8 mink, 2 red foxes, 1 beaver, 1 marten, 1 wolverine

A chill east wind and a penetrating drizzle made the little cave by the side of Big River seem particularly dismal, yet in a sense it was an encouragement. Whoever had built the place had presumably made his way upstream from the coast, so we ought to be able to make it downstream.

The rain continued as we plunged on between rock dykes thirty or more feet high plowed up by the ice during the spring melt. Windy, who hated rain, scrunched up under my pack and consequently failed to give timely warning of a rapid that nearly proved to be my nemesis.

Sweeping around a bend, we were confronted by a two-mile-long cascade. Steep rubble banks prevented us from landing, so Charles pulled on the Lockwood's starter cord. When the motor caught, he gave it full throttle and headed into the maelstrom.

We were in the final chute when the canoe struck a ledge, stopping so abruptly I was almost pitched over the bow. The stern instantly swung around, and the river began pouring in. Without conscious thought, I jumped overboard.

Freed of my weight, the bow shifted enough to allow Charles to lever the stern around with his paddle until the canoe was again heading downstream. Although pulled off my feet by the current, I managed to cling to a gunwale and so was able, very slowly, to haul myself back aboard. I lay in the bottom of the half-filled canoe coughing and retching until Charles guided us through the pool below the rapids to a safe landing on a little island.

The strike had cracked another of the canoe's ribs (we had already sprung or broken five or six) and ripped another hole in the tattered canvas covering. We had also come close to losing Windy, who, trapped under my pack, had nearly drowned.

We bailed out the canoe and continued on our way, but our hearts were not in it. At least, mine wasn't. As we passed through a lake-like expansion filled with gravel-covered islets, I demanded we go ashore and camp for the night. Desolate as these islets were, they were at least dry and firmly moored! Despite or perhaps because of my close call, I slept like a dead man.

Next day the high banks which had so constrained us subsided to reveal a new landscape: a dun-colored expanse of pond-dotted tundra visibly tilted toward the east. We were descending onto a coastal plain—one which some eight thousand years earlier had been sea bottom.

In mid-morning we were greatly heartened to spot a pair of inuksuak on the northern shore. These, the first we had seen since leaving Nueltin, assured us we were back in a land of Eskimos.

A few miles farther on, we surprised a yearling buck and seven does standing thigh-deep in the river. I headed the canoe toward them while Charles levered a shell into the chamber of his rifle. However, before he could shoot, the little herd exploded in the most extraordinary manner. The does leapt up the bank and began running in frantic circles, sometimes crashing into one another. The young buck fled at full gallop along the shore to where an outcrop jutted out above the river. Leaping to the top of this obstruction, he unhesitatingly flung himself over the edge to crash sickeningly onto the rocks below.

We *heard* leg bones snap! When we reached him, he was thrashing about helplessly in the water. Charles thrust a knife blade between two neck vertebrae to end his agony.

His behavior had seemed manic to me: as if a devil had been

riding him. When I said as much, Charles pointed to something on the dead buck's back.

"There's your devil!"

I saw a gaudy yellow fly about an inch long crawling over the deer's still quivering flank. It was a warble fly: an incubus against which the deer have no defence except panic-stricken flight.

The single warble fly had evidently been responsible for the suicidal action of the buck and the frantic behavior of the does. Charles remarked that one warble, or its closely related cousin the bot fly, could stampede an entire herd. During a consequent visit to the barrenlands, I had occasion to remove a pint sealer-full of warble maggots—each of them almost as large as my little finger—from under the skin of a single infested caribou. I also found thirty-seven bot fly larvae in the throat and nasal passages of another victim. It is not difficult to understand why these flies should inspire manic behavior in their hosts.

A rising northwesterly breeze prompted us to hoist sail. We sped eastward at a good clip, relishing the thought of the banquet we would have when we made camp that night. Skimming through two minor stretches of whitewater, we came into another broad stretch clogged with gravel islands pushed up by the spring ice. When Charles spotted something odd on the right bank we went ashore to investigate.

The object proved to be a twenty-two-foot seagoing canoe overturned on top of a stony ridge. Flat rocks had been placed along its keel to help keep it in place when winter gales blew. Clearly it would never float again. Wind and weather had stripped off most of its canvas covering, leaving its cedar staves to crack and splinter under the sun. On the chance that it might cover a cache made by a white man, we stripped off the anchoring rocks and turned it over.

Underneath were several bundles wrapped in rotted-out deerskins. With something of the anticipation of children on Christmas morning, we opened one. The wrappings parted to reveal four soapstone pipe bowls; a rusted tin of tea; another of tobacco; a battered tin plate; a pair of wooden snow goggles; an iron spearhead; and a pile of unidentifiable debris, presumably of softer objects destroyed by the chisel teeth of lemmings.

The provenance of this "cache" should now have been obvious to us, but it was not until we broke open the largest bundle, whose coverings were so decayed they fell apart at a touch, that we realized we were dealing with a grave. The large bundle contained the semi-mummified body of the occupant, legs jackknifed into the fetal position, heavy skull crowned by a mat of jet-black hair.

Hurriedly, we put everything back as near as we could to the way we had found it and wasted no time pushing off.

"Bad luck, you fool around with somebody's grave," Charles muttered grimly. "Must have been a real big fellow too. His people sure gave him lots of stuff to use where he was going."

A cluster of inuksuak four or five miles farther along marked a former encampment, presumably the one to which the dead man had belonged. It contained five tent rings, all over twenty feet in diameter; four sets of kayak supports; and a number of beehive-shaped rock piles built to shelter meat storage pits. Oddments lying about included part of a wooden meat tray, a toy sled, countless caribou bones, and the massive skull of a muskox. Bundles of twigs squirreled away in crevasses amongst the rocks gave the illusion of recent occupancy, but Charles thought the site had been abandoned for a long time.

We brewed tea and fried steaks in marrow fat over a fire fueled with some of the cached twigs. They burned hot and almost smokeless, and we were grateful for this gift from the past. We were equally grateful for the assurance that whatever obstacles still lay ahead of us on Big River, they could not be insurmountable.

Flooding out over the coastal plain, the river now began

dissipating its strength amongst innumerable island-filled channels. As we picked our way amongst these, we came upon a second habitation site at a narrows which offered a splendid crossing place for migrant deer.

The stony shore and immediate hinterland were white with caribou bones. Most were of considerable age, but some were of animals recently killed. We soon discovered that hunters had camped behind a low ridge nearby where the tents would have been out of sight of the crossing. Here we found a ten-gallon gasoline drum we naively hoped might contain fuel, but of course it was empty.

Charles "read" the story of this camp as deftly as he read whitewater: "Four or five families, maybe twenty people, been here all last winter. Come to spear deer in the fall and put down enough meat to last 'til spring. According to all them meat caches, sure don't seem like nobody went hungry. Only been gone a little while. Likely gone to the coast to trade at Tavanni."

Now the river widened into a lake dotted with caribou swimming aimlessly about. Since it was a warm day, I thought they were just cooling off, until Charles explained: "Flies really after them today. Driving them crazy. Be a good time to make a hunt on the water, but the meat's kind of poor now 'cause the deer is too much bothered to eat."

A brisk sou'easter set us back as we entered another lake-like expansion, so we stopped for a brew-up. While Charles looked for twigs and moss to make a fire, I went for a walk.

The uncircumscribed expanse of tundra surrounding me was windswept and sun-drenched. Glinting gold and green, it bore an uncanny resemblance to the plains of south Saskatchewan I had roamed as a youngster. It was just as vitally alive. Every pond swirled with waterfowl impatient to begin the great migration. Loons, Canada geese, snow geese, spiky-tailed old squaw ducks, curlew, plover, and sandpipers of a dozen species honked, mewed, gabbled, and bustled about beneath a canopy of gull wings.

As I walked along an ancient beach left behind by the receding waters of Hudson Bay, I met several fat, orange-coated ground squirrels who shrilled their *sic-sic-sic* calls at me before flicking their tails and plunging into their shallow burrows. Except for the gaudiness of their coats, they could have been mistaken for Saskatchewan gophers. One had only to visualize bison instead of caribou to make these arctic prairies seem almost one with the southern plains.

I returned to the canoe, drawn by a tantalizing odor. Charles had found another cache of dwarf birch twigs and was roasting the brisket from the suicidal buck. Not to be outdone, I fried up two large bannocks, using most of our remaining flour. We gorged as if there would be no tomorrow then, torpid as ticks, sipped tea while the embers cooled.

Charles became talkative, revisiting some of the traumatic events that had occurred before my arrival at Windy Post. I found some of the stories so disturbing that, when he suggested we pitch the tent and get some sleep, I was apprehensive of what dreams might come, so I persuaded him we should continue on.

Night had fallen by then and the wind had died down, giving way to a heavy mist. We paddled onto the lake in almost impenetrable darkness, our only light the momentary flare of a match as I checked our compass course.

For a long time the blackness and eerie silence remained nearly absolute. Then, with heart-stopping abruptness, we were set upon by a flight of phantoms! They were jaegers, a kind of predatory gull whose scimitar wings and trailing tail feathers brushed our heads as they swept around us, piercing the night with their raucous shrieks. They vanished as mysteriously as they had appeared.

Before dawn we fetched up on a stony beach, where we did not attempt to pitch the tent but were content to unroll our sleeping bags on the gravel.

Unbeknownst to us, we had landed on a narrow isthmus being used by insomniac deer as a thoroughfare. Some of these blundered so close we had to shout to make them stay clear. Then a white fox gave me fits by scuttling across the foot of my sleeping bag. Finally I was violently awakened from fitful sleep by the crash of a .30-30 as Charles fired a warning shot at what he thought might be a wolf investigating the meat in the canoe.

I might have had a better rest bedded down on a city street.

While I got breakfast, Charles went exploring. Not far off he came upon an elaborate, stone-built "hide" Inuit hunters had anciently used to ambush passing deer.

"Only had bows and arrows," he reported, showing me a quartzite point he had picked up. "When they got guns I guess they never needed that place no more. Bunch of weasels living in it now tried to chase me out."

As we were preparing to depart, Charles spotted a seal on an offshore rock to the south of us. This time he set off to stalk it from the land, painstakingly creeping closer until he was no more than a hundred yards from it. He took careful aim over the repaired foresight but, just as he squeezed the trigger, his elbow slipped. The seal slid into the lake and swam placidly away.

The bullet had had no effect, but the sound of the shot was magical. Seal heads popped up all over the bay. Charles blazed away furiously and fruitlessly until he ran out of ammunition, then came running back to the canoe for more; but I stood in his way. Only ten shells remained to us, and we were an unknown distance from any point of resupply. The target practice had to end.

Charles took my intervention well, though he flung the offending rifle into the canoe with a fervent malediction: "First thing I do when we get to a trading post, I throw this overboard and get a good one!"

So ended our association with the river dogs.

Although at the time I was sorry we failed to get a specimen, now I am glad. Had we managed to kill one, its skin and skull would have been minutely studied at some academic sanctum and then, properly identified and catalogued, another living mystery would have been laid to rest amongst a multitude of dusty relics and desiccated facts.

Science would have been served ... and so would Death.

CHAPTER TWENTY-THREE

KUMIUT

BEYOND THE BAY OF SEALS, BIG RIVER SPREAD itself to half a mile in width, becoming shallow and boulder-studded, though still running very fast. For the umpteenth time I was thinking to myself that any attempt to travel upstream would be a Herculean task, when Windy sounded his whitewater alarm. No rapids were in evidence, but far ahead of us we could make out two peculiar-looking objects seemingly suspended between wind and water. As we drew closer they resolved themselves into two very large canoes crawling upstream under sail.

In great excitement Charles started the kicker and headed us full tilt for the strangers, then had second thoughts. Not having encountered human beings since leaving Windy Post and not having even seen an unfamiliar face this side of the Cochrane River, both of us suddenly felt apprehensive. Although reason told us there was probably nothing to fear, primordial instinct suggested otherwise. Who *were* the strangers in these big canoes? Where were they from? How might they react to us?

Charles slowed the motor and nodded toward an islet in midstream.

"Maybe we better wait there 'til they come up." It was not a question, but a declaration.

We headed for the islet, landed, and scrambled to its crest, where, after some hesitation, Charles fired a shot into the air and I waved a paddle in invitation to the strangers to come to us on ground of *our* choosing.

There was no acknowledgement.

Propelled by inadequate sails made of old canvas patched with deer skins, the canoes were making barely perceptible progress. An hour passed before they were abeam of us, hugging the north shore a quarter-mile distant and giving no indication of being aware of our existence. Tension mounted until it became too much for Charles and he fired another shot, this time over the heads of the strangers. They could hardly ignore this direct challenge. Reluctantly, it seemed to me, one canoe began angling out into the stream on a diagonal course directed toward our islet. As it inched its way closer, Charles identified the occupants as Eskimos.

The canoe crawled crabwise toward us, steered by a powerful-looking man with long black hair streaming in the wind. A second, younger man in the bow was paddling energetically to offset the leeward drift. Two women sat amidship, one of them cradling a child. All were dressed in a motley mixture of store clothing and skin garments. They looked to be a wild and uncouth lot.

Their canoe, a twenty-two-foot seagoing model, nosed ashore tentatively on our islet, and the young man leapt overboard to hold the bow in place. None of the other occupants shifted position or even glanced in our direction.

We all seemed frozen in a strange tableau. Charles, rifle still in hand, hunkered down on the crest as if he were part of the islet. The strangers seemed totally absorbed in contemplating the contents of their canoe: rusty metal drums, old stove pipes, broken crates, bundles of deer skins, a clutter of driftwood—and a shiny rifle leaning against the helmsman's thwart, where it would be handy in case of need.

Since nobody else appeared ready to break the impasse, I slid down the slope and with a gesture offered the young man my help in hauling the canoe ashore. When he stepped back in alarm, I nervously stuck out a hand and announced, far too loudly, "HELLO! MY NAME FARLEY! HOW YOU DO DO?"

Do do? Yes, that is what I said. Whereupon the older man in the stern looked me keenly in the eye, smiled the ghost of a smile, and replied in Inuktitut. Stymied, I turned to Charles for help. Ostentatiously laying his rifle aside, he joined me.

What ensued was not markedly dissimilar to a meeting between two unfamiliar wolf packs. All eyes were on Charles and the older Inuk: two alpha males sizing each other up. However, whereas wolves engage in body sniffing, Charles and the Inuk limited themselves to verbal sniffing, the gist of which Charles later passed on to me.

"Says his name's Inoyak, then he say his father's name and his grandfather's. So I tell him my father's name and say my *atatok* [adopted father] was Ihalmiut. So then he says he is Kumiut— that means River People—but he knows about the Ihalmiut, so that's all right. He don't ask no more question about who I am, but he sure must have wondered who *you* is.

"Then we talk a while about the deer: how many we seen; how fat they is. Stuff like that. He say he's going to that camp we saw yesterday to hunt deer and spend the winter. I tell him we're going to Tavanni."

Charles and Inoyak walked a few paces away, leaving Inoyak's son, Alekahaw, and me to get along as best we might. Neither of us could understand a word of the other's language, so we grinned a lot then built a little fire over which to hang the tea billy. Inoyak's two wives, one of whom was old and deeply wrinkled, the other still young and pretty, remained where they were, unmoving and watchful. Charles later remarked with some relish: "They never seen but a couple other whites before, so I guess they didn't want to take no chances with you. Or maybe Inoyak didn't want them to...."

With Charles translating I learned that the Kumiut wintered

in the interior, relying mainly on deer, but in early summer they moved to the coast, where they hunted seals, sometimes white whales, and even an occasional walrus. Inoyak said that in his father's time there had been more than a dozen camps along Big River and its twin stream, the Th'anne, some with as many as fifty people.

"He says them Kumiut never lived on Edehon 'cause there was too many trees there so that was Indian country to them. He says they lived good before traders and white trappers come onto the coast, but after that the people started dying off.

"That dead fellow we found under the canoe was his uncle, one of the biggest men on the river. Now there's only four camps left and maybe forty people. I guess you and me is lucky we meet them before they all be gone."

Inoyak and his companions had been alarmed to see us coming *down* Big River. No strangers had come that way for generations but the Kumiut knew that Indians had descended the river in times past, and remembered that there had sometimes been trouble between the two peoples.

Intrigued by, and a bit jealous of the Kamiuts' ability to bring big canoes up this formidable waterway, I asked Charles how they managed it.

"Mainly because they don't care how long it takes. And the canoes is mostly empty going upstream. Just somebody to steer and maybe some old folk or sick folk. Sail when they can, and when they can't they line them up. Don't do much paddling. Don't haul much freight in them either. Most of the people, and the dogs, walk along the shore carrying most of the gear on their backs. They don't have kickers 'cause gas costs too much, so it takes them a lot of time. But Eskimos got lots of time."

I could now see a string of little figures plodding along the northern shore—fifteen dogs and six human beings—all toting packs. They seemed not to be in any hurry. In fact, their progress seemed more of a leisurely outing than hard traveling.

While we had been talking, the consort canoe had crawled half a mile farther upstream. Inoyak was probably anxious to rejoin her, but did not wish to break away until we had indicated a similar desire. Charles eventually got things moving by giving the women a small packet of tea, which they accepted silently and without looking at him. Inoyak reciprocated with the gift of a pair of eider ducks, after which the Eskimo men got back into their canoe and we pushed them off. The big sail bellied sloppily. As they slowly drew away, Inoyak called out to suggest we stop at his cousin's camp a little farther downstream.

I watched them go with the feeling that an immeasurably distant past was slipping away from me just as I was becoming aware of its existence. I so much wanted to know more about these people out of another age, but the opportunity to spend real time with them would not be mine for another year.

Shortly after leaving the islet, we could probably have shot a seal that was sleeping on a bar in the river . . . had it not turned out to be a doe caribou who had found herself a fly-free sanctuary on which to take a nap. She raised her head negligently, looked at us without concern, then returned to her slumbers.

We landed well above the camp of Inoyak's cousin, taking pains to make considerable fuss so the inhabitants would be warned that strangers were arriving, then walked slowly and noisily toward two tents: a skin topay and a battered canvas wall tent.

A woman peered out through the door flap of the topay as we approached, then vanished and two men emerged. One was Inoyak's cousin, Hanna, a handsome if somewhat flat-faced fellow of middle years clad in worn deerskin clothing. The other was Eetuk, a burly, white-haired elder wearing a faded red cardigan and ragged woolen pants.

This time it was Charles who did the honors on our behalf, extending his hand while mumbling a brief explanation of who we were and where we were from.

The two men could not conceal their uneasiness at hearing we had come from Big River's headwaters. They glanced past us at our canoe and would, I suspect, have been relieved had we returned to it forthwith. When we made no move to do so, Eetuk bravely invited us into the wall tent which was his family's home.

Its furnishings were minimal, consisting principally of a rumpled pile of deerskins serving as the communal bed, a rusty shotgun, a rustier axe, a deer spear, and an ancient wind-up gramophone. A hodgepodge of odds and ends strewn over much of the floor served as playthings for five rambunctious puppies and as a nursing station for their suspicious mother, who showed me a lifted lip as I gingerly stepped past her.

We were diffidently welcomed by Eetuk's robust wife and by a pixie-faced charmer of a ten- or twelve-year-old daughter. They bobbed their heads at us before hustling outside to join Hanna's wife, who was firing up a stove made from an old gas drum, preparatory to cooking us a meal.

In the Ontario town from which I came, Eetuk's daughter would have been considered little more than a child. Here she was a young woman in full bloom, which is how Charles evidently perceived her. Perhaps she fevered his mind with memories of his lost Pama and thoughts of Rita. Although he did nothing overt, he could not keep his eyes off her. I was not the only one to notice. Both Eetuk and his wife observed, and appeared pleased by Charles's all-too-evident interest in their daughter. And why not? Charles was a young man of obvious ability and means, and there could have been few like him left in the wasted Kumiut community.

We four men made ourselves comfortable on the pile of deerskins while dinner cooked. When we handed our tobacco pouches to Eetuk and Hanna, they loaded their pipes then passed them outside to their wives, who lit and enjoyed the first several puffs before smilingly handing them back. It was a small but, I thought, significant gesture of mutual affection and regard.

At length Eetuk's wife brought in a battered copper pot filled with steaming caribou ribs. Hanna's wife contributed a wooden tray heaped with boiled tongues and ready-cracked marrow bones. I was a trifle worried that the suckling bitch might challenge me for possession of a bone, but she contented herself with fixing her pale, amber eyes on my mouth while drooling steadily until I relented and flung her a bone of her own.

By now caution and reserve had vanished, and we were being pelted with questions. Forced to act as translator, Charles hardly had a chance to swallow, so he withdrew into his normal taciturnity leaving me to muddle along as best I could. I resorted to pictography. Using a page torn from my notebook I sketched a river seal and asked for its Inuit name. This led to a heated discussion totally beyond my comprehension so, to occupy myself, I idly drew a pipe in the seal's mouth. Happening to glance at the sketch, Eetuk burst into laughter. The others crowded close to take a look, then followed his lead until they were almost literally rolling on the floor.

I was astonished, then alarmed, as Hanna began to choke, and tears rolled down Eetuk's furrowed cheeks. Hanna's wife had to flee the tent, a hand stuffed into her mouth to stifle her mirth.

In the midst of this hullabaloo (in which the dogs had joined with vigor) the door flap was flung aside and two burly young men appeared, each with a rifle in his hand.

"Now you done it!" Charles muttered in my ear, though, as it turned out, all I had done was establish for myself an instant and stellar reputation as a comic.

The young men were Hanna's and Eetuk's sons. They had been several miles upriver hunting when our canoe went by and had run all the way home. Eetuk's boy, who seemed about eighteen, was the wildest-looking youth I have ever encountered. He had the build and carriage of a bear standing upright. His lank, ebony hair hung in a thick fringe, front and back, curtaining his black and glittering eyes. Mouth and chin projected wolfishly, and hard running had left foam upon his lips.

Someone showed him the seal sketch, whereupon he unleashed a screech which sent the puppies scrambling and a shiver down my back. Then, plunging a hand into a bag slung around his neck, he hauled out a half-plucked ptarmigan and thrust it at me: unmistakably a friendly gift.

Momentum built with the arrival of several people from a nearby camp. Soon all hands, young and old, were engaged drawing fanciful animals on pages torn from my notebook and, when paper ran out, on flat stones. For pencils they used the lead noses of bullets. The creatures they drew included a lemming wearing a white man's peaked hat; a bear aiming a rifle at a surprised Inuk hunter; a hare downing a mug of tea; a bearded animal of inscrutable ancestry bearing some resemblance to myself paddling a canoe backwards down a rapid; and a grinning dog-fox peeing into somebody's cook pot. The mirth these and many other images evoked was unrestrained.

As night came down, we all adjourned to the larger space enclosed by the conical topay, where Eetuk was prevailed upon to produce his drum. This was a skin-covered hoop somewhat resembling a large tambourine. It had a wooden handle with which it could be twirled while being struck on the rim with a short stick. Having first treated us to a deprecatory song about his inadequacies as a hunter and as a lover, Eetuk's mood shifted, becoming more somber as he leapt about with great agility, pounding the drum and chanting plaintively. His dimly seen presence dominated us, and it was not hard to believe he was a shaman possessing a magician's powers, as Charles claimed.

I felt as if I had been transported to a primordial time when human beings had been only one of many creatures sharing a common world more or less on a basis of equality. At one and the same instant I felt like an alien, while experiencing the extraordinary impression that I was somehow returning to an ancient home.

Hours later, lying sleepless in my bedroll waiting for the dawn, my blood still echoed the beat of Eetuk's drum.

We were warmly invited to stay for a prolonged visit, and I would have dearly loved to do so, but Charles would not hear of any delay. Churchill, and Windy Post, were clamoring for him. We had to go.

Eetuk warned us of a bad rapid close ahead, around which we would have to portage, and we had not gone a mile before Windy sounded the alert. We went ashore for a look but, finding no very serious obstacle, elected to run it, which we did with ease. When we reached steady water below, we exchanged some condescending remarks about the timidity of Eskimo canoe men.

Shortly thereafter Windy sounded off again. This time we ignored him and, on rounding the next bend, found ourselves about to be engulfed by a torrent of whitewater thundering down a steep-walled canyon. We had no time even to react before being swept into one of the worst rapids on Big River. We got through it somehow, but in a considerably humbled state of mind.

"Next time," Charles said with conviction, "we going to listen to what them people tell us."

High clay banks hemmed us in for several miles then fell away to reveal a single tent perched on a low hill in the midst of a doleful sweep of rock-strewn country resembling a giant's gravel pit. We went ashore to meet a family of four: a youngish man named Koonik, his wife, and their twin six-year-old sons.

This was a poverty camp. Koonik had neither canoe nor kayak, and there were no deer this close to the coast. He and his family were existing on what fish they could catch from shore with handlines. They told us they had been left here by Inoyak to await the arrival of Koonik's father-in-law in another seagoing canoe. When would he arrive? Nobody knew. He would come when he came.

The wife, a hospitable woman with one extraordinarily blue eye (she may have been blind in it), offered us fish soup. We countered by giving her a hind quarter of deer meat, which she accepted as graciously as if she had been a queen receiving homage from her subjects.

Koonik borrowed a pencil and a piece of paper from me with which to write a letter for us to take to his father-in-law, urging him to hurry up. Painstakingly he drew a series of syllabic symbols that looked to me like hieroglyphics, then, apparently stymied for the right "word," he cast the paper aside and asked for a lift to the coast so he could deliver his message in person.

This was fine by us, for it meant we would have a guide the rest of the way to Hudson Bay and, perhaps, on to Tavanni, although when we inquired how far away Tavanni was, Koonik looked bewildered and shook his head.

"Funny thing," Charles said. "I ask Eetuk how far Tavanni was too and he act like he never heard of the place. Maybe they got a different name for it."

Koonik's wife was not anxious for him to go, and the couple had a heated argument to which their three dogs contributed doleful howls until the wife silenced them with a sibilant hiss. Her hiss seemed to affect Koonik equally powerfully, sending him hustling down to our canoe, where he climbed into the bow without so much as a backward glance at his spouse.

I was now able to sit amidship, with nothing to do but enjoy the passing scene. The sun came out and things warmed up, which turned out to be a mixed blessing. Charles and I had not bathed for many days, nor had we washed our clothing. Nevertheless, we were not in the same league with Koonik, whose winter-worn deerskin clothing had become an almost integral part of him. But it ill behooves the pot to call the kettle black.

Koonik was a willing worker, and he and Charles settled into a paddling rivalry which sent us flying downstream. Stretches of whitewater were fewer and less formidable as Big River, apparently intent now on flooding the entire landscape, broke up into proliferating channels. Koonik directed us into one that flowed along the north mainland shore and, late in the afternoon, suggested we take a break on an island of heaped-up boulders.

Although only a few feet above water level, it was sufficiently high to afford a view over what was evidently a broad estuary and, at a distance of several miles, to see the gray sweep of truly big water extending to the eastern horizon.

Hudson Bay at last! Through binoculars I could even pick out two tiny black rectangles a mile or so inland from the coast which I took to be the buildings at Tavanni.

"Might as well use what gas we got," Charles shouted happily. "We're almost there!"

The relentless current which had held us in its grip for so many days now eased, allowing the Lockwood to propel us sedately over the broad saltwater estuary. Halfway across we came upon a pod of six or seven belugas—white whales—the creatures from which the Thlewiaza took its name. As long and as slim as our canoe, they shimmered like white ghosts in the shoal water within a stone's throw of us. I would have been happy to have spent the rest of the day with them, but we were too near our long-sought objective to delay. As we got closer, it seemed a very queer-looking outpost of the Honourable Company. Here were none of the neat and shiny red-and-white-painted buildings which bear the HBC's hallmark. Instead, we beheld two slouching shacks covered with black tar paper. Nonplussed, I pointed at them.

"Tavanni?" I asked Koonik.

He did not answer, but only waved a hand vaguely in a northerly direction. Charles steered for shore, and as the canoe nosed up on the beach a mob of men, women, and children came pouring out of several tents, shouting cheerfully. Our guide tumbled ashore and, after grinning a thank you at us, vanished into the largest tent with the crowd at his heels.

Charles and I were left to stand and stare.

"Don't look like no trading post to me," said my companion dubiously.

"Well, let's go see if anybody's home."

CHAPTER TWENTY-FOUR

TAVANNI NOT

WE SAW NO SIGN OF LIFE AS WE APPROACHED
the larger of the two buildings, from whose chimney smoke was rising. Small and rather daintily
curtained windows on either side of a heavily planked door
stared unwinkingly. The door did not open. Charles had fallen a
few paces behind, which told me the initiative was all mine.
Hesitantly I knocked.

"Come in, goddamn it!" boomed a cheerful voice.

The door swung open to reveal a large man clad in long
underwear. His face was completely smothered in lather and he
was waving a shaving brush at me with one hand while stuffing
false teeth into his mouth with the other.

"Heard your kicker a while back. Figured to scrape off the
whiskers and put on me best bib and tucker so's I'd look half-
human, but you come on too quick. Don't often get somebody
from outside. Just the natives and they don't hardly count...."

He broke off to glance apologetically at Charles.

"*Huskies*, that is. Shut the door and set you down. Kettle's on
the boil and you byes is likely hungry?"

Self-consciously running a hand through my own scraggly
beard, I introduced Charles and myself.

"I guess you're the trader here, Mister...?"

"Lush. Jarge Lush," he replied, wiping away the lather with a huge yellow towel. "Trader? No, me son. I'se just a common trapper."

"Oh. But there *is* a trader at Tavanni, isn't there?"

"At Tavanni, yiss, bye, but Tavanni's a hunnert and fifty mile up the coast. Nary trader here."

Charles and I exchanged alarmed glances.

"So, how far are we from Churchill, Mr. Lush?"

"Me name is Jarge. Churchill's a hunnert and twenty mile to the south. Say, where the hell you byes come from anyhow . . . the moon?"

When I explained that we had come from Nueltin Lake, he was incredulous at first. During the seventeen years he had lived at the mouth of Big River, no stranger had come down it. Indeed, he had never heard of anyone traveling *up* it beyond Edehon Lake. However, he knew about the Schweders at Windy Post and so was prepared to accept us for what we claimed to be, although he remained baffled as to why we should have thought we would emerge on the coast at Tavanni.

"Lard Jasus, byes, you'se a long ways off course. Suppose this *was* Tavanni, where'd you think you was goin' to go from there?"

I explained that we had hoped to buy grub, gas, and oil to carry us to Churchill.

George Lush burst into uproarious laughter.

"In *that* little pisspot of a canoe? In the fall of the year? Lard livin' Jasus, byes, even seals gets drowned out on the Bay those times. No, me sons, you'd best think again."

"What do you think we ought to do?" I asked anxiously.

"Best make up your minds to stay where you're at 'til after freeze-up. Then the Huskies could sled you to Churchill. They'd be right glad of the chance to make a dollar. Times is right hard 'round the Bay this year. The Company's big boat, *Nascopie*, hit a rock and sunk on her way into the Bay and their smaller one, *Neophyte*, busted her shaft. So everybody's short of most everything.

"In a good year I could've fitted you out for a boat trip down to Churchill if you'd had a boat fit for it, but I can't 'cause I'm short of damn near everything myself. Only place you might be able to find a boat would be Eskimo Point fifty mile to the nor'ard, and the worst fifty mile on Hudson Bay! Don't you even think about it! Anyhow, 'tis time for a scoff."

Further discussion was postponed while George bustled about serving the meal he had been cooking when we arrived. It centered on a slab of boiled bacon spiced with *cloves* and, miracle of miracles, a succulent pie made with molasses, canned butter, and dehydrated apples. Whatever shortages might be plaguing the region, George Lush did not seem to be suffering from them.

Dinner over, I fetched our jug of bug juice, and the three of us were soon immersed in the all-engrossing arctic pastime of exchanging gossip and telling tales. Although I had not given the outer world much thought for several weeks, I was somewhat curious to hear what had been happening during my absence. George owned a powerful battery radio but had little interest in outside affairs.

"You wants to hear all that bullshit as goes on out there, you listen in yourself... but *after* I be pounding me ear in bed!"

So we talked about things that really mattered, such as the shortage of caribou the previous autumn; the price of fur, past, present, and future; and the heinous activities of the Mountie stationed at Eskimo Point who was "hell bent" on halting the production of home brew.

Some people react to a long absence from social contacts by becoming almost mute. Charles was such a one. George Lush was the opposite. Our presence burst his vocal floodgates wide open. He was still talking full-bore at midnight, when Charles and I slunk off to pitch our tent and get some rest. George seemed miffed that we refused a warm offer to share his double bed with him. Not only did it have a box spring but, he told us proudly, it was topped with an "honest-to-God Beautyrest mattress," which had been shipped at great expense all the way from Winnipeg to Churchill by rail, then forwarded by boat.

"Plenty room for all three of we," he had insisted hospitably. "An' I don't care as I has to sleep in the middle."

Born in Newfoundland, George had emigrated to Canada when he was just sixteen looking for a job. In 1930, while still a teenager working as a dishwasher for a rail gang at Churchill, he had met the Buckholtz brothers, Olie and Karl, who, for undisclosed reasons, wanted to disappear. They took George with them to Big River, where they built a shack.

The brothers set out long traplines into the interior: one up Big River and the other up the Th'anne. George, who was inclined toward domesticity, remained at home while the others were off tending their lines. Whenever Olie or Karl returned to the shack, he would enjoy a few days of rest and recreation with George.

This comfortable arrangement endured until one ill-fated day when Karl and Olie both returned on the same day. Both expected to have their creature comforts and pleasures ministered to, and neither was prepared to take second place. In consequence, the odd little ménage à trois at the mouth of Big River disintegrated. Karl and Olie departed in different directions, this time for good, leaving George on his own.

He did not long remain so, but took a crippled Eskimo youth named Arlow as his companion. Arlow learned to speak English and picked up sundry other skills. Nevertheless, he *was* a "Husky," and George yearned for the company of his own kind. Which may explain the warmth of our reception.

With a good deal of help from the Kumiut, George became a fairly effective trapper, though the biggest part of his income came from another, if related source. He constituted himself the Kumiut's middleman, buying their furs, which he shipped out of the Territories to be sold surreptitiously in Winnipeg. Since he held no trader's license, this was illegal, but he was quite unapologetic about it, insisting that "the poor Huskies" got more from him for their fur than they ever would from the monopolistic Hudson's Bay Company.

George owned a superb team of dogs. The leader, a giant white bitch, was fond of putting her paws on his shoulders (George was nearly six feet tall) and licking his ears. For water transport he had a twenty-four-foot canoe fitted with an eighteen-horsepower kicker. Mostly he used the big canoe for trips up the lower reaches of Big River, taking it to sea only during the finest stretches of summer weather.

Over the years he had transformed the original shack into a four-room house nearly as cosily equipped and furnished as those of many a proud housewife in suburbia. The living room, heated by a coal stove, contained an overstuffed chesterfield and two armchairs upholstered in bold floral patterns; a console radio; a gramophone; and a corner knick-knack cupboard. Rose-patterned wallpaper added an almost voluptuous touch.

The *pièce de résistance*, however, was the bathroom. It boasted a cast iron tub, a washstand, and an indoor toilet connected to tin stovepipes that delivered the waste outside, to be disposed of by a family of white foxes George had encouraged to become part of his ménage. He cherished the silky little creatures and was careful to ensure that visiting Eskimos did not trap in the neighborhood.

George maintained a separate building in which he stored the supplies he brought in once a year from Churchill by chartered schooner. A glance inside made it evident that the loss of the Hudson's Bay Company's supply ships had worked little hardship on George Lush. The place was bulging with goods of every kind. Having expressed disapproval of our meager outfit, George delved into this cornucopia to supply us, gratis, with various items of badly needed clothing.

"Summer's over, byes. Dressed like you is, you're like to freeze your knockers off, an' that'd be a crying shame."

He took every opportunity to reiterate that any attempt we

might make to reach either Churchill or Eskimo Point in our eighteen-foot canoe would be suicidal.

"The bestest thing, me sons, is stick with me 'til winter. Us'd have the foinest kind of time."

This was a generous offer but, apart from the fact that we did not have the time to spare, we suspected there might be a catch. When we turned it down, George took the rebuff badly and increasingly became a prophet of doom.

"You wants to go out there on the Bay and drown'd yourselves, I supposes that's your own damn-fool business. But don't you say as I never told you so!"

When we said we had decided to try for Eskimo Point, where it might prove possible to persuade the Eskimo owner of a little motor schooner to make a passage south to Churchill, George snorted and shook his head. It was a hell coast, he told us, bordered by tidal flats never less than three or four miles wide consisting of muck studded with boulders and strewn with shards of ice-shattered rock which would prevent us from getting ashore except at high tide. According to George, there was really only one place between Big River and Eskimo Point where we might safely land, and then only if conditions were just right. This was at the mouth of the McConnel River.

"Suppose a blow catches you before you gits to Eskimo Point and you can't claw into McConnel River, then you've had the biscuit, byes. And this time of the year it'll more'n likely be starmy. Fog. Rain. Snow. At low tide you'll have to stay so far to seaward you'll lose sight of land entirely. No, byes, don't you try it...."

To escape his jeremiad, we went to visit the Kumiut camp, where we found Koonik about to return up Big River with his father-in-law's family. We did not envy them the journey. They would probably have to line their big canoe most of the way to Koonik's camp, wading knee- to thigh-deep in the river. However, this prospect did not seem to bother them. On the contrary, the two men, three women, and four children in the party were as ebullient as if they had been embarking on a picnic excursion.

"Can't hardly wait to get into the deer," was Charles's comment. "They don't like the sea. Rather be up in the country."

He paused to look out over the ominous gray void of Hudson Bay.

"Me too. Only we got no choice."

It was blowing hard from nor'east next morning and the Bay was seething with whitecaps. No small craft could have lived in it. Resigning ourselves to being weather-bound, I went hunting ptarmigan while Charles occupied himself methodically dismantling and overhauling the Lockwood. I found no ptarmigan but saw and envied countless flocks of waterfowl streaming southward. There could be no doubt that summer was at an end. Autumn in the arctic is not much more than a brief interlude. Winter would soon be seizing the land—and sea.

The weather remained impossible through the next several days, and the waiting began to wear on everyone's nerves. Windy brought matters to a head. One evening after a late supper George banged a tin pie plate into the sink and announced, "You byes is welcome to stay so long as you got to, but keep that goddamn bird outta my house. He shits on my floor one more time and the dogs get him!"

With which he stomped off to his Beautyrest, leaving us to twirl the radio dial in search of a weather report.

To our delight we found a forecast amongst the stutter of static, one suggesting there might be passable weather over the Hudson Bay region the following day.

We woke next morning to find a light westerly blowing *off* the land. The big easterly sea that had been running was declining. Hopeful, if apprehensive, we decided to try our luck. We told George of our decision, and somewhat grudgingly he provided us with a "whore's breakfast" of coffee and cigarettes.

"No use to give you nothin' else 'cause if you're bound and determined to go out on the Bay you're goin' to feed the fishes anyhow."

Eventually he relented and gave us a loaf of his excellent bread together with a boiled sea duck to eat en route—should we feel like eating.

The canoe was already loaded, which is hardly the right word since in order to keep her floating as high as possible, we had stripped her of every pound of disposable weight, including most of our personal gear and one of the two sleeping bags. George agreed to send our belongings on to Churchill when an opportunity arose, but thought we were overdoing our efforts to reduce weight.

"You're cuttin' her too fine, byes. Not even a rifle! How the hell you goin' to eat after you gits wrecked?

"Full tide by five o'clock," he added as Charles prepared to start the Lockwood. "Make damn sure you gets ashore at McConnel River when the water's high or you'll be out on the Bay 'til hell freezes over."

With which he turned his back and stomped back to his house.

Two years later George Lush would be carried out of it and taken by schooner to Churchill suffering from intestinal troubles. He never returned to Big River.

Our departure was not as dramatic. The tidal flats at the mouth of Big River extend several miles to seaward and, although the tide was rising, the Lockwood's tail fin ticked ominously on unseen rocks as we sought deeper water. By the time we found it we were four or five miles offshore and had lost sight of the low-lying mainland. Meanwhile the sky had darkened and the wind was rising and veering to the southwest.

We were pitching through a nasty chop with spray breaking over the bow when Charles shouted, "Maybe...oughta go back...try later..."

I did not feel heroic. "Goddamn right!" I yelled. At which he pushed the tiller hard over and a moment later we were pounding into a head sea back toward Big River. But then solid water, as opposed to mere spray, began coming in over the bow—more water than we could handle no matter how hard I bailed. As a wave broke full over me, Charles opened the throttle and turned downwind.

Seeking refuge in Big River's entrance was no longer an option, nor could we hope to reach the coast to the west or the northwest until the tide rose sufficiently to flood the intervening flats.

Wind-driven spray now became a serious problem. Exposed to the weather as it was, the Lockwood's spark plug could handle freshwater spray, but salt water could and did short it out and kill the motor. The first time this happened I thought my heart would stop. However, by drying the hot spark plug with his hand, Charles got the motor going again. Temporarily. It stopped at least a dozen times during the succeeding hour. Each time it did so the canoe blew off to the eastward, where the nearest land was more than five hundred miles away. The sensation of being helplessly carried out to sea was almost too much to endure, but endure we must.

Charles finally solved the ignition problem by stripping off his canvas parka and wrapping it around the head of the engine. As a consequence he soon became chilled to the bone, for the air temperature was only a few degrees above freezing. I was somewhat better off because we were taking so much water that I had to bail almost continuously and the exercise helped keep me warm.

Every few miles we encountered an out-thrust tongue of rocks, a kind of natural groin which forced us seaward. These perilous detours into the growing turmoil of the Bay outraged every survival instinct. I felt as if we were connected to the land by an unseen elastic filament stretched to the breaking point. Charles must have felt something similar because he began cutting too close to the ends of the barrier reefs, until we struck one while running at full throttle.

Although the shear-pin broke, it was not able to entirely save the propeller, one of whose twin blades was badly twisted. While I tried frantically to prevent us being blown seaward, Charles hauled the motor in over the stern, replaced the pin, and hammered the blade back into some semblance of its proper shape. This took perhaps twenty minutes, during which time we blew a further mile or two out into Hudson Bay. It felt like a thousand miles, and I thought we were finished. So we probably would have been had not the Lockwood started again at the first pull. Nevertheless, the distortion of the propeller resulted in considerable loss of power, and we were able to inch our way back toward the unseen land only by means of the combined efforts of the kicker and our paddles.

Land was only occasionally visible as a diffuse and wavering line of darker gray. Looking toward it was rather like peering at the edge of a mirror upon which a few flyspecks floated. The flyspecks were in fact gigantic boulders rising out of an otherwise-unseen coastal bog. They were of no use in helping us determine where we were in relation to McConnel River, or anywhere else.

By five o'clock, when we should have been abeam of that river, we were still literally and figuratively at sea. Though we crowded in as close behind the rising tide as we safely could, the enigmatic loom of the still-distant mainland had nothing useful to tell us. Not daring to go farther in, we blundered on toward the north.

Periodically the Lockwood ran out of gas. To prevent salt water getting into the tank while refueling, Charles had to haul the engine inboard. This took precious minutes during which we would be blown seaward. The third or fourth time this happened he bawled at me, "Guess...missed McConnel River...only chance now...Eskimo Point...*if* we see it."

We knew we simply *had* to get ashore somewhere, and soon. Neither flesh and blood nor the indomitable old Lockwood could endure much more. The tide was now almost full, and at this juncture we saw what looked like a low butte floating on the northwestern horizon. Resolutely Charles headed in toward it.

"Watch out for rocks!" he yelled unnecessarily.

My best efforts to obey were not enough to save us. Minutes later a big comber lifted the canoe then dropped her with a sickening crunch upon a reef of kelp-slimed boulders.

Thank God for the kelp! Without it she would assuredly have been shattered. Both of us leapt overboard to drag her forward until we could wedge her between two half-submerged rocks where we could hope to prevent further damage until the tide turned and began to fall.

Hudson Bay's tides run large and swift. Thankfully, the canoe was soon high and dry and we were able to examine her wounds. Several more ribs had been broken and a long strip of canvas hung from her bottom, but she would live to float again—when the incoming tide returned long hours later.

Night was falling, but it was not yet dark enough to veil a dismal scene. The retreating waters uncovered a stinking waste of mud and rocks shot through with shallow rivulets of icy water. This desolation extended from the isolated reef upon which we were marooned as far as we could see in all directions.

The cold was stupefying. Our clothing was soaked. The only shelter that might have been available to us would have been under the upturned canoe, but we did not dare turn her over for fear the rising tide would catch her like that, so we unrolled our one sodden sleeping bag on the wet floorboards and huddled into it.

Eventually I shivered myself into a half-doze—to be awakened by a pelting rain that froze as it fell. This was too much for Windy, who had squeezed himself under the tiny foredeck. He scuttled aft to spend the rest of that dreadful night squished against my head.

It was indeed dreadful—though nothing to what it would have been had we been adrift on the unforgiving wastes of the Bay.

The tide began to rise and by 2:00 a.m. the canoe was afloat, yet we dared not push off until the light returned. The cold was intense enough to form a skim of ice on our container of drinking water; however, I had no desire to drink or to eat. I was too cold even to piss.

Dawn breaking under the edge of a leaden overcast revealed what we optimistically took to be a ragged shoreline, though it would prove to be a range of distant hills some miles inland. Charles wrapped the starter cord around his right hand—his fingers being too stiff to grasp it—and the engine caught on the second try. We were under way, but the sou'west wind, which had fallen out during the night, began to rise again, and soon the sea was building.

Almost immediately we encountered another finger reef. This one forced us well over a mile to seaward before letting us past. It was followed by another, and yet another. Rain drove down, became sleet, and finally obscured the world in snow squalls. After several hours of this dicing with the devil, we were stopped by a reef stretching eastward farther than any of its predecessors.

Our resolution failed. The prospect of being rendered helpless by a conked-out engine and swept out to sea as we attempted to weather this barrier was too much to face.

Fortunately it was a relatively narrow reef so, in our desperation, we determined to lift over it. This required both of us to go overboard and haul the canoe through a jumble of rocks and a smother of breaking seas. At length we stumbled upon an islet composed of slippery boulders projecting a foot or so above the chaos. Hauling ourselves out on this queasy eminence, we lay like a couple of exhausted seals.

As if on cue, the rising wind, now blowing half a gale, tore a hole in the storm scud to reveal a cluster of white buildings on the horizon several miles to the northwest.

Eskimo Point was finally in view, but we had still to reach it.

Scrabbling the rest of the way across the reef we launched the canoe. But this time the Lockwood refused to start. There was nothing for it but for one of us to jump overboard and become a living anchor. This became my task while Charles tried to work a miracle on the outboard. Standing waist-deep I found myself barely able to prevent the canoe from blowing out to sea, and I gave way to panic. I screamed that we must abandon her and try to make our way ashore on foot.

Charles would have none of that.

"Be drowned before we got halfway!" he shouted in reply. "Hang on, Farley! Engine's *got* to go!"

My grip on the gunwale was slipping when the kicker finally caught. Charles had to help me back aboard with his free hand while steering with the other. With the motor running at full throttle, it took us an hour and a half to make good the distance we had lost. Meanwhile a snow squall blew over and Eskimo Point vanished from sight.

Wind and waves were increasing steadily and I could no longer hear what Charles was yelling so I crawled aft.

"Not going to make it this way!" he shouted. "Only chance we got now is cut straight for shore!"

Too numb to reply, I only nodded. The canoe swung into the steep troughs and headed across the flats, which were being drained both by the falling tide and the pressure of the offshore gale.

I thought it could only be a matter of minutes before the Lockwood smashed into the rocks, but I no longer cared all that much. I only wished that, one way or another, the ordeal would end.

At long last came a rift in the storm scud, revealing a shoreline less than a quarter of a mile distant. And almost unbelievably it was *solid land* fronted by sandbanks as high as houses, covered with waving grass.

Soon thereafter our dauntless little vessel took the ground— not on rending rocks but on a bed of yielding sand.

Charles and I clambered stiffly ashore, dragged her well up beyond reach of the hungry seas, and turned her over. That done we both stood motionless, like clockwork toys whose springs have run down.

I do not know how much time passed before Charles half-whispered the simple epilogue:

"Well, I guess we done it."

PART SEVEN

AFTERMATH

CHAPTER TWENTY - FIVE

CHARLES

LEAVING THE CANOE WITH ALL OUR GEAR stashed beneath it, Charles and I happily walked across some miles of muskeg to the little settlement of Eskimo Point, which consisted of a Hudson's Bay Company store, two mission stations, an RCMP post, and the tents and shacks of a score of coastal Eskimos.

For a while it appeared we would be marooned here until November, when a dog team might be found to take us two hundred miles south to Churchill. Certainly there was no way we were going to be able to complete the journey by water, not under our own steam at any rate. As Charles put it with unusual fervor, "You see me heading onto Hudson Bay in a canoe, you shoot me first!"

Nor were we able to persuade the native owner of a motor schooner, who was even then preparing to haul it out for the winter, to attempt the passage.

"You too late," he told us firmly. "Ice come soon."

Without much hope I sent off a shortwave radio message from the Company post to the officer in charge of the Canadian section of Fort Churchill. Colonel Donald Cameron had been my C.O. during the Italian campaign. He still remembered me and, noblesse oblige, arranged for an RCAF Norseman on floats to pick us up.

So it came about that Charles, Windy, and I arrived at Churchill on time, and in some style.

Other journeys now awaited us.

I needed to return to Ontario to begin my second year at university, and Charles could barely contain his anxiety to get back to Windy Post, partly because (as he now openly admitted) he was afraid Fred "don't keep his promise."

There were difficulties to be overcome. We learned that Johnny Bourassa had crashed his yellow banana, and though he himself had survived more or less undamaged, the old Anson was a write-off and Peace River Airlines was out of business.

Although Johnny's luck and guts had carried him through the war years, luck was running out.

On May 18, 1951, he took off from Fort Reliance at the east end of Great Slave Lake flying a single-engine Bellanca on skis. His destination was a nameless lake not far from Ennadai where he was to pick up two prospectors.

An hour out of Reliance, the weather closed in and falling snow cut visibility almost to the vanishing point. For a time Bourassa continued eastward on a magnetic compass bearing, but magnetic variation interfered and he unwittingly drifted well to the south of his intended course.

To make matters worse his radio failed, preventing him from getting a position fix. With the ceiling down to a few hundred feet, he turned the little Bellanca and fled in what he believed was the direction of Fort Reliance. However, when snow began blotting out all sight of the ground below, he wisely decided to "set down" until the storm abated.

He made an emergency landing on what he took to be a frozen pond but which in reality was a patch of very rough ice near the southern shore of Wholdaia Lake, a vast and convoluted body of water 150 miles west of Windy Post.

It was a hard landing. By the time the Bellanca clattered to a stop, both skis had been shattered, leaving the plane unable to take off again until they could be replaced. Johnny hauled his small tent and emergency supplies out of the cabin, made camp in a patch of scrubby spruce, and prepared to wait out what had become a tearing blizzard.

He waited in the expectation that when the weather cleared an aerial search for him would begin. Perhaps he believed this would be "a piece of cake" and he would soon be found. What he did not realize was that he was almost a hundred miles south of the flight plan he had filed before leaving Fort Reliance, and nearly as much to the east of where he believed himself to be.

The storm abated, to be followed by warm days and good flying weather—yet no planes appeared in the high sky and there was not even a distant vibrato of aircraft engines. Two weeks dragged by, and Johnny must have realized the search would soon be abandoned. He waited another few days and then, when there was still no sight or sound of a search plane, he scribbled a note, which he left in the pilot's seat, shouldered his pack, and set out to *walk* to Fort Reliance.

No tyro, he must have been aware of the odds against him. Break-up had now begun, and the Land of Little Sticks had become a morass of raging rivers, overflowing lakes, saturated muskegs, and sodden snowdrifts. Even caribou struggled through it with difficulty. At best, a man on foot could manage only a very few miles a day.

The fact that Johnny set out for Reliance, two hundred miles distant, instead of trying to reach the army station at Ennadai or the settlements on eastern Lake Athabasca, all three of which were much closer to the downed Bellanca, shows how far astray he was in his own mind. Eventually he must have realized he was lost in a vastness so nearly absolute there could be no escape.

Three and a half months later the abandoned Bellanca was spotted from the air by a photo-survey plane. The RCAF mounted another search for the missing pilot, although in truth nobody expected him to be found alive. In the event, the searchers did not find even his body.

The collapse of Peace River Airlines had resulted in its commitment to the Keewatin Zoological Expedition being transferred to Gunnar Ingebritson's Arctic Wings.

We sought out Gunnar, to be told he had not received any instructions to pick Harper up in mid-September, nor would he be able to do so since he was fully booked to the end of that month.

Charles went off to stay with his father and siblings in Churchill. At Colonel Cameron's request, I agreed to spend a few days at the military camp preparing a report on the country Charles and I had traveled through. Early one morning the colonel unexpectedly called to tell me an RCAF Lancaster would be leaving for Ottawa in an hour's time and had room aboard for me.

It was an offer I could not refuse, even though it meant departing without saying goodbye to Charles. I wrote him a quick note, then hustled out to the airfield.

Windy rode with me to Ottawa and on to my parents' house in Richmond Hill, where he spent the winter living the life of Riley on chopped steak and chicken parts. In the spring of 1948 he accompanied me back to Churchill and into the barrenlands again. Although his flight feathers had regrown by then and he could fly well, he refused to go his own way—and one autumnal morning I emerged from my tent to find him lying dead beside the doorway without a mark upon him. Perhaps he had no wish to go "outside" with me again.

Charles, stranded in Churchill, was not only worried about what might be happening at Windy Post, he was increasingly concerned about what would happen to the Ihalmiut if no ammunition reached them before the migrating caribou abandoned the barrens for the winter.

Soon after he and I had arrived at Churchill, we had gone together to the RCMP detachment headquarters to apprise the authorities of the Ihalmiut's precarious situation. There we were told not to worry, that if necessary a police patrol would deliver a plane-load of emergency supplies. Charles was not reassured.

"I think the Mounties figure I'll look after the people, then they don't have to make a patrol," was how he expressed his fears.

After my departure his unease increased. He pestered Ingebritson so intensely that the pilot finally agreed to attempt a flight on September 14.

With drums of spare fuel taking up nearly half the cargo space, the Norseman lifted off carrying less than a thousand pounds of "payload." With Charles's guidance Gunnar found the way to Nueltin despite a heavy overcast and splashed down heavily on the bay below Windy Post.

Francis Harper was not at all pleased to see the plane. Flatly denying that he had ever authorized a change in the agreed-upon October 20 pick-up date, he refused to accept any responsibility for this flight, which left the Schweders on the hook for the charter fee. Not only did he refuse to leave Windy at this time, but now that the post had been resupplied he also decided to postpone the expedition's pick-up date until November to give himself plenty of time to see the southbound passage of the rutting caribou bucks.

Gunnar warned him that freeze-up would almost certainly arrive before then, and that the consequential "no-fly" interval, during which bush planes could not operate either on skis or floats, might delay a pick-up flight well into December. Harper was adamantly determined to remain.

So Gunnar returned to Churchill laden with nothing except the gear I had left at Windy Post before setting out down Big River. He was convinced, as he told me later, that Harper was "crazy as a coot. I'd have liked to leave the old bugger there for good, but I couldn't do that to Charley and the kids."

This new change in plan was not all bad news for Charles. He was at least assured of another load of supplies when Gunnar did return to pick up Harper. He also had hopes of persuading Fred to fly out then, thereby resolving the conflict between himself and his brother over Rita, which, as he had feared, had not been resolved during his absence.

Meanwhile he had to get Windy Post back into shape while making preparations for the oncoming winter. These included laying up quantities of fish and deer for people and dogs, gathering wood for fuel and repairs, and preparing his outfit for the trapping season. He also had to deal with Harper's demands upon his time and substance, demands which became ever more imperious as the days drew on.

Windy Post was not a happy home. On October 19 Charles wrote in his diary: *Oh God give me strength and courage so that I can do it.*

Taking Rita with him, he spent as much time as possible away from the cabin, sometimes at a fish camp on Simmons Lake, sometimes on deer-hunting trips out on the barrens.

Heavy snow arrived late in October. Early in November Charles and Rita were able to set off for the north by dog sled to see how the Ihalmiut were faring, and to prepare the traplines. They found the Ihalmiut had exhausted the limited supply of ammunition Charles had been able to bring back for them on the September flight, without being able to secure sufficient deer to ensure their survival through the remainder of the winter.

Not until December 4 was Arctic Wings' Norseman, now on skis, able to return to Windy, bearing a skimpy load of supplies for the post put aboard by Fred Schweder Sr. It also brought a letter from Fred telling Charles there appeared to be no likelihood of a government patrol being made, and instructing him that unless trapping prospects were exceptionally good he should abandon Windy Post and bring himself and his brothers out to Churchill on Harper's flight.

The weather was dubious that day. Anxious to get back to base, Gunnar allowed Charles less than an hour to make up his mind what to do. In the event, the decision was taken out of his hands when Harper concluded he needed all the Norseman's cargo space for his own equipment and specimens, which now included several hundred pounds of caribou antlers. There would be no room for the Schweder boys.

In some ways Charles was relieved. But he was also apprehensive that without the promised government supplies he might not be able to provide for many hungry, perhaps starving, Eskimos. Black memories of the previous winter came crowding back upon him.

Although as the December nights grew longer, fears for the future dominated Charles's thoughts, things did not go too badly at Windy Post during the remainder of the month. Charles and Fred established a kind of truce, and Harper's departure had removed an onerous presence as well as a serious drain on dwindling supplies. However, when, near the end of December, Charles went north to run his trapline he found the Ihalmiut already short of food. Though he was able to give them some additional ammunition, very little now remained in the land for them to shoot. Furthermore, there were very few foxes to be trapped.

In January of 1948 Charles, accompanied by Anoteelik, reluctantly undertook the long sled trip to Duck Lake for more supplies and—echoes of the previous grim winter—to again report the Eskimos were starving. A message to this effect was duly transmitted to Churchill by the Hudson's Bay Company outpost manager.

By the end of February, supplies at Windy Post were in perilously short supply, and the cabin was besieged by needy Ihalmiut for whom Charles could do little or nothing. His resources, both internal and external, were almost exhausted.

By mid-March he had reached the end of his tether. With Fred, Mike, Anoteelik, Rita, and two dog teams, he set out to break trail across the still-winter-bound barrens. In early April, after an epic journey, the little group reached Churchill.

I spent the winter of 1947–48 sporadically attending university classes while devoting much of my time to organizing a new expedition to the barrenlands. I persuaded a biology student, Andy Lawrie, and a young photographer, Bill Carrick, to join with me and Charles in making a study of and a film about the caribou, and I arranged with the Arctic Institute for a small grant-in-aid-of. All seemed to be going well until the federal Department of Northern Affairs reviewed the matter and concluded it should itself undertake the caribou study. Lawrie and I were offered minor roles in the Department's plan, with the clear implication that, should we refuse, we would be denied official permission to go north. The Arctic Institute thereupon withdrew its support of my proposal.

Having no real choice in the matter, we accepted the Department's fiat, and in mid-May of 1948 Lawrie and I flew to Churchill, where we found Charles working on a construction site. Although he was willing and indeed anxious to accompany us, his father now refused to let his eldest son and most lucrative source of income do so.

Learning that Lawrie and I would be flying to the Kazan country, the RCMP asked us to take in a load of "relief supplies" for the Ihalmiut that had been sitting in storage since the previous autumn. Dutifully we added a drum of dried milk, a sack or two of white beans, a couple of camp stoves, and a bundle of axes to the load aboard Gunnar Ingebritson's Norseman, and took off.

Lawrie and I spent that summer in the Ihalmiut country. In October I flew south to Brochet to study caribou and wolves on winter range. My employment with the Department, and my potential career as a biologist, ended in January of 1949, when I was fired for paying too much attention to the situation of the Idthen Eldeli and the Ihalmiut, and not enough to science.

Early in the winter of 1949 Charles was hired, on the strength of my recommendation, to Colonel Cameron, to guide a military expedition from Churchill to the northern end of Ennadai Lake, where a radio and weather station was to be built for the Royal Canadian Signal Corps. Charles took his trapping outfit and dog team with him, and Anoteelik was also allowed to go along.

Until 1949 the interior barrenlands had been accessible only to canoes and dog teams or to float- and ski-equipped aircraft. None of these would have been able to move the tons of supplies needed to establish the new station. Nothing less than a ship, or a train, could have done the job.

A train now came into being at Churchill. It was composed of Caterpillar tractors towing strings of heavy sleds. Such "cat trains" had been used in the boreal forests before but had never operated in the Keewatin Barrens, which in winter resembled a congealed ocean corrugated by frozen waves. The military intended to penetrate this icy void to a distance of about three hundred air miles, which would be more like four hundred over the ground, with the tractors having to pick their way across unmapped country, navigating largely by compass. They would, however, have Charles Schweder as their pilot.

Early in January four D-6 tractors, each towing a string of heavily laden freight sleds with a heated caboose for the crews, ground their way out of Churchill. Traveling day and night, the lumbering argosy crawled northward along the coast of Hudson Bay for a hundred miles before swinging westward into a frozen wilderness which had never seen their like before.

Charles and Anoteelik reconnoitered ahead by dog sled. Blizzards halted progress for days on end. Breakdowns required repairs to be effected in the open at temperatures as low as minus forty degrees Fahrenheit. One of those who made the journey remembered: "It was kind of like Scott might have felt trying to reach the South Pole. Only *he* never had D-6s to haul his grub and gear."

The journey took seventeen days and nights. On reaching the objective the sleds were hurriedly unloaded and the train turned back for Churchill. Charles accompanied it as far as the Kazan, where he dropped off with his dogs and outfit, intending to spend the remainder of the winter trapping foxes along his old line to the north, using the Kazan travel camp as his base.

He was alone because Anoteelik had left the train at the construction site, where some of his Ihalmiut relatives had appeared. When these people had returned to their own winter camps, Anoteelik had gone with them.

Charles's hopes of again becoming part of the land and of a cherished way of life proved short-lived. There was now a different ambience in the camps of the Ihalmiut. He was welcomed into their snow-banked, deerskin topays, but perhaps because of what Anoteelik had to tell them, was no longer regarded as one of them. Furthermore, he had lost his once-faithful acolyte, Anoteelik, who had joined the family of Owliktuk, one of the most effective of the Ihalmiut survivors. Ano would follow Charles no more.

Unendurably lonely, Charles drove his team south to Windy Post—to find a dark, dank wooden crypt concealed under mountainous drifts. He burrowed down to the cabin but found it had become a snake-pit of the mind, writhing with intolerable memories of Pama and of his mother, Rose. Unable to bear the place, and yearning disconsolately for Rita, he soon fled north again to his tiny trapping cabin near the Kazan.

When, a few weeks later, the cat train made a second trip to Ennadai, Charles joined it for the return journey to Churchill. Never again would he see Windy Post, nor would he ever return to the land of the Ihalmiut.

In Churchill Charles relapsed into subservience to his father as a wage-earner for a family which was soon enlarged by the arrival from Germany of Fred Schweder Sr.'s sister, Freeda (as she signed herself).

Freeda became the domineering mistress of the household, and a singular character amongst Churchill's rich assortment of characters. She is said to have openly and proudly acknowledged having worked in a Nazi camp for the "re-education" of gypsies and other such benighted people. Certainly she showed little empathy for the native people she encountered in Churchill.

Until as late as 1952 Charles still hoped to return to what, in one of his infrequent letters to me, he called "my country."

His father was implacably opposed. Fred Schweder Sr. believed Charles could make a better living in Churchill. And he was probably correct, in money terms, for the palmy days of the fur trade were certainly drawing to an end.

In the early spring of 1952 something occurred to revive Charles's hopes and dreams. He was offered a job with another expedition bound into the barrenlands—an investigation of southern Keewatin by the Canadian Geological Survey. Despite his father's opposition, Charles seized this opportunity.

It brought him little joy.

During the ensuing summer he was flown to a score of sites, mostly well to the east of the Ihalmiut country, where he served as cook, chore boy, and general factotum to a party of geologists and other scientists. He had no time to wander on his own. As he put it in one of his last letters to me: "I might just as well stay in Churchill. At least some of my own people is there to talk to."

He stopped writing soon thereafter, and for a time I lost track of him.

Nineteen fifty-four brought another major disruption into Charles's life. He was separated from Rita by the threat of criminal action unless he took himself out of her life. When, soon afterwards, Fred Schweder Sr. found it expedient to leave Churchill in a hurry and flee to Winnipeg, Charles went with him—fleeing from his own demons.

In Winnipeg Charles met a woman who was able to assuage at least some of his needs. He took her back with him to Churchill, where she produced eight children—six of them by 1961.

For the remainder of his life, Charles worked at whatever was offered, wherever it was offered. He was by turns a construction worker on arctic DEW Line sites; a miner in northwestern Ontario; a laborer in Churchill; and, for a good portion of the time, one of the unemployed. The monthly Family Allowance payments for eight children, together with relief and other social subsidies, made it possible for him and his family to survive in their cramped and cluttered Churchill home.

He lived his final years in ill health, within sight of the barrenlands. Sometimes he would take a few rusty old traps and make his way to the edge of the great plains—to the verges of what had once been his country. And perhaps in his mind he again became a man of the land.

Charles Schweder died at Churchill in 1994.

A stranger in a strange place.

CHAPTER TWENTY-SIX

RITA

B Y 1947 THE FRONTIER VILLAGE OF CHURCHILL had become a squalid garrison town dominated by the U.S. and Canadian military presence at nearby Fort Churchill. Much of its hurriedly built assemblage of gimcrack shacks was occupied by camp followers of one kind or another. There were a few Chipewyans confined to an abysmal ghetto, but the majority of the inhabitants were transient whites, often of dubious antecedents and shadowy professions.

On reaching Churchill in the spring of 1947, Fred Schweder Sr. had rented a shanty for himself, his youngest son, Norman, and his two attractive daughters, twenty-year-old Mary and eighteen-year-old Else. The subsequent arrival in 1948 of Charles with Fred junior, Mike, and two Eskimo children crammed the shanty to the bursting point.

Fred senior viewed Rita and Anoteelik as unexpected and unwanted bodies for him to feed and shelter. Both were banished to an old tent during the summer of 1948, and Anoteelik spent the first half of the following winter sleeping in a snow house of his own contriving. Both were expected to earn their keep—and more. Of the two, Rita may have received somewhat better treatment, not only because of her relationships with Charles and Fred junior but also because she had greater potential earning power than her brother, who had been put to work as a sweeper in the government grain elevator.

As we have seen, Anoteelik escaped from this servitude by returning to his own people. Rita was afforded no such opportunity although, had she been, it is by no means certain she would have accepted. After her experience in the winter of 1946–47, working as a drudge in the Schweder household may have seemed preferable to life in the Kazan camps.

Rita was nothing if not adaptable. She had to have been to have survived her first six years, and she continued to be. She was baptized into the Roman Catholic church by the local Oblate missionary, and even began a sometime attendance at the local day school, where she did well when she was present. Much of her time was consumed doing the Schweder family's chores, and the rest was increasingly at the disposal of soldiers whose playground the village of Churchill was. Despite her obvious youth, a good number of men in uniform took a fancy to this, the first Eskimo they had ever encountered. Rita responded, for she had reason to believe that only by doing so could she avoid the fate which had engulfed her mother, sister, younger brothers, and so many others of her people.

Her situation was not improved when Fred Schweder Sr. became a bootlegger and his house became a rendezvous for soldiers on pass looking for a good time. Rita was expected to treat the customers well, and if she failed to please, she was at risk. One day Mike Schweder found her hanging by the neck from a beam in an outhouse. No official investigation of this incident was ever made, and Rita would never afterwards say whether it was attempted suicide or something worse.

She quit school in Grade 4 after having been sexually assaulted by a school employee. Although this incident *was* investigated by the RCMP, no charge was laid.

Rivalry between Fred junior and Charles for Rita's affections continued. This, and conflict between Charles and his father's customers, eventually drove Charles to take Rita out of his father's house and try to make a home with her elsewhere. Else, who was sympathetic to the plight of the Eskimo girl, later claimed Charles wanted to marry Rita but was prevented from doing so by Fred senior, who, apart from rejecting the idea on racial grounds, seems to have been afraid a marriage would attract unwanted attention from the authorities because Rita was still very much a minor.

This was indeed so obvious that some of the few moral stalwarts in town did complain about the situation to the police, and in 1954, when she was eleven or twelve years old, the authorities belatedly intervened in Rita's life.

The RCMP informed Charles he must either hire a housekeeper or send Rita to live with a decent family; otherwise, he would find himself facing charges of molesting a minor.

One of those outraged by the situation was Amelia Pratt, a Cree married to a Saulteaux employed by the military at Fort Churchill. Both were activists in native causes. They now took Rita into their own extended family. However, when it became apparent that Charles was not going to sever his connections with her, the Pratts decided to send her to a boarding school where she would be beyond his reach.

In the autumn of 1955 the Muskeg Special carried Rita south to Hudson Bay Junction, from which she traveled west to St. Michael's, a Roman Catholic residential school for natives at Duck Lake on the Saskatchewan prairies, a thousand miles from Rita's homeland.

Here she was a stranger and alone. There were no other Eskimo inmates. Now almost fully developed physically, Rita retained the effervescent attractiveness of childhood without having acquired any effective means of protecting herself against those who would exploit it. And there were many such in St. Michael's, where she was abused, sexually and otherwise.

During the winter that followed, Rita began having what staff members of St. Michael's described as "fits." When, in the spring of 1957, she attempted to commit suicide, perhaps for the second time, St. Michael's shipped her off to Winnipeg as a problem to be dealt with by the Manitoba authorities.

Sent to a Winnipeg hospital to undergo psychiatric assessment and treatment, she experienced one of the happiest interludes in her life. The staff there made much of her. As she would later tell me, "They sure liked having a Eskimo girl. First one they ever see. That's when I make up my mind to be a nurse if I can."

Early in January of 1958, after having enjoyed the best Christmas she had ever known, she was returned to Churchill with a diagnosis of severe epilepsy, for which a heavy dosage of barbiturates had been prescribed. She was nevertheless able to get a waitress's job at Torchy's Café. She lived with the Pratts and it was in their crowded home that I found her that summer on my return from a harrowing journey into the barrenlands to investigate the fate of her people.[1]

What I saw and heard at the Pratts' was shocking, though it did not come as a complete surprise. During my travels with Charles, I had harbored suspicions as to the nature of his relationship with Rita and had even, reluctantly, considered the possibility that he might have been her lover. But I had chosen to suppress such suspicions, partly because of my high regard for the man but also because such treatment of a child was virtually unthinkable according to the mores of the world in which I had been reared. So I had concluded that Rita was Charles's daughter and that his concern and affection for her were paternal.

Now I had to grasp the nettle.

Rita, who by then was fifteen and had not seen me for ten years, greeted me as if we had parted only yesterday. I wrote in my journal:

[1] See Farley Mowat, *Walking on the Land*, Key Porter Books, Toronto, 2000.

She bounced all over me like an irrepressible puppy. When I told her I had recently met her brother Anoteelik, his wife, Aijai, and their two small sons at Eskimo Point she was ecstatic. She had not known for sure if he was even still alive. "I go see them right away!" she cried. But all the time we talked her hands never stopped trembling and her eyes were as black and unrevealing as pools of asphalt.

She talked without apparent bitterness and with a kind of childish naïveté of her life since leaving Windy Post. It was such an appalling story that I might have rejected its worst aspects had they not been confirmed by the Pratts and others.

At Mrs. Pratt's urging, Rita exposed not only many of her psychic scars but some of her physical ones as well, including a six-inch scar on her scalp from a gash inflicted, she told me, by one of the Schweders wielding a skillet to teach her a lesson in obedience.

While in Churchill on this occasion, I had intended to get in touch with Charles. I changed my mind when I was told that only a few weeks earlier he had accosted Rita from a taxi being driven by his brother Fred and tried to pull her into the vehicle. She had fled to the Pratts' house, where she succumbed to such a severe seizure that Mrs. Pratt was forced to pry the girl's mouth open in order to drag her tongue out and so prevent her from swallowing it and choking to death. Mrs. Pratt then had to skewer Rita's outthrust tongue with a fork to prevent her re-swallowing it while she was being driven to the nursing station. The doctor there recommended she be returned to hospital in Winnipeg.

Unable now to stomach the prospect of meeting Charles, I went to see Northern Service Officer Bill Kerr, a newly appointed representative of the Department of Northern Affairs who had been sent to Churchill as part of an attempt to rectify the federal government's long neglect of the Inuit. I intended to tell Kerr about Rita's recent trouble with Charles, but he already knew about the incident and had, in fact, reported it to the police. Furthermore, he was in the process of arranging for her return to hospital in Winnipeg, "as much to get her out of harm's way as to see what can be done for her medically. The trouble is there is no use laying charges because she's a native and no jury up here would convict without witnesses." This was a phrase I would hear again.

Kerr was also aware of Rita's hopes of some day becoming a nurse, or at least a nurse's aide. When I offered to write a supportive letter, and a synopsis of her history as I knew it, for submission to the Minister of Northern Affairs, he accepted gratefully.

I sent this letter off to the Minister in September. In November I got a response from Kerr's replacement, Robert Kennedy, in which he wrote:

"Rita, or Kunee as you prefer to call her, arrived back in Churchill yesterday [from Winnipeg]. We have finally managed to have her officially recognized as an Eskimo. With that legal stumbling block removed, we are now in a position to attempt to make up to Rita for the years during which we ignored her.

"The psychiatrist to whom she was sent in Winnipeg reported that Rita's epilepsy does not appear to proceed from any specific cause—and certainly not from a physical one. She is back on one of the barbiturates in an attempt to keep her emotions from boiling over too frequently.

"I have recommended to Ottawa that she be given a chance at nurse's aide training—possibly at the Ottawa Civic Hospital. There she could be treated, if necessary, by a psychiatrist while her training is in progress....

"In the meantime she is living with an Eskimo family in Camp 20....

"I'm afraid we know very little more about her background ... certainly much of it must have been sordid. I doubt very much that any charges will be laid in connection with her maltreatment. There were no witnesses, and no jury will convict without some supporting testimony. For the sake of the girl it is probably better to forget the past and concentrate on trying to make her future worthwhile....

"Best regards.

"(R.L. Kennedy) Northern Service Officer"

Camp 20 was by no means as bad a place as the ominous name might suggest. It was principally a center for dealing with increasing numbers of Eskimos who were being sent south for medical treatment, mostly of tuberculosis, or being returned to their distant arctic homes. It also housed some Eskimos who were working at Fort Churchill, and a number who had no homes at all. Rita was amongst the latter. Since she had at last achieved official identity, it had been deemed best that she should live with other Eskimos rather than with the Pratts.

My next news of her came in an unofficial letter from Kennedy dated May 28, 1959.

"I thought you might like a little recent news of Rita. She has had a difficult time since you last saw her but a good many of her troubles are self-inflicted, or perhaps more accurately, as a result of her past unhappy experiences over which she had no control, but you know as much about her past as anyone.

"It proved impossible to get training for her in a hospital because she lacked the minimum education and because of her emotional troubles. She lived with an Eskimo family in Camp 20 for several weeks last winter but this did not work out too well. It's amazing how many men from Churchill and from Fort Churchill find Rita's charms overwhelming. Quite frankly both I and the head of the household in which she lived became tired of throwing men out of Rita's bed around breakfast time.

"Fortunately she evinced a desire to visit her brother [who is now] at Rankin Inlet. Once she arrived her brother made a great fuss over her—so great in fact that his wife became quite upset. Rita was given a room at the school, but a small house was hurriedly built for her after she fell asleep with a cigarette in her hand and narrowly avoided burning down the school.

"Enter Arloo. You may remember him from your Ennadai Lake days.[2] Arloo moved into the house with Rita and before long she announced they were to be married. She made a quick trip to Churchill to pick up the balance of her possessions (plus a mild dose of V.D.). Upon her return to Rankin the date was set and the guests invited. Everyone showed up at the ceremony except Arloo who went hunting instead. About two weeks later, however, he relented and the ceremony was finally performed.

"Now comes a piece of good luck which may be the salvation of both Rita and Arloo. Don Grant, the Rankin N.S.O., scraped together enough material to create a coffee shop and installed Rita and Arloo as proprietors. The venture is financially sound and provided Rita remains happy things stand a good chance...and so, Mr. Mowat, your protégé may well be the first Eskimo entrepreneur in Keewatin."

I tried to keep in touch with Rita by letter, but she wrote only rarely. In June she sent me a neatly typewritten note.

"Well I just came back from hunting with my brother and his wife...but they eat the same thing [ptarmigan] all the time so Arloo and I stay only for one week for hunting because I didn't like the little bugs running around our bed.... And besides I had to go and see the doctor for a needle for my baby which I'll be getting in November.

"I never got a letter from the Pratts any more, I think they are mad with me because I left them.... I'm happy here in Rankin with my brother and Arloo. This is not a very good letter because I haven't anything to say right now."

This was followed in mid-August by a handwritten note.

---

[2] Arloo was a brother of Anoteelik's wife, Aijai. Together with other Ihalmiut survivors, he had been sent to a Department of Northern Affairs rehabilitation camp at the newly established mining town of Rankin Inlet on the west coast of Hudson Bay, 280 miles north of Churchill.

"Arloo and I don't work at the coffee shop anymore now...
because the doctor said it wasn't good for my baby.... So I'm
happy at home again and Arloo is working at the mine.

"I keep on writing to the Pratts and they never answer back so
I think I'll stop writing to them all now. I write to Elsie
[Schweder] and she is only one who'll answer my letters. That's
only one who is the nicest in the Schweder family, but the others
I don't want to know them any more. Even though Charles saved
my life I thank him for that but not more."

Though I wrote several times thereafter, she never replied.
When I tried to find out from others what was happening to her,
responses were vague to nonexistent. Nobody seemed to know
or, if they did, they were not inclined to say. Not until I revisited
Churchill in 1966 was I able to assemble some bits and pieces of
the final chapter of Rita's life, and even these hardly amounted to
more than disjointed fragments fraught with rue.

The tenuous connection she had re-established with her own
people through Anoteelik, Aijai, and Arloo failed to hold.
Sometime in 1961 she gave up the attempt and, taking her baby
with her, left Arloo and returned to Churchill.

For a time the staff at Camp 20 did what they could for her, but
there were frequent staff changes and Rita slipped through the
cracks and was lost to view. The Pratts moved away. Presumably
Rita never re-established connections with any of the male
Schweders, but she did maintain an ephemeral contact with Else,
who lived down the road from the jerry-built cabin which had
become Rita's home... and which welcomed a succession of men
who contributed to her precarious livelihood and to that of the
three children she produced.

When her life became too bleak to be borne, or when she felt
another epileptic seizure coming on, she sometimes phoned
Else, who would offer what help she could. Once or twice Else
tried to interest town officials in Rita's plight, even urging them
to take Rita's children into public care. This they failed to do until

one dark winter's day when an easterly blizzard was savaging Churchill and the temperature had fallen far below zero.

Sometime in the blackness of the storm's passage, Rita went out into the night—and did not return. When the blizzard ended, a search was made, and her lightly clad body was eventually discovered beneath a drift.

The official verdict was that she had frozen to death while in the grip of an epileptic seizure. The unofficial one was that, drunk or drugged, she unwittingly stumbled out into the blizzard and became lost in it.

No one will ever know.

But it may be that, following an ancient usage of her people when life became of no further worth, a child called Kunee chose to go walking on the land.

AUTHOR'S NOTE

Some critics may take exception to my use of such terms as *Indian, white man, Eskimo,* and *half-breed.* No offence is intended. These were the names in general usage, often by the people themselves, during the times of which I write. I have not felt it necessary to arbitrarily alter these terms because they may now be considered politically incorrect.

The sources drawn upon in this book are, for the most part, acknowledged and identified in the text. A number of the quotations from Charles Schweder's diaries are from notes made after reading the originals; others come from journals which he gave to me at the conclusion of our 1947 journey together.

INDEX

Aijai, 335

aircraft, 14, 73–78, 201, 319, 320–21, 324

Alekahaw, 293

Amadjuak Lake, 275

Angakouk, 23, 52–53, 68

Angela, 209–10

Angikuni Lake, 275

Angleyalik, 24–25, 36, 42

Anna Karenina (Tolstoy), 95

Anoteelik, 82, 224–25
    and Charles Schweder, 96, 113–14
    on Ennadai Lake expedition, 327, 328
    as entertainer, 224–25, 231
    and Fred Schweder Jr., 234
    Fred Schweder Sr. and, 331–32
    at Hekwaw's camp, 42–43, 44, 61
    as hunter, 67, 222, 230, 234
    on Little Lakes trip, 229–31
    in Rankin Inlet, 337
    return to Ihalmiut, 328, 335

Anson aircraft, 14, 73–74, 75–78

Arctic Institute of North America, 5, 326

arctic prairie, 229, 232, 239, 247, 287–88

Arctic Wings, 5, 10, 13, 322, 324

Arloo, 338

Arlow, 305

Baffin Island, 275

Baker Lake, 73–74

bannock, 32, 57, 66, 88, 114–15, 144, 150

barrengrounds, 3–4, 98, 103, 326. *See also* arctic prairie

Barrenland Band, 181

beaver, 145–46

Bedford House (Deer Lake Post), 152

Belikari, 42, 44, 61

Bellanca aircraft, 320–21

beluga whales, 301

Big Bend, 45, 47

Big Opening (Nueltin Lake), 126–27, 215

Big Point (Nueltin Lake), 118–21, 216

Big River expedition, 207–8, 237, 240, 244–45

Big River (Thlewiaza River), 244, 257–66, 270–74, 277, 283–91, 299–301. *See also* Big River expedition; Kasmere's River
  caribou on, 259–60, 262, 265–66, 269–72
  on coastal plain, 284–85, 286–89
  portages on, 265, 294
  rapids on, 248–50, 258, 260, 262, 264–66, 283, 299
  seals in, 271–75, 289–90

birds, 101, 102–3. *See also individual species*; Chief; Windy
  migrating, 82–83, 85, 123–24, 308

blackflies, 180, 274

blowflies, 95

Bones (dog), 166, 167, 178, 215, 228
  and birds, 187, 189, 191
  fear of abandonment, 168, 172, 179–80
  fear of water, 173, 199

bot flies, 285

Bourassa, Johnny, 14–15, 73–74, 75, 78, 320–22

Brochet, 54–55, 57, 135, 152–55

Buckholtz, Olie and Karl, 305

"bulldog" flies, 180

cabins. *See* dwellings

caches, 148–49
  Ihalmiut, 46, 229–30
  as supply source, 124–25, 216
  theft from, 52, 66
  trappers', 44–45, 46, 50, 58

Cameron, Donald, 319, 322

camps, 45, 55. *See also specific camps*
  Hekwaw's, 43–44, 48, 61
  Idthen Eldeli, 119–20, 137–40, 177, 266
  Ihalmiut, 236–37, 328
  Kumiut, 286, 307–8
  at Putahow River, 64–65, 67

Camp 20, 337, 339

Canada jay (whisky-jack), 143, 169

Canadian Geological Survey, 329

canoes, 106. *See also* Lockwood outboard motor
  freighter, 94, 114, 245
  of Idthen Eldeli, 179, 263
  of Kumiut, 285, 291–92, 294
  lining upstream, 294, 307–8
  loading, 165–67
  maintaining, 104, 107, 125
  paddling, 106, 148, 249
  poling, 141–42
  under sail, 125–26, 268–69, 273, 285, 291–92
  seagoing, 285, 291–92, 306
  tracking, 168, 197–98
  in whitewater, 151, 177–78, 191, 248

caribou, barrenground ("deer"), 3–4, 95–96, 99, 130–35, 326. *See also* la Foule; pemmican
  on Big River, 259–60, 262, 265–66, 269–72
  butchering, 90
  decimation of, 134–35
  fawning grounds of, 131
  and flies, 95, 284–85, 287
  hunting of, 101–2, 178–79, 287, 289

importance of, 42, 224–25
mating season of, 132–33
migrating, 58, 67, 98, 133,
    259–60, 289
at Reindeer Lake, 152
reverse migration of, 132, 250
shortages of, 139, 179, 210
as swimmers, 243, 265–66, 269,
    270–71
Caribou Hills, 88, 103
Carrick, Bill, 326
cat trains, 327, 328
Chamberlain, Hairy Joe, 15
Charles Rapid, 197–98
Charlie Lake, 279, 282
Chief (hawk), 186, 205–6
Chipewyan Falls, 171
Chipewyan people, 119–20. See also
    Idthen Eldeli
        at Churchill, 331
        epidemics among, 55, 57, 139,
            145, 151, 154
        homeland of, 21, 193
        paddles of, 249
        Charles Schweder and, 67
        at Windy Post, 35
Churchill, 11–12, 331. See also Fort
    Prince of Wales
        military at, 12, 319, 331
        racism in, 336
cigarettes. See smoking; tobacco
clothing, 32, 139–40, 155, 214, 306
coastal plain, 284–85, 286–89
Cochrane River, 148–51, 167–68,
    171–72, 177–78
Cook, Alphonse, 35, 151
cooking, 33–34, 144, 209–10, 262. See
    also bannock; ponassing

Cree language, 138
Cree people, 8, 19, 129, 151, 154
crows, 168

deer. See caribou, barrenground
deer flies, 180
Deer Lake Post (Bedford House),
    152
Dene. See Chipewyan people;
    Idthen Eldeli
Deneygun, 149
Denikazi, 119
Depression, Great, 22
The Desperate People (Mowat), 201–2
Dettani, 149, 165
disease. See specific diseases; epi-
    demics
    in dogs, 42, 49
dog food
    caribou as, 33, 44–45, 63, 86,
        101–2, 230–31
    fish as, 57
    oatmeal as, 60, 65, 66
dogs, 97–98, 192, 194, 306. See also
    Bones; dog food; Scamp
    diseases of, 42, 49
    feeding, 96, 99
    food shortages and, 52, 66
    as guards, 148–49, 179–80
    for hunting, 179
    inexperienced, 38–39
    Kumiut, 296, 297
    as pack animals, 44, 228
    Charles Schweder and, 21, 44
    at Windy Post, 33, 86, 221
dragonflies, 180
Dubawnt Lake (Tobontua), 131,
    155–56, 181

Dubawnt River, 4
Duck Lake, 37, 51–53, 64–65, 177
ducks, old squaw, 88, 98, 102,
    287–88
dwellings, 45, 46, 76–77
    on Big River, 277–78
    Etzanni's, 174–75
    Jonsson's, 64, 127–28
    Kasmere's, 192
    La Pensie's, 169
    Lush's, 306

eagles, 106–7, 168
Edehon Lake (Edehontua), 263,
    266–70
Eetuk, 295–96, 297–98
Egenolf, Joseph, 156–62, 165, 167
    and Etzanni, 174, 175–76
    and Idthen Eldeli, 157, 160,
        162, 263
    and Kasmere, 181, 194–95
"Endymion" (Keats), 100
Engola, 25, 36, 42
Ennadai Lake, 326–27
epidemics
    in Brochet area, 55, 57, 151, 154
    and Cree people, 151, 154
    and Idthen Eldeli, 119, 145, 154
    and Ihalmiut, 41–42
eskers, 89–90, 142, 143, 199–200, 209
Eskimo Charlie. See Planisek,
    Janez
Eskimo Point, 238, 304, 313
Eskimo Post (Fort Hall), 146,
    187–90, 193
Eskimos. See Ihalmiut; Inuit;
    Kumiut; Utkuhilingmiut
Etzanni, 174–76, 181, 194

falcons, 121, 185–87, 190–91, 196. See
    also Chief; Windy
Farley, Frank, 2
Fidler, Peter, 152
firewood, 46, 79, 86, 99, 176
    on arctic prairie, 247, 260,
        261–62
fish, 85, 102–3, 106, 107. See also indi-
    vidual species
fishing
    on Cochrane River, 169
    Idthen Eldeli and, 140, 210–11,
        213–14
    Ihalmiut and, 42
    Kumiut and, 299
    with nets, 106, 210, 213–14, 223,
        228
    at Windy Post, 32, 104, 107,
        223, 228
flies, 140, 167–68, 171, 179–80. See
    also individual species
flu. See influenza
Fond du Lac, 188
forest, boreal, 136–37, 147. See also
    spruce trees; treeline
forest fires, 171–73, 176
The Forsyte Saga (Galsworthy), 261
Fort Hall (Eskimo Post), 146,
    187–90, 193
Fort Hall (Thanout) Lake, 145–46
Fort Prince of Wales, 263
la Foule, 3, 44–45, 79, 130–32,
    251–53, 263
foxes
    arctic (white), 26, 229,
        279–80, 289
    as pets, 306
    trapping of, 49, 325

free-traders, 28–29, 153, 154–55, 169, 241
frogs, 99
furs, 32, 77. *See also* fur trade
fur trade, 23–24, 134, 145, 146, 241–42. *See also* Hudson's Bay Company; Revillon Frères
    Eskimo Charlie and, 279–81
    George Lush and, 305–6
    Idthen Eldeli and, 134, 263
    wartime collapse of, 29, 37, 139, 241–42
    at Windy Post, 35

Gallagher (aircraft mechanic), 14, 74, 75, 78
gardening, 158, 161
geese, 88, 213, 274, 287–88
Government of Canada. *See also individual employees*
    agents of, 157, 211
    Department of Health and Welfare, 55, 202, 233, 236
    Department of Northern Affairs, 326, 335–38, 338
    and Idthen Eldeli, 169, 181–84, 211
    neglect of Ihalmiut by, 233, 235, 236, 324–25, 326, 335
    treaties with, 169, 181–84
Grant, Don, 338
Grave Rapid, 196
graves
    desecration of, 236–37, 285–86
    Idthen Eldeli, 144, 145
    Ihalmiut, 236–37
    Kumiut, 285–86
grayling, 106, 169

Great Depression, 22
Great Slave Lake, 160–62
ground squirrels, 288
gulls, 83, 102, 121, 288

Hall, Herbert, 187–88
Hanna, 295, 296, 297
Harper, Francis, 6–7
    and animal killing, 15, 83, 99, 100
    arrival at Windy Post, 77–78
    and Brochet trip, 108–9, 114
    conflict with, 107, 116, 201, 204–5, 240, 243
    intolerance of, 82, 83–84, 95, 222
    and Farley Mowat, 6, 221, 223
    racism of, 11
    return home of, 323, 325
    Charles Schweder and, 108–9, 114, 237, 240, 324
    and Fred Schweder Jr., 226, 235, 243
    as scientist, 5, 76, 100–103, 107
    and seals, 108, 223
    and Robert Yule, 203–4
Harris, Husky, 15
hawks, 95. *See also* Chief; Windy
Hearne, Samuel, 4, 119
Hekwaw, 42, 43–44, 48, 61, 68
Henderson, Frank, 55
Hicoliguak Lake, 275, 276
Hidden Valley, 118
Highway, Joe, 35, 58, 129, 130, 244
Hudson Bay, 301, 309–15
    dangers of, 303, 307–8
    tidal flats of, 307, 309, 312, 314, 319

Hudson Hotel (Churchill), 12
Hudson's Bay Company (HBC),
   151–53, 241–42
   boats of, 303
   at Brochet, 152, 153, 154–55
   and other traders, 154–55,
     305–6
   posts of, 20–21, 26, 152, 187, 238
   at Simmons Lake, 23–24, 241
   at Windy Lake, 20–22, 23, 241
hunting
   of caribou, 101–2, 178–79, 287,
     289
   dangers of, 271
   by Idthen Eldeli, 177–78
   by Ihalmiut, 46
   methods of, 129–30, 270,
     279–80, 287, 289
   at Windy Post, 32, 86, 87–91
Hyslop, Robert, 158

ice, 117–18, 121–22
Idthen Eldeli (People of the
   Deer), 137–38. *See also specific*
   individuals; Chipewyan people
   Barrenland Band, 181
   beliefs of, 160, 175–76, 183, 212–13
   and caribou, 134–35, 178–79,
     263, 270
   decimation of, 135, 151
   epidemics among, 119, 145, 154
   and Europeans, 151–52, 194
   and fur trade, 134, 263
   government and, 169, 181–84,
     211
   hardship among, 139, 140, 149,
     210–11
   and Ihalmiut, 188–89

Misty Lake Band, 149, 165,
   174–77, 181
   Farley Mowat and, 326
   and seals, 275
   travels of, 181, 263
   and Treaty day, 165, 170
Idthentua (Reindeer Lake), 19,
   133–34, 151–52, 181
Ihalmiut (Caribou Eskimos), 21–22
   beliefs of, 120
   and caribou, 42, 270
   clothing of, 32
   deportation of, 238
   dwindling of, 41–42, 116
   epidemics among, 41–42
   Eskimo Charlie and, 279–81
   family life of, 25
   famine among, 47, 49–52, 55,
     58–69, 104, 115, 203, 322–23,
     325
   fate of, 334
   and fur trade, 23–25, 35, 146,
     187–89, 193
   government and, 236
   and Idthen Eldeli, 188–89
   Farley Mowat and, 326
   Schweder family and,
     41–42
   and seals, 275–76
   and Second World War, 35
   shelters of, 43, 121
   trade with, 121
Indians. *See also* Chipewyan
   people; Idthen Eldeli
   and Inuit, 294
   racist attitudes toward, 8, 20,
     22–23
influenza, 55, 57, 139, 145, 154

Ingebritson, Gunnar, 10, 13, 322, 323, 324
Ingebritson, John, 12–14, 73
Inoyak, 293, 295
insects, 85, 138–39. *See also individual species*
Inuit. *See also* Ihalmiut; Kumiut; Utkuhilingmiut
    on Big River, 287, 289, 291–301
    caribou hunting by, 287, 289
    dwindling of, 41–42, 116, 294
    in Keewatin, 4
    seal hunting by, 275–76, 294
    in Thelon River area, 279
inuksuak, 98, 229, 284, 286
Itkuk, 25, 36, 42–43, 44, 61
Itooee (Sandy) Lake, 142, 199–200, 211

Jackfish Lake (Lac Brochet), 149–50, 173–74
jaegers, 288
jay, Canada (whisky-jack), 143, 169
Jonsson, Ragnor, 39, 52–53, 128–30, 151
    cabin of, 64, 127–28, 214

Kakumee, 188–89, 193
Kakut, 193, 236–37
Kala, 42, 44, 61
Kasmere, 181–87, 192, 193–95
Kasmere Lake (Theitagatua), 145, 191–92
Kasmere's (Thlewiaza) River, 137, 141–45
    Charles Rapid, 197–98
    Grave Rapid, 196
    Mud Rapid (Tebanaycha), 199

Nilee-Deesee Rapids, 141–42, 205
    portages on, 143, 144, 145, 190–91, 198–99, 208
    Spruce Falls, 199
    Sucker Rapid, 198–99
    Tebannay Chah Rapid, 143
Katelo, 47, 60–61, 63, 66, 68
Kazan Camp, 45, 61–63, 66
Kazan River, 4, 6, 203
Keewatin Territory, 4
Keewatin Zoological Expedition, 5–6, 74, 84–85
    Farley Mowat fired from, 107, 201, 204
Kemp, H.S., 158
Kennedy, Robert, 336–37
Kerr, Bill, 335–36
Kogaluk River, 275
Koonik, 299–300, 301, 307–8
Koudjuak River, 275
Kumiut (River People), 287, 289, 291–301, 305–6
    family life of, 296–97, 299–300
Kunee. *See* Rita

Lamb, Tom
    and famine relief, 56, 59, 203
    grave desecration by, 236–37
    and Farley Mowat, 201–2, 237, 239
    and Charles Schweder, 201, 205, 233, 235, 238, 241
    and Fred Schweder Jr., 233
Lamb Airways, 200, 227
Land of Little Sticks, 21, 22, 232
La Pensie, Louis, 169
La Pensie Lake, 169

Lawrie, Andy, 326
lemmings, 26, 94
lighting, 34, 77
Little Lakes, 25, 47, 227, 228–31
Little River, 91, 92–93, 102
lob-sticks, 124, 180
Lockwood outboard motor
 (kicker), 113–14, 146, 167
  repairs to, 147–48, 168, 173,
   180, 308
  and shear pins, 142, 177–78,
   311
  spark plug of, 191–92, 310
Long Carry Lake, 180
longspurs, 88–89, 98
loons, 88, 287–88
Lopeezin, 149
Louis, 138
Lush, George, 302–9
lynx, 187

Madees, 138, 139, 209–14
Mallet, Thierry, 181–84, 190
Many Islands Lake. See Nueltin
 Lake
maps, 208, 244, 246–47, 259
mergansers, 88, 102, 142, 199–200
Metis, 11, 22–23, 28, 35, 116
mice, 84, 221
military
  in Brochet, 153
  in Churchill, 12, 319, 322
  at Duck Lake, 177, 230
  at Ennadai Lake, 326–27
  Charles Schweder and,
   326–28
Mink Rapid, 168
missionaries, 153, 156–58. See also

Oblate Fathers
  and native people, 20, 160–62,
   175–76, 181
Misty Lake, 57, 148–49, 176–77
Misty Lake Band, 149, 165, 174–77,
 181
mixed-race relationships, 20, 169,
 280. See also Pama; Rita (Kunee)
Moiestie, Peter, 133–34
Moiesty, Rose. See Schweder, Rose
mosquitoes, 103–4, 106, 127, 143, 200
Mowat, Farley, 242, 326
  arrival at Windy Post, 76–79
  books by, 201–2, 334
  in Churchill, 2, 73
  clothing of, 139–40, 155, 306
  and dogs, 96, 97–98
  and Francis Harper, 6, 221, 223
  as hunter, 90, 101–2
  and hygiene, 172–73
  and Idthen Eldeli, 326
  and Tom Lamb, 201–2, 237, 239
  return home, 322
  and Rita, 84, 225, 334–35,
   338–39
  and Charles Schweder, 104,
   107–8, 215, 334, 335
  and Fred Schweder Jr., 102–3,
   235
  and Fred Schweder Sr., 9–10
  as scientist, 84–85, 94–96,
   100–101, 102, 326
Mud Rapid (Tebanaycha), 199
Muskeg Special, 2–3, 9

Nahzee, 140
Nettsilling Lake, 275
Never Cry Wolf (Mowat), 201–2

Nilee-Deesee Rapids, 141–42, 205
Nileen, 141, 178, 206–9
Norseman aircraft, 201, 319, 324
Norway rat, 7
Nueltin Lake, 10, 124–27, 136–37,
  214–16, 245–48. *See also* Jonsson,
  Ragnor
    Big Opening, 126–27, 215
    Big Point, 118–21, 216
    Hidden Valley, 118
    in spring, 98, 117–19

Oblate Fathers, 153, 157–58. *See also*
  missionaries
Old Junk (Tomlinson), 224
Oquinuk, 59, 66
Owliktuk, 328

Padlei, 238
Pama, 25, 36, 42–44, 61, 116, 216–17
The Pas, 2, 7–9
Peace River Airlines, 14, 320. *See
  also* Bourassa, Johnny
pemmican, 134, 152–53, 159
People of the Deer (Mowat), 201–2
plain, coastal, 284–85, 286–89
Planisek, Janez ("Eskimo
  Charlie"), 277–78, 279–83
poison bait, 74, 129–30, 280
Pommela, 35, 236, 237, 239
    Charles Schweder and,
      49–50, 54–55, 57–58, 230
ponassing, 142–43, 146, 200, 209
portages
    on Big River, 265, 294
    to Brochet, 147
    on Kasmere's River, 143, 144,
      145, 190–91, 198–99, 208

to Thanout Lake, 180
Povungnituk River, 275
prairie, arctic, 229, 232, 239, 247,
  287–88
Pratt, Amelia, 333, 334–35, 338, 339
ptarmigan, 75, 78–79, 88, 95
Putahow River, 59, 64–65, 67,
  209–14

rabies, 49
radio, 26, 34, 64–65
ravens, 99–100, 121, 168, 170–71,
  189–90, 252
Redhead, 187
Red-head House, 145
Reindeer Lake (Idthentua), 19,
  133–34, 151–52, 181
religion, 278. *See also* missionaries;
  Oblate Fathers; Roman
  Catholic Church
residential schools, 333–34
Revillon Frères, 19, 105, 145, 181, 190
Rita (Kunee), 36, 82, 222, 331–40
    abuse of, 332, 333, 335
    authorities and, 332–33,
      339–40
    in Churchill, 331, 337, 339
    as conflict source, 68, 115–16
    death of, 340
    at Hekwaw's camp, 42, 44, 61
    Tom Lamb and, 205
    marriage of, 338–39
    medical problems of, 334,
      335–36
    and men, 332, 337, 339
    Farley Mowat and, 84, 225,
      334–35, 338–39
    in Rankin Inlet, 337–39

at school, 332, 333
and Charles Schweder, 44,
62–63, 96, 329, 332–33, 335
and Fred Schweder Jr., 65,
104, 226–27
Fred Schweder Sr. and, 331–32,
333
status of, 336–37
suicide attempts of, 332, 334
in Winnipeg, 334, 335
robins, 82, 88–89
Roman Catholic Church, 20. *See
also* missionaries; Oblate
Fathers; residential schools
Royal Canadian Air Force, 319,
321–22
Royal Canadian Mounted Police,
322–23, 332–33
Royal Canadian Signal Corps, 153,
326–27
Royal Ontario Museum, 5, 74
ruddy turnstone, 100

St. Michael's School, 333–34
St. Pierre du Lac Caribou, 153
sandflies, 180
sandpipers, 100, 101, 287–88
Sandy (Itooee) Lake, 142, 199–200,
211
Sandy Rapids, 171–72
Scamp (dog), 44, 48, 97–98, 228
schools, 8, 210, 332, 333
Schweder, Charles, 80–81, 155–56,
206–7, 238, 296. *See also*
Schweder family
and Anoteelik, 96, 113–14
canoe skills of, 247, 258, 264,
283

childhood of, 20, 21–22, 23
in Churchill, 322, 326, 328–29,
330
as cook, 262
generosity of, 81, 136
as guide, 326–28, 329
and Francis Harper, 108–9,
114, 237, 240, 324
as hunter, 271–73, 274–75,
289–90
and Ihalmiut, 24–27, 36, 116,
235, 324, 328
and Ihalmiut famine, 53, 55,
58–69, 115, 288, 322
and Keewatin Zoological
Expedition, 79–81, 84
and Tom Lamb, 201, 205, 233,
235, 238, 241
marriage of, 329–30
as mechanic, 147–48, 168, 173,
180, 308
and Farley Mowat, 104, 107–8,
215, 334, 335
and Pama, 25, 44, 63, 116,
216–17
return to Windy Post, 323–24
and Rita, 44, 62–63, 96, 329,
332–33, 335
and Fred Schweder Jr., 64,
115, 325
and Fred Schweder Sr., 26–27,
28, 36, 150, 328–29
and Rose Schweder, 64, 115,
240–41
as trader, 41, 109, 237
as trapper, 24–25, 33, 36–37, 45,
48–49, 237
and white men, 154

in Winnipeg, 23, 329
Schweder, Else, 32, 33, 36, 331
    and Rita, 333, 339
    as trapper, 37–40
Schweder, Fred, Junior, 81–82, 222,
    233–35
    and Brochet trip, 114
    as hunter, 234
    and Ihalmiut, 46–47, 63
    and Tom Lamb, 233
    and Farley Mowat, 102–3,
        235
    racism of, 43, 47, 234–35
    and Rita, 65, 96, 104, 116,
        226–27, 234–35
    and Charles Schweder, 64, 115,
        226, 234–35
    as trapper, 33, 45, 58, 63
Schweder, Fred, Senior, 19–30
    as bootlegger, 332
    in Churchill, 331
    and Eskimo Charlie, 280
    as father, 28, 36
    as fish camp operator, 55
    as free-trader, 28–29
    as HBC employee, 20–22,
        23–24, 25–26
    and Ihalmiut famine, 55, 59
    and Kasmere, 194–95
    Farley Mowat and, 9–10
    racism of, 22, 27, 35, 333
    and Rita, 331–32, 333
    and Second World War, 27,
        34–35
    as trapper, 19, 36–37
    at Windy Post, 30–35, 40
    in Winnipeg, 22–23
Schweder, Freeda, 328–29

Schweder, Mary, 9, 10, 37, 331
    family responsibilities of, 32,
        33–34, 36
Schweder, Michael (Mike), 82, 96,
    222, 242
    and Ihalmiut, 46–47
    and Charles Schweder, 67,
        113–14
    as trapper, 58
Schweder, Norman, 9, 331
Schweder, Rose (Moiesty), 19–20,
    22, 29–30, 150, 240–41
Schweder family, 96, 328–29. See
    also individual members; Windy
    Post
    in Churchill, 325, 331
    and Rita, 335, 339
    at Simmons Lake, 242
    tension among, 104, 115–16,
        221, 225–27, 234–35, 324
scoters, 88
Seal Hole Lake, 249–51, 257
Seal River, 275
seals, freshwater
    in Big River, 271–75, 289–90
    Francis Harper and, 108, 223
    in lakes, 275–76
    stories of, 244, 275–76
Second World War, 1, 27–28, 29,
    34–35
    and fur trade, 29, 37, 139,
        241–42
shamans. See Etzanni; Pommela
Shieff, Israel, 153, 154
shrews, 84
shrimp, 98
Simmons, Del, 105, 241
Simmons Lake, 240–42

HBC post at, 23–24, 105–6, 235–36
sleds, 44, 54, 87–88, 97–98, 228. *See also* dogs
smallpox, 119
Smith, Windy, 15
Smith House Bay, 89
smoking, 82, 88, 138, 296. *See also* tobacco
snow blindness, 39
snow buntings, 95
sparrows, 101, 102
specimens
 killing, 15, 74, 83, 84, 99, 100–101
 preserving, 84, 85, 95
spring, 85–91
 air travel in, 75–76
 canoe travel in, 116–19, 121–22, 124–27
 migrating birds in, 82–83
 nights in, 66, 82–83
 sled travel in, 87–88, 97–98
 at Windy Post, 82–83, 91–92
Spruce Camp, 98
Spruce Falls, 199
spruce trees, 79, 103, 180, 260, 261–62
storms, 229
 on Big River, 262
 on Hudson Bay, 313
 at Jackfish Lake, 173
 at Nueltin Lake, 122, 128
 at Windy Lake, 98–99, 116–17
strychnine, 74, 129, 280
Sucker Lake, 199
Sucker Rapid, 198–99

summer nights, 209, 288
swallows, 121

taiga. *See* barrengrounds
Tavanni, 244, 287, 293, 300, 303
tea, 138, 143, 177
Tebannay Chah Rapid, 143
Telequoisie (Telee), 138–39, 140–46, 149, 155
 as cook, 142–43, 146, 150
tents, 82, 261, 296. *See also* topays
terns, 123–24, 199
Th'anne River, 275, 294
Thanout (Fort Hall) Lake, 145–46, 180–81, 187–90
Thlewiaza River. *See* Big River; Kasmere's River
Thompson, David, 151–52
thrushes, 82, 88–89, 101
timberline, 124
tobacco, 138, 144, 149, 177, 229–30. *See also* smoking
toboggans, 54. *See also* sleds
Tomlinson, H.M., 224
topays, 43, 298
traders, 193, 294. *See also* free-traders
 illegal, 280, 305–6
 missionaries as, 157
Trafford, Jim, 28
traplines, 45, 48–49, 325
trappers, 15, 58, 129. *See also* individual trappers
 equipment of, 46, 129
 white, 134, 151, 193, 279–80, 294
The Travels of Marco Polo, 150, 261
travois, 44, 228
treaties, 169, 181–84

Treaty day, 165, 170
treeline, 239, 260
Tseekunee, 149
Tulemaliguak Lake, 275
tundra. *See* barrengrounds
Tyrrell, Joseph and James, 4

udzi, 193
United States Army, 7
United States Office of Naval
    Research, 5
Utkuhilingmiut (Soapstone
    People), 279

Walking on the Land (Mowat), 334
Waller, Sam, 8
warble flies, 95, 284–85
warblers, 101
waterfowl, 88, 287–88, 308
weasels, 95
whisky-jack (Canada jay), 143, 169
Wholdaia Lake, 320–21
Windy (hawk), 207, 215, 228, 243,
    269, 274, 308
    in later life, 322
    misadventures of, 225, 245,
        261, 283–84, 312
    as whitewater alarm, 247, 248,
        257, 260
Windy Lake, 104, 105, 116–17, 224
Windy Post, 76–77
    abandonment of, 325, 328
    dogs at, 33, 86, 221
    fishing at, 32, 104, 107, 223, 228
    food shortage at, 50, 52
    and fur trade, 20–22, 23, 28, 29,
        35

hunting at, 32, 86, 87–91
life at, 31–34, 221–28
meals at, 32, 33, 47, 84, 107,
    224
native people at, 35, 50, 52,
    325
as Nueltin Post, 28–29
in spring, 82–83, 91–92
supplies for, 104, 166, 245, 324,
    325
in winter, 31–33
Windy River, 91, 102, 105, 106
winter
    preparations for, 46
    travel in, 37–39, 51
    at Windy Post, 31–33
Wolf Island Lake, 179–80
Wolf Knoll, 89–90, 99
wolverines, 48–49, 278
wolves, 89, 94, 100, 246, 326
    on Big River, 252, 274
    hunting of, 129–30
    and traplines, 48–49

Yule, Robert
    grave desecration by, 236–37
    and Idthen Eldeli, 211
    and Ihalmiut, 233, 235, 236–37,
        238
    and Ihalmiut famine, 55–56,
        59, 203
    and Farley Mowat, 202, 237
    racism of, 55–56
    and Charles Schweder, 241
    at Windy Post, 202–3, 227, 239